Jimmy Tibbs is one of t ... ng trainers. Aged 11, he st ... st Ham Amateur Boxing C ... es before turning profession ... guidance of Terry Lawless and Mickey Duff.

He won 17 of his 20 fights before being imprisoned for his role in gang violence in London.

At the age of 35, having served nearly five years in jail, Jimmy was given a second chance in boxing and started training the likes of Charlie Magri, Frank Bruno and Lloyd Honeyghan.

By 1983, Magri was a world champion and Jimmy had started to get a firm reputation as a trainer who could get the best out of his fighters.

Jimmy extended his stable of world champions through some incredible talent such as Chris Pyatt and Nigel Benn, the latter winning all seven of his world title fights under Jimmy's tuition. There were also sadder times such as training Michael Watson for his fateful fight against Chris Eubank – the closest Jimmy ever came to retiring.

At the age of 67, Jimmy is still training champions, including British and Commonwealth middleweight champion, Billy Joe Saunders.

JIMMY TIBBS

SPARRING WITH LIFE

Sport Media

JIMMY TIBBS

SPARRING WITH LIFE

I'd like to dedicate this book to my dad for making me the man I am today.

SPARRING WITH LIFE

Written by Jimmy Tibbs with Paul Zanon

Edited by Chris Brereton
Production: Lee Ashun, Simon Monk

Published in Great Britain in 2014
Published and produced by: Trinity Mirror Media,
PO Box 48, Old Hall Street, Liverpool L69 3EB.
Managing Director: Ken Rogers
Publishing Director: Steve Hanrahan
Executive Editor: Paul Dove
Executive Art Editor: Rick Cooke
Sales and Marketing Manager: Elizabeth Morgan
Senior Marketing Executive: Claire Brown
Senior Book Sales Executive: Karen Cadman

Photographic acknowledgements:

Front cover image: Nicola Collins
Other images: Press Association, Team Pictures Limited,
Martin Bowers, Mirropix, Ron Peck, Gianluca Di Caro,
Hugh Glendinning, Andy Gray at www.boxingportraits.com
Every effort has been made to trace the copyright. Any oversight will be rectified in future editions at the earliest opportunity by the publishers.

Printed and bound by CPI Group (UK) Ltd, Croydon, CR0 4YY

ISBN: 9781908695857

Contents

Acknowledgments

TOO MANY TO THANK

When I went to prison, I left my wife with hardly anything and if it wasn't for my friends and family she would've really struggled. Therefore, some people deserve paying tribute to. People like Dennis Doherty, who always looked out for my wife and kids by constantly checking they didn't go short and he always made sure my kids had Christmas presents.

Then there's Bobby Reading. Here's one example of what he did for me while I was behind bars. Bobby wanted to contact my wife one day but had no success. Aware that she did not have a working telephone, he wanted to make sure that she was able to make calls in case of an emergency and to have people to talk to while I was inside.

He consequently paid for her phone to be set up and he

also insisted he paid all the bills while I was away. I couldn't believe it.

Roy Lane, Micky May and Fuzzy (Kevin Hussey) also need a specific mention. They used to visit me regularly, bring my wife and kids down and make sure my mum was able to visit me in prison.

I also owe a lot of gratitude to the people who took the time out of their busy routines to share their anecdotes without whom this book would have never happened.

Wayne Alexander, Frank Bruno, Tony Burns, Mickey Cantwell, Teena and Nicola Collins (Nicola – thanks for the front cover photo!), Dennis Doherty, Johnny Eames, Jimmy Flint, Colin Hart, Dean Hollington, Mo Hussein, Kevin Hussey, Roy Lane, Gerry Sullivan, Ray Lee, Colin Lynes, Micky May – RIP, Jim McDonnell, Barry McGuigan (thanks for a great foreword!), Colin McMillan, Kevin Mitchell, Ron Peck, Dean Powell – RIP, Chris Pyatt, Jimmy Yellop – RIP, Bobby Reading, Billy Joe Saunders, Frankie Simms, Benny Stafford, Freddie Luke Turner, Danny Williams and Martin Bowers – I owe you a very big thank you for allowing me to use your boardroom at the Peacock Gym and making me feel like it was my own house, no matter how busy the gym was.

My wife Claudette deserves enormous praise for putting up with me through thick and thin and being a rock for me when times were tough.

To my dad – you have been an inspiration all my life and still are. To my mum – RIP.

I also need to say a few words about my ghostwriter.

Over the past 10 years or so I've been approached by various publishers and individuals who have all wanted to tell my life story. I was always told it would make for a good read and it would be something to leave my family in years to come.

However, something always told me not to do it and that went on for about 10 or 12 years. Then one day I was at the gym and my son said to me, "I don't know why you don't get your book written." I replied, "I've been asked on many occasions to have it written, but I don't really fancy it."

He said, "I've got a man for you. His name is Paul Zanon. Let me introduce you to him."

We met a couple of days later at the gym and after a little chat, I instinctively knew that if my book was going to be written, this was the man I wanted to do it.

I told my story the best I could and he's been a great help putting the words together the way he has. I'm really pleased to have known him, not because he's written my story, but because he's become a friend.

It's been a pleasure to work with him.

Jimmy Tibbs, April, 2014

On a trip to India in March, 2013, I walked past a faded fast food signpost which read, 'Tibbs Frankie – The Original Frankie'.

I took a photo of it and sent it to Jimmy's son. On the flight home I was thinking about various boxing interviews I needed to conduct for the Daily Sport on my UK arrival, but the photo kept appearing in my thoughts with the same question, 'I wonder if Jimmy would be willing to have his story written by me?'

I contacted his son and the rest as they say is history. Jimmy is a man of incredible integrity and I feel honoured to have stepped into his world and been able to walk through his incredible life and achievements.

But be under no illusion – there are many more champions still to benefit from his guidance and I'm sure Jimmy will continue to spread his wisdom both inside and outside the boxing ring. He is a friend, a fighter and a teacher. Cheers Jim.

I also owe a big thanks to the team at Trinity Mirror Sport Media, especially my editor, Chris Brereton, for patiently guiding me through the minefield and hurdles associated with getting a book of this depth together and also to Steve Hanrahan for having opened the door of opportunity.

Paul Zanon, April, 2014

Foreword

BARRY McGUIGAN

"Left jab, straight right hand, double left hook.
Whack, whack… whack, whack!
Slip, slip, roll.
Left hook, right hand, finish with the jab.
Whip, whip, whack!"

This is just a little taster of a pad session Jimmy Tibbs would put me through when we trained back in the late 1980s.

His growling, hard exterior and sharp, direct East End accent was mesmerising and it came as no surprise to me that he went on to train a long list of British, European and World champions.

After losing to Steve Cruz in the late summer of 1986 and having been out of the ring for nearly two years, I started working with Jimmy in 1988 as part of my comeback.

I was still in a phase of contemplation as to whether I wanted to jump back into the ring and dedicate my life again to the toughest sport of all; professional boxing at the top level.

I decided my goal was to step up a division and be a super featherweight champion of the world. I needed people around me to not only inspire me but to help me realise I was genuinely good enough to recapture my old form and become champion again.

I was on a mission to prove something to myself and Jimmy was an essential ingredient in helping make that happen. After three good stoppage wins, my quest to regain world honours was cut short by a cuts defeat to Jim McDonnell in 1989.

At the age of 28, I wisely decided that enough was enough and retired, but Jimmy had never doubted me and still believes that if I had fought on I would have been a champion of the world again.

I have a number of stories I could share of my time with Jimmy but there is one episode which I still laugh about today. Jimmy had a good friend called Frankie Simms, who was a massive boxing fan and who I got to know as he would often come down and see me train.

Jimmy is a man with a colourful past and a great sense of humour. One day I had managed to lose the keys to the gym and asked my brother Dermot if he had them. He replied, "Sorry Barry. I don't have them." Jimmy replies, "I ain't got them", and then Frankie looks at me and after about a five-second gap says, "I don't know why you are all looking at me for. I'm a bank robber, not a petty thief!"

We all broke out into a fit of laughter and to this day the

story still makes me laugh when I reminisce.

In a day and age where a number of boxers seem to be talking mostly about securing their 'legacy' and certain trainers are often involved in more trash talking than the boxers themselves, it is consoling to know that there are a few good guys left.

Jimmy Tibbs is definitely one of them.

He has immense integrity as a boxing coach and a mentor. I was lucky enough to have him in my corner and it is a privilege to be asked to write this foreword to his book.

Barry McGuigan
WBA world featherweight champion 1985-1986

Round 1

EAST LONDON

"And in the blue corner, weighing in at an even seven pounds and seven ounces, hailing from the heart of the East End of London, let's hear it for Jiiiiiiiiimmmmyyy Tiiiiiiibbbbbsss."

It would be another 19 years before I would get used to that kind of introduction, but on September 9, 1946, I was welcomed to this world by the doctor at Howard Road Hospital as James Edward Patrick Tibbs.

I would soon become known as Jimmy. At the time of writing this book, there's four generations of Jimmy Tibbs alive and kicking.

I grew up on Fox Street in Canning Town, E16.

It was an old place that was so crooked you couldn't even close the front door, never mind lock it. The house was very run down and if you needed to use the loo, it was located at the back of the yard. That was not so bad during the summer months, but on a cold winter's day, with the rain pelting down, the experience became more challenging.

As kids we would all chip in with the household chores but it was my mother who was forever scrubbing the house and making sure that it was spotless. She made it home.

Living in a house in itself was considered a luxury by many. After World War Two, many East End families were left without homes due to the mass bombings and were consequently placed into temporary housing for accommodation – we referred to them as 'prefabs'.

One solution which addressed the shortage of housing was the construction of a number of multi-storey flat blocks. Many still litter the Canning Town horizon now. They started to sprout up everywhere and most of them looked awful.

They were very uniform and a poor substitute for what many had been used to a few years before their houses had been bombed. Although I couldn't appreciate how lucky we had been to live in a house back then, as I look over my shoulder now, I'm very grateful.

As a kid, there were only two radio stations to listen to – Radio Luxembourg and the BBC. Standing about two feet high from the floor, the radio was hardly compact, but it would be like a magnet as we sat close, listening to whatever blared out from the speaker.

During the 1950s, the production of electrical goods such as televisions, radios and washing machines became massive but the majority of the people in the East End didn't have a telephone, so if you had an urgent message you would write a short telegram which would then be hand delivered to whoever you needed to contact.

Most of the messages that the Tibbs had to relay were usually within a few miles, so me and my brothers turned into human telegrams on many occasions, running around the area and making sure that mum and dad knew who needed to speak to them and why!

We did eventually have a phone installed in the house when I was about 12. I still remember the first three numbers – 476 Canning Town.

Funny how certain memories stick in your head for no apparent reason.

For the first six years of my life I grew up under the reign of King George VI, who passed away in 1952 and who was followed by Queen Elizabeth II.

As a kid I don't really remember much about the Queen's succession but I do have distant memories of people being sad on one day and then soon after there were street parties all over a smoggy East End, with the Union Jack hanging out of every window and banners going from roof to roof as we celebrated the Queen coming to power.

This was Britain's biggest party following the end of World War Two and the whole of the country came together to celebrate.

As I say, I only have vague recollections of the East End partying that day. I would certainly remember the Queen's 25th year anniversary though, and for all the wrong reasons.

But more of that later...

The London docks provided me, my friends and my family with a good source of income. Just before I was born, the Luftwaffe bombed the docks, causing an incredible amount of damage, but by the time I was growing up in the 1950s they were buzzing again as London rebuilt itself after the devastation of war.

The number of ships and boats coming in and out from the British Commonwealth was incredible. Imports and exports were at a peak, with tons of sugar, tea, whiskey, bananas and pretty much everything you could think of being loaded and unloaded.

The docks were more vibrant and energised than ever before as young men from all over the country, and especially the East End, flooded to the area looking for work – which was incredibly easy to get.

I, like most likely lads from the East End, had my own stint of working at the docks. As kids we had grown up in the scrap metal game, but by the age of 16 I fancied a bit of a change and went to work as part of the 'shore gang' down the Royal Albert docks.

You needed to be 18 to work down the docks, but I lied about my age as I needed to earn a living. I was getting good money for clearing out the dunnage down in the hold of the ships. Dunnage is the protective material used to wrap valuable cargo during transportation and once a shipment had been taken out, there would be loads of it left.

As with my time working at the scrapyard, there were no hard hats, gloves or boots, you just went below, got stuck in and did your job.

As a boat docked, the packages would be lowered by crane or thrown off to the dockers. They would in turn, using their trolleys, transport them to their trucks and then drive off to the client. The boat would then move on and the next in a long line would squeeze in and start the process all over again, but with a different product.

You certainly knew when a ship was being unloaded because there was so much shouting going on.

These were the days before mobile phones or walkie talkies, so the man in the crane communicating to the docker on the quay would have to shout and make signs. This was not only to let you know of the arrival, but to keep everybody safe as there would be cargo swinging around and goods being thrown around all over the place.

The line of cranes all along the dock seemed never-ending and with the nonstop smoke being churned out from the tug boats, along with the shouting from the senior dockers, the atmosphere was electric.

For many East Enders, those docks were home.

Even before I started working there I can remember as a kid, hundreds of men walking on their way to the docks for all kinds of work. Dockers, welders, you name it. The place had its own culture, and if you speak to any old East Ender still alive now about happy memories of the 1950s, I guarantee you they will give you a story or 10 about the docks.

I am proud to say that I was a part of true East London heritage on a number of fronts.

When you see the old black and white photos of fruit stalls and fires burning out of metal bins in the 1930s and 40s,

90 percent of the time they were shots from the market on Rathbone Street.

We lived a stone's throw from there and it wasn't just a place to buy a wide choice of goods, it also acted as a place where people would hang out, swap some stories over a cigarette and a cup of tea, and catch up on the latest gossip. My nan had a fish shop and two fish stalls and my dad's side of the family had a fruit stall down the other end.

Everybody down there knew me and my brother Johnny. We were a couple of livewires as kids and were always known for messing about, causing a bit of trouble and having a bit of fun.

Everybody knew each other down the market. In its prime, you had a problem getting from the White House pub down to the Barking Road. You would be shoulder to shoulder with pretty much everyone, but there was no tension amongst the shoppers – it was simply packed!

Certainly more packed than any modern day supermarket. People would travel from all over the East End to come to Rathbone Street. Wanstead, Poplar, Barking, you name it – simply because the market had it all. Maybe not in comparison to the product range of today's supermarkets but it had it all in terms of atmosphere and culture. It was especially brilliant at Christmas time and you couldn't have create a better scene if you'd tried.

Fruit stalls were open all night and market traders with fingerless gloves would hover over open fires, trying to keep their hands warm as people got into the seasonal spirit.

The sounds of Bobby Darin and Elvis Presley coming out

of the record store could just about be heard over the buzz of activity in the market and the sound of the hard-selling street traders calling you in with their shouts.

Although Rathbone Street market didn't have the selection of the modern day Amazon website, as kids we always found everything that we ever needed, and if we behaved ourselves, my mother would even buy us a present.

One year, probably around 1954 or 1955, I asked my mum for a trumpet for Christmas. Without hesitation she found a big plastic one down the market and popped it into a big sock with some apples, pears and nuts. I was over the moon! I played that trumpet until it fell apart. Some would argue that I've been blowing my trumpet ever since.

Despite the fact that my childhood was so soon after World War Two, my mum's side of the family were in the fish trade and my uncles Gerry and George (Bogey as he was known) owned a greengrocer's stall and shop respectively, so we never went hungry. Not only did the family businesses provide us with food on the table, but as kids we had the opportunity to earn a pound note. I worked at the fish stall and my brother worked with my uncle Gerry at the greengrocers. I don't think we were cut out to be market traders, but we certainly had some fun being part of the famous Rathbone Street market culture.

****

Hygiene was always a big thing in the Tibbs household and although taking a bath once a week may not seem like the height of cleanliness, we were top of the leaderboard in the 1950s.

We'd get the old tin bath out, put a bit of Daz on our hair and you were good to go. Bit different to the power showers of today, but it still had the same outcome.

My mum always made sure that we were immaculately presented at school. Sometimes too immaculately! The first school I attended was St Helen's Primary and on one occasion my mum had decided to dress me and my brother in identical shirts – loud Hawaiian ones.

We were only about 10 or 11 and the headmaster spotted us a mile away at morning assembly wearing these shirts hanging out over our long trousers, and called us up to the front. We thought we were in trouble, but he was loving it! He announced to everybody how smartly dressed we were and that we were an example of how a student should present themselves. Something also tells me he was having a bit of a laugh.

I'm sure that my smart clothes also helped me get out of trouble on a number of occasions. I remember as a kid absolutely loving our school dinners and when the bell rang to let you know dinner was ready, you were supposed to walk to the dinner hall in an orderly manner. I never did though! I used to race through the playground past the headmaster's office and get to the food as quickly as possible. On one occasion as I was racing past the headmaster's office, he shouted out, "Oi – Tibbs. Get over here." I thought to myself, 'I'm in trouble here and probably gonna get hit'. I walked over to his office, knocked on the door, and he said,

"Come in Tibbs." He turned to the other teachers and said, "Look at the way he's dressed. Look at the way his mother keeps him. You can go now." I thought to myself, 'Phew!'

My dad was building up the family scrap business when I was a little kid, and by the time we moved to Tarling Road (just round the corner from the current day Peacock Gym), he was well on his way to being a successful business-man. The sky was now the limit when it came to luxuries – which meant having a loo inside the house as well as one in the garden.

On a serious note though – my parents provided us with everything we needed, we never went short on any front and at a time when rationing was still in full force, I would say that put us in a minority.

It's worth mentioning that the family scrap business did not become a success overnight. We all worked very hard at the yard, but in those early days when me and my brothers were young kids, it was my dad who worked non-stop to make it a fruitful business and to make sure our family had a regular income.

One day he located a piece of council owned property and they let him open a scrapyard in Ordnance Road, opposite Rathbone Street market.

My dad managed to get a reputation very early on for being a fair and honest trader and within a short time he started to get regular work from a number of companies. Soon after, he found another piece of council-owned land in Star Lane and the scrap business continued to thrive there as well.

The days of scrap being delivered to us with hand pushed carts, barrows or horses were long gone with the quantities we were now dealing with.

Lorries would pull up to the yard with hundreds of tons of scrap metal each week, with popular items being batteries and cars. The Ford Motor Company, based in Dagenham, were our biggest customer at the time and were booming themselves, so we had no problem in shifting anything which came our way.

When I started to work there at the age of 15, I remember the place being non-stop, and health and safety certainly not being a consideration.

As well as having a great sense of humour, my dad was a disciplined man who got you to use your common sense, which was the best protection available. Nowadays you would be decked out in steel toe-capped boots, hard hats and padded clothing.

Some people moan about these regulations these days, but trust me, it's a good thing they exist. You can't just walk into a scrapyard and get a job today, you could however in those days, and within a very short time you could be handling potentially deadly equipment.

At our yard, we used to have mechanical shears about 10 feet long, which would cut the metal into any sizes required – six inch blocks, 10, 18 etc, or whichever measure Ford or the client specified. The blocks would then be weighed and a man working the magnet would pick it up and put it on the lorry.

This would continue until the lorry reached its weight limit and it was then driven to Ford. We would do about two or three loads per day and that would be considered a good day's work.

There was a specific skill set needed to operate the machinery, otherwise you could seriously injure yourself. You had to know where to place the metal under the shears and when to let go of it. The scrap game was a very dangerous business for a novice. When you are dealing with shears and cranes and magnets carrying tons of metal with big chains hanging down, you had to literally watch yourself.

Batteries provided us with good trade but cars were the bread and butter of the business. We would stick the car on the weigh bridge – making sure we gave the correct monetary value to the person bringing in their car – the crane would then rip the bonnet off, pick the car up by the engine and give it a good shake until the engine fell out. Remember – nobody was wearing hard hats! The engines would go on one side of the scrapyard and the shell of the car on another.

When there was about 100 cars stacked up, we would call in a guy called Percy Leaman to compress everything, take the blocks away and then we would start the process all over again.

The engines would be melted down on site to get the aluminium from them. In fact, lighting up the melting pot at 5am would be one of my first jobs when arriving at the yard. It would take about half an hour before it was ready and we would then start chucking metal into it to make liquid aluminium which would eventually become 'ali bricks'.

Although I used to stop working at 1pm, I became so used

to working outside that I didn't need a watch to check the time, I could tell by looking at the sun what time it was and when it was time to finish.

As I mentioned earlier, the scrapyard was a dangerous place to be and I got tagged on a number of occasions. Most of those were just cuts and bruises but I can still clearly remember one particular time, whilst loading up some scrap from Ford's, the tailgate of the lorry caught my arm and the pain was incredible. It happened so quickly and it was agony. A real reminder that you were never far away from a serious injury. I didn't want to let my dad know I was hurt so walked away like an old dog and sat down in intense pain as my arm swelled up and bruised instantly. I genuinely thought I'd broken my arm.

To this day I still have a lump on the bone of my arm where the tailgate came down on me. Not ideal at the time as I was an amateur boxer trying to keep himself in peak condition. I eventually stopped working at the scrapyard when I was 19 as I had to dedicate myself 100 percent to the sport of boxing.

****

My dad always made sure that we had a holiday each year, taking us down the South coast in his white Austin Wolseley to places like Devon, Hastings, Camber Sands – basically anywhere with sea and sand. It was fantastic and even back then I knew that we were lucky as children.

My memories as a little child are mainly about me and my

brother Johnny. We were always together as kids. We boxed together, went to school together, hung out in the market and played football in the street – inseparable. As we grew older, my two brothers, my sister Eileen and I became a very tight unit. If anybody wanted to start a fight with any one of us, they had to pretty much take the lot of us on.

I was also lucky to be part of a large extended family. My dad had three brothers and three sisters, one of whom was called Eileen, and my mum had one brother and two sisters. Aunt Eileen died when she was very young.

I remember the moment it happened clearly. We were living in Tarling Road and we received the call. The phone went and my mum answered it and she was very upset and started crying and turned to my dad and said, "Your sister's just died Jim." They lived in Clarence Road at the time, only a few minutes away, so my dad put his jacket and hat on, and ran over straight away.

I've never really thought about it before, but I'm guessing my sister being named after my aunt was done as a fitting tribute. My aunt was a lovely person who was taken from us way ahead of her time.

Most of my family were based very close to where we lived so I had loads of cousins within a short walk, with the bulk of them being from my dad's side of the family. All very good people. My dad's dad (my grandfather), was called George and during the war he'd bought a farm down in Raleigh, when it was proper countryside. He then moved to Barking and, soon after, East Ham. He was a bit of a character and was always very good to us, but he was also a very strict man. You only had to make one mistake and you were on your toes! He looked like my dad, but not as big though.

My father was a well respected and very likeable man in the East End. Still is now! Known as 'Big Jim' by many, in his prime he was 6 feet 3 inches tall, weighed a lean 17 stone and had hands like shovels. He was a very quiet man who never started any trouble but could handle himself if put in a situation.

I only have one memory of him involved in a fight with a man about the same size as him in a pub. They took their jackets off, the other guy chucked the first punch and my dad ducked it and hit him with an uppercut and knocked him spark out.

I was only about 10 at the time but I remember my mum holding my younger brother in her arms. The moment the guy regained consciousness, he received a far more painful onslaught from my mum, by way of a verbal whiplashing. He promptly apologised to her, and she reiterated, "You got what you deserved!"

My father had a lot of presence about him. He never laid a finger on us as kids. He only had to look at us or say something and we knew he meant business. If he said you could go out to play and be back in two hours. He meant two hours – he allowed no deviation on the time he set!

My mother, Kate, was an incredibly hard working individual. She loved her family and would never want to see any harm come to us, but being a very proud woman, she also taught us to stick up for ourselves. When I was at St Bonaventure's there was a lad called Charlie Stone who was the same age as me and was also a good boxer.

We must have been about 13 or 14 at the time. Whenever I went to visit my nan in Credon Road I would drop in and see him and we would spar in his alleyway. One day we were deep into a nice sparring session and I looked up and saw his dad telling him to hit me. Soon after, we found out that we were to be matched up in a bout at school. A couple of days before the fight, as my mum was working on the fish stall, Charlie's dad came over to her and sparked up a conversation. Within a couple of minutes he said, "I hear your boy is boxing my boy Kate." She said "That's right." He said, "Don't worry, I won't let my boy hurt him." She replied, "Hurt him? HURT HIM??" She went berserk! She wouldn't have anybody saying a bad thing about the family.

I went on to beat Charlie. Twice in fact. She didn't mind when I got beaten in the boxing ring, that was accepted. What she couldn't tolerate was people being rude and paying no courtesy. I consequently grew up living by similar principles.

Funnily enough, as a kid I was actually very quiet. Don't get me wrong, I wasn't shy. I was like any other lad in terms of messing around and I got in trouble like most kids in my area at the time but on the whole I was always a polite lad. That's the way I'd been brought up.

Being born in 1946 meant I grew up around mass debris from buildings which had been bombed but not yet condemned as a result of World War Two. As a kid you never thought anything different. As far as I was concerned, it was part of our culture and neighbourhood. In fact, I have some good memories of grabbing a few potatoes from the greengrocers stall with my mates, lighting a fire amongst the debris of the buildings and throwing on a couple of spuds as a snack. Why not?

In terms of undetected or unexploded bombs – we were aware of them, but I guess we thought it would never happen to us. Thankfully it never did. I remember a hand grenade being found amongst the debris of a house near us in Canning Town. They sent the guys from the bomb squad down to diffuse it and no fuss was made. As a kid, until you have experienced pain or tragedy, you just look at the bright side of life and embrace everything as good. At the age of 10, me, my brothers and my mates embraced the debris as modern day kids would embrace a computer games console.

As the years would go by, the sites of exploded bombs or piles of debris would be replaced by housing or large office buildings. Back then we could never have imagined that Canning Town would one day have the likes of Canary Wharf looking down on us.

The environment around you changes, but your memories are there for life.

East Enders are a tough and proud bunch and although we had to rebuild our lives and homes, the experience never fazed us, it just added strength to an already tough group of people.

Therefore, bombs were never a concern for me as a kid, they were just part and parcel of life.

However, when I encountered them a few years later as an adult, the story would be quite, quite different.

Round 2

LEARNING MY TRADE

"Jimmy – I've been training lads at West Ham Boxing Club for 30 years, and you're the best."
– Jackie Gubbins, boxing trainer, 1962

Canning Town is a tough area. Boxing is a tough sport. The partnership works well.

Most people tend to take up boxing or football in this part of East London and over the years some great boxers and footballers have come out of here.

Believe it or not, but I was actually a good footballer at one time. I went for trials at West Ham United with Frank Lampard (senior) at Cumberland Road School. I never got through unfortunately, but Frank did and the rest is history. His son ain't a bad player either. I decided instead to dedicate myself to boxing and I've never regretted it.

Boxing is a poor man's sport. Rich kids don't tend to want

to box at an early age as the parents don't introduce them to it and it's usually not part of their culture.

The rich kids will go and watch boxing and love the energy surrounding the sport, but they don't really participate at a serious level. Many people in the East End have boxed to fuel their hunger. Not for the sport, but literally to get food on the table. In the 1920s, the likes of heavyweight champion Jack Dempsey would ride underneath the carriage of a train for about three days, just to get a few cents to buy some food. By the time he was facing his opponent, the motivation to win was so great he would be like a wild animal.

It's been argued that people lose their hunger to fight when food is plentiful. It's at that point that you need the guidance of a good trainer to keep your passion and motivation focused and your skills developed.

Boxing is one of the best disciplines in the world.

The training and dedication needed to succeed runs on a similar parallel to military routines and I would go as far to say that boxing has saved lives and will continue to do so while it's integrated into society.

I believe it should never have come out of the schooling system either – the benefits for young kids are there for all to see.

The opportunities for personal development – not just for fitness – but for building social skills through meeting and mixing with people and for travelling and understanding different cultures is incredible.

How would a boy from Canning Town back in my day ever have got the chance to travel to somewhere like

Liverpool in the 1950s? I didn't even know where Liverpool was back then – I'm serious! Boxing at school made me respect people and got me respected at the same time.

In my opinion, boxing should be reintroduced back into schools, especially in the East End, because the kids seem to have nothing to do these days.

It seems that they hang around in the playgrounds smoking and eating badly. You see them playing a bit of football and cricket, but cricket's not a sport for an East Ender!

Just for the record, you need to be very fit and dedicated to be a good cricketer, I'm just saying that it's just not a sport associated with the East End.

You also never find many bullies in boxing, as the regimented approach to training doesn't provide a comfortable environment for them.

As with most sports, for those wanting to do more than just train, success at the top level is difficult to reach and takes a lot of hard work and dedication.

If 100 kids turn up at the gym, there's probably about 10 who have the potential to develop to a higher level.

Out of those juniors, one or two might make a senior boxer and if you're very lucky, one of those two senior boxers might turn pro. Of those who do turn pro, very few will become champions and of those champions, even fewer will become world champions.

The dedication, commitment and physical effort needed to become a boxer at the highest level is unique.

It might well be the most disciplined sport in the world – it is certainly the toughest and it gives a lot of people some crucial life skills that many youngsters would still do well to learn and live by.

****

The first school I ever attended was called Clarkson Street at the age of four, followed soon after by St Helen's, in Plaistow, which was a convent school. I was there from the age of about five up to 11.

And it was here in 1956, when I was 10, that I would have my first ever boxing experience.

It was a rainy day when our headmaster, Mr Welsh, decided to take a few of us into the assembly hall and have an informal boxing tournament.

Moving four benches together, he made a boxing ring and matched us up with somebody to spar with. I remember him pairing me with a ginger haired lad called Booth, who was a hell of a lot bigger than me, but that didn't stop me having a right tear up with him. Mr Welsh was laughing and loving the spirit the both of us were showing.

That was the moment I fell in love with boxing.

At the age of 12 I then went to St Bonaventure's in Forest Gate, which was an all boys school, with about a thousand kids attending.

My mates also went here and we all boxed – in fact, you didn't have a choice in those days as it was part of the curriculum. Boxing was no different to English, arithmetic or geography and unless you had a letter from your parents saying you were sick, you had to take part.

The same guys I was friends with then are still my mates now. As the saying goes, "birds of a feather flock together."

Although the teachers were very hard with their students, I got on extremely well with them. Mind you I did play a few games, so it wasn't always their fault! When I started boxing for St Bonaventure's, the teachers always used to come and watch me wherever I was fighting and that gave me great encouragement.

I respected their support and in turn started to behave myself. I would say I was lucky growing up as a kid as I never got around people who were a bad influence on me and I always had good people to steer me in the right direction.

With the bug in my system, there was no shortage of inspiration on my doorstep to help fuel my enthusiasm and a gentleman by the name of Terry Spinks was a principal figure when I grew up.

An incredible fighter, he was born and bred in Canning Town and he became an East End hero when he won the gold medal in the 1956 Olympic Games. When he boxed, Canning Town was empty. Terry was a great role model as well as an excellent boxer. He used to walk to his opponent's corner before a bout and shake their hand – pure class. God knows what he made of all the trash talking and bragging that has evolved over the years.

When I was an amateur, Terry Downes was also a big boxing idol for me. A few years later, I would box at the Royal Albert Hall as a pro and on one occasion while crossing paths in the changing room after one of my fights, he gave me some great advice on how to improve on my existing skills and how to use the ring space to my advantage. I've never forgotten his kind words or the lessons he taught me.

Terry would go on to challenge for the world title twice and shared the ring with some all-time boxing legends such as Willie Pastrano and Sugar Ray Robinson. From my perspective, to see a couple of ordinary Londoners progress so far in a sport I had fallen in love with was just the extra boost I needed to dedicate myself 110 percent for the next 12 years.

Unlike some parents' perspective on boxing, mine were totally behind me. Although my father never trained as a boxer, he loved the sport and saw pretty much every fight I had, both at amateur and pro ranks.

At 11 he took me down to West Ham Amateur Boxing Club and left me to it. He could see I was happy and in his eyes, that was the most important thing.

As a kid who hadn't yet entered his teenage years, any encouragement for my boxing was very important. I distinctly remember being picked up by the words of one former teacher during a brief period when I was feeling a little low. I was attending St Bonaventure's at the time but I would often see old teachers from my old Clarkson Street school as we lived opposite it.

On this particular day, I was off school recovering from a nasty dose of Asian flu and I was sitting on the wall outside my house when my old teacher, Miss Leevy, crossed the road and came over and asked me how I felt. I said, "I'm just getting over the flu, but I feel better." I told her I was now boxing and she said, "Look after yourself and get well.

Stick with the boxing. You'll go far." I'm a grandfather now but I remember that moment like it was yesterday and it certainly gave me a boost in the right direction.

****

I felt confident as I stepped into my first proper boxing ring. Of course I was nervous but that's good as it keeps you on your toes. I've seen kids crying in the dressing room because they couldn't get in the ring and at that point realising it just wasn't for them. I knew this was for me and at 11 I knew I was already willing to put in the time and make the necessary sacrifices.

I loved every aspect of boxing. Everything from the early morning six-mile runs in the freezing cold, through to punching the big heavy bags with that distinctive gym odour. If I woke up the morning with my muscles aching after a good workout and sparring session I would smile, knowing that I had just improved my boxing game. I couldn't wait to return for more every day.

Some people think boxing is similar to street fighting and often ask how I could go into a ring and want to smash somebody's face in.

This is a good time to make the clear distinction.

Boxing can be compared to chess. For every attacking move, there's a defensive counter. When you go into a ring you usually don't know anything about your opponent's personal life and you're fighting under supervised and timed conditions and that is nothing like your average drunken street brawl. As an amateur, the aim is not far off fencing, in terms of wanting to get in and out of your opponent's personal space to score points.

If your opponent throws a jab, you might want to slip it, step back, or roll and counter with a hook. The thing to remember is that all this happens in a split second and your mind and body need to be supremely conditioned to cope with the punches, but to also get to grips with the timing. The strategy involved in boxing is intense and the discipline that comes with it helps to develop an individual outside the ring as well.

My routine at the gym was quite simple – train hard for a few hours on Mondays and Wednesdays and then get the 69 bus back home from Plaistow, where the gym was. The trainers used to watch your progress and if you showed any talent, they would invite you to train on Sundays with the seniors. Quite soon after I started training, I was asked to join the Sunday sessions, which was a great boost to my self-esteem so early on.

As training progressed, and within only 12 months, I went on to win my first Schoolboy title in Shoreditch Town Hall. My mum and dad were there, and although my dad did not show a great deal of emotion, I knew he was proud. However, I almost didn't take part in that fight!

On the morning of the bout, my mum made me a massive bacon sandwich, but as a kid I thought nothing of it. I was fighting in the seven stone category and the thought of making weight had never entered my head. A few hours later, I stepped on the scales and the man in charge of monitoring the weights (Billy Cable) was furious as he checked and double checked before shouting out, "Tibbs. You're two pounds overweight! Get down to the boiler room."

I sprinted down to the boiler room and was skipping away, when another kid who was sitting on the top of the boiler looked down and said, "Hello mate, what's your name." I told him and he replied, "I'm boxing you!" We carried on as normal and I beat him later that night. Pat McCann was his name and he came from Liverpool. He ended up turning pro with the same manager I had a few years later.

I ended up winning a plaque for my efforts. There was an opera going on at our school, St Bonaventure's, and they stopped the production to announce "James Tibbs has just won the Schoolboys Championships of Great Britain", and they all stood up and clapped their hands. So I was told anyway! I went on the year after to become Schoolboy champion again, but this time round it was different. I was a boxer the first time round, whereas second time round I was a puncher. I always remember this man came up to me angry and said, "What's the matter with you? All you want to do is knock everybody out!" I wasn't intentionally trying to knock people out, I just took the opportunities in the ring as they became available.

I was actually a box fighter all through my career including as a professional – I could fight when I needed to fight and box when I needed to box.

The Schoolboy final was at Stanmore Airport Hanger. My dad was supposed to be there and never having missed any of my bouts I was somewhat surprised not to see him in the crowd. But I had a fight to be getting on with and without hesitation, or my dad in clear view, I jumped into the ring. As the bell sounded for round one, I saw him walking in with a mate of mine, Teddy Robins, and they took their seats. Within five seconds I had knocked my opponent out and they were off again!

I distinctly remember my first amateur loss against a boxer called Graham Siney, who boxed for Hornchurch. He beat me on his own club show with a close decision, and then I had a return immediately and beat him on my home show. Jackie Gubbins, my trainer, was good to me after the loss. He said, "You won that but never got the decision." He gave me advice on how to beat him next time, and it worked!

Jackie made the whole experience feel like water off a duck's back and knew how to motivate and encourage me sufficiently for me to want to get back in the ring as soon as possible.

****

During the summer of 1960, the Olympics were being hosted in Rome and I was approaching my 14th birthday. Some 18-year-old lad called Cassius Clay had won the light heavyweight gold medal but in all honesty I didn't really know anything about him – although that would change soon enough.

The 1960s were branded 'The Swinging Sixties' but the East End was still suffering from post-war poverty. Whilst other areas of London had recovered at an incredible rate, many families in the East End were still living in corrugated iron housing shelters, which had now been transformed into barely liveable houses. The environment pushed the East End closer together as many tried to work out why they had been the victims of under-investment from the government.

Consequently, more and more people turned to boxing as a possible route to escape. Thankfully, my motivation to box was inspired by a deep-rooted belief that this was something I could actually become very good at, as opposed to the environment I grew up in.

I had entered the sport aged 11, achieved a number of amateur boxing accolades by 13 and then left school at the age of 14 to go into full-time work.

I did however realise a short while later that heavy labouring and intense boxing training don't mix well and that I would need to take better care of myself if I wanted to progress as a genuine boxing prospect.

Before my dad had the scrap business up and running at full steam, he used to work down the meat market. After nagging him to death asking if I could also get a job there, he took me down and got me a job in the poultry factory in Smithfield. I used to get up at four in the morning and finish about one or two in the afternoon and then I'd go training down the gym. I worked there for about six months and got on with everyone really well. When I used to box all the porters and other staff used to come and watch me.

Anyway, one day I was working away and just collapsed. They took me over to St Barts hospital and they said, "There's nothing wrong with you, just exhaustion." So I stopped working at the meat market and starting working for my nan in the fish business for a little while and then from there I moved into the scrap game.

By the age of 16 I won the National Ambition Boxing Championships (NABCs) but this was not without the help of my trainer Jackie Gubbins. Jackie was like the old man from the 'Rocky' movies and was a big reason for me winning so many accolades at amateur level.

Just when you started to doubt yourself, he would say something to make you feel indestructible. I remember being in the NABCs and the matchmaker was very concerned that I was fighting a lad called Reid, from south west London, who has just beaten the two Finnegans (Chris and Kevin – who later became recognised at world level). I was sitting with Jackie and he said to me, "Jim – I've been training boys at West Ham for 30 years, including Terry Spinks, Ron Barton and many other top guys, and you're the best. Now go out there and win this fight!"

He gave me such a pump-up that when I got in that ring I felt like Sugar Ray Leonard. I out-jabbed and out-boxed this lad, and won the bout convincingly. I'd like to state that as much as I was delighted with that compliment, I certainly didn't rate myself as the best, certainly not in comparison to the likes of Terry Spinks, Ron Barton and Billy 'The Kid' Davis.

After my successes at schoolboy level, I progressed to the Junior ABA finals at the Royal Albert Hall. The top fighters in Britain were all present such as Mark Rowe and Pat Dwyer. I got beaten in the finals by a Scottish boy, his name was Curry. No excuses, I didn't box him well. I remember looking at my dad and seeing him a little disappointed. You learn to live with the defeat. Again, it comes down to who's around you to help you get through it quicker.

****

I kept boxing, kept progressing and I really enjoyed it throughout my teenage years. By the time I was a senior, a fella called Chazzer Chapman was my matchmaker and his passion for the sport was unparalleled.

If it wasn't for him I would never have travelled the length and breadth of the UK and beyond.

He knew how to put on a good show and had a very warming personality about him which helped gain everybody's confidence. I can't think of a single person who ever had a bad word to say about him.

When I was 17, Chazzer took a group of us from West Ham Amateur Boxing Club to Paris, to take on their team in a tournament. It was one of the first times I'd been on an aeroplane and I had a big following, including my dad, my uncle, cousins and a number of mates including Frankie Simms and their support meant everything to me.

The whole of the West Ham team had got beaten and our trainer Jackie Gubbins came over to me and said, "Come on Jim. We've gotta have a winner tonight." And I won! Chazzer put my name on the map when I didn't even really need it and I'll always be thankful to him for that. I also remember my dad and uncle went to the Moulin Rouge on that trip and had bought back some programmes which my mum had the right hump over because most of the women featured were in the nude!

We had a return match with the team from Paris a few months later at West Ham Baths and they only had a big middleweight for me to fight but I still beat him comfortably. All good memories.

I also went to Copenhagen with the London boxing team and was drawn against a southpaw who wanted to stand and fight, but I thought to myself, 'Not tonight mate!' and I jabbed his head off instead, winning convincing.

I remember the hotel distinctly, not for any other reason apart from the quilt! Growing up in England, I was used to having sheets and blankets and I looked at what was on top of the bed and thought, 'What's this?!' It was lovely! That was the first time in my life that I'd slept on a bed with a quilt. However, another first I experienced was not so pleasant. The 18-hour journey home on the ferry tackling the high seas was more of a test than the fight I had just won. Rocking backwards and forwards and side to side put everybody's stomach to the test, apart from my dad's!

By the time we reached the UK we were all green and the mention of a fried breakfast would have put us all over the edge but dad was as fresh as a daisy.

****

I was now 17 and coming up for the senior ABAs. I had matured into a sharp boxer, weighing 11 stone, touching 6 feet in height and I was now ready for the seniors. In those days you would box as a novice, intermediate or 'open'.

Open meant that you could box anybody in the country or in the world come to think of it. I passed the novice category, had one intermediate fight and then went straight into open. When fighting at that level, you couldn't fight every week. They had to bring in people from all round the country and abroad. West Ham was recognised as one of the best boxing clubs in the world then so I boxed Italians, French, Spanish and a number of other nationalities.

Just before the London area finals, I was handed a great opportunity to spar with Billy Walker, who was a much loved British boxing idol.

As a junior amateur boxer, I distinctly remember the likes of Ralph Charles and Billy – as the headlining senior amateur bouts – having their names printed on all the posters at West Ham Baths. At the bottom of the poster it would sometimes have, 'Also featuring Jimmy Tibbs – junior boxer' and I used to think to myself, 'I'd love to see my name headlining on the bill one day as a senior'. That day came against Pat Dywer!

One day, Chazzer walked into West Ham Amateur Boxing Club and said to me, "Do you want to fight Pat Dwyer? It's a club show at West Ham Baths." That's one thing you never say to a fighter, "Do you want to fight?" because if he'd have said do you want to fight King Kong I would've been up for the challenge.

That's why they should always ask the trainer. The guys in the changing room asked if I was mad. When I went home and told my dad, he said, "Well you better get in that ring and fight him then."

At the time, Pat Dwyer was known for knocking people out and was often chosen to be filmed by the BBC because of his knockout power.

Although I lost the bout, I gave him the fight of his life and beat him all over the place in the last round especially. It was a great experience and certainly helped mould me into a better boxer.

Back to Billy Walker. Bert Spriggs, who used to run the Duke of Fife back then, was friends with somebody who knew George Walker, the brother and manager of Billy. George asked if I would like to have a spar with Billy, who like myself, was an ex-West Hammer. We sparred for a couple of rounds and as heavyweight pro versus a middleweight amateur, he didn't take any liberties. With his mop of blonde hair and boyish good looks, his nickname was 'Golden Boy', and he certainly was of the heavyweight division in the UK. He had just turned pro and every time he fought at Wembley, the place sold out.

I also sparred with Johnny Pritchett before the London Area finals for what turned out to be a magical training experience. Legendary radio and television boxing commentator Reg Gutteridge, who came from a boxing family, had seen me fight and – as a friend of Johnny – called up and asked if I would like to spar with him because he was getting ready to fight Wally Swift and they wanted partners with a good left jab.

I passed the phone to my dad and he agreed on the

understanding that Johnny did not take any liberties.

Consequently, I went over a couple of days later to the Butcher's Arms in North London, where Bobby Neill had all his fighters training, and sparred a couple of rounds with Johnny. After moving around the ring and feeling comfortable, I threw a left hook under his elbow, which made him drop his arm and then I slipped a left hook over the top. Over he went! I assumed he may have been off balance...

Reg Gutteridge was so pleased with the sparring session at the Butcher's Arms that he asked me to go away with Johnny on his training camp up in the North of England. My dad agreed as long as it was on the same terms.

I distinctly remember staying in Johnny's mum's house and being treated like one of the family. On the first day of camp, using the same punch combo, I sent Johnny to the canvas again!

Although Johnny went down, when he got up, he never took any liberties and he went on to beat Wally Swift and become a great British and Commonwealth champion. Unfortunately, I sprained my ankle soon after arriving at camp and had to come home. It was a great learning curve though, all doing our road work together and experiencing the life of a pro boxer as a teenage amateur and as corny as it sounds, I was living the dream. I was a massive fan of Alan Rudkin, who went on to become British, Commonwealth and European champion, not to mention challenging for the world title on three occasions, so to be on the road with him and Johnny was priceless.

My intention was to fight in the London ABA finals, but

before getting there I needed to focus on trying to win the North East London Divisional Championships.

The finals were held yet again at West Ham Baths, where I fought and beat a guy called Mickey Cain from Canvey Island, who would later go on to turn pro with Terry Lawless. I had three fights that night, with very little time in between each bout and Mickey was without doubt the strongest. I always remember him telling me after, "I won the last round" and I told him, "Maybe – but I won the first two!" I'd fought him three times over the years and he was a very tough fighter. You had to be on the top of your game to beat him and thankfully I was each time. Mickey was a very nice guy who later finished with a pro record almost identical to mine at 16-3-1.

****

There was a group of us who were hot favourites to win the senior ABAs. Myself, Mark Rowe, Ronnie Smith and Eric Blake. Mark Rowe was knocking people out, I was knocking people out and in *Boxing News* each week there would be a feature on at least one of us. Eric Blake was a very good fighter and went on to fight in the Olympics. I remember on one occasion when I fought him that he hit me with a right hand and I saw stars.

To this day, that's the hardest punch I've ever received. I managed to pull myself back together and beat him, and Mark Rowe would go on to beat him twice.

Me and Mark both won our London area titles and each

week, all the talk in the amateur boxing world was about who was going to win the London ABA finals.

Tibbs or Rowe? Rowe or Tibbs? Tibbs or Rowe?

Then we both got beaten!

There was only three of us in the semi-final and Ronnie Smith went straight through because Eric Blake hadn't turned up on the evening. Perhaps he was ill, but I never did find out. However, me and Mark went on to have the battle of all battles.

In my mind, in the build-up to the fight, I always knew it was going to be a hard night and I'm sure he was thinking the same.

We had both trained very hard and on the night we never stopped for three rounds. First round, I came out and had my strategy all set. I circled round him, throwing out a single jab, followed by a double and then threw the right hand, left hook and finished off with another jab, while he was trying to close me down and get me on the ropes.

Anybody who knows Mark Rowe also knows that he was a great body puncher, but that particular night I was genuinely not disturbed by his power.

First round was mine, but by the second round my eye had blown right out making it tough to see and that consequently made it a close round. As bad as my eye was the doctor didn't dare stop it, although in this day and age the fight would have been stopped without a doubt.

Mark won the third and final round, clinched the decision and consequently progressed to the next stage of the competition.

I had no complaints about the result, I shook his hand and congratulated him on his victory.

Mark was one of the strongest amateurs I'd ever fought and, just to clarify something, he has mentioned in other publications that we also fought when we were about 12. That's not true.

We were about 15 and I beat him at East Ham on a club show. The reason I know I was 15 is because Billy Walker (the trainer not boxer) had seen me fight against Mark and consequently asked me and my dad if I would spar with the professional boxer Brian Bissmire.

He's a good lad Mark, so I don't mean anything by clarifying this, but also want to point out that I couldn't have been sparring with Brian Bissmire at the age of 12!

Mark went on to have a good pro career, fighting 47 times, losing only eight times and becoming middleweight Commonwealth and British champion.

In terms of the ABAs, Ronnie Smith went through. He was a true man at that stage, with man strength, whereas, at the age of 17 I was pretty much a grown-up kid and he probably would have beaten me. Even though I turned pro at 19, I don't think I reached my 'man's strength' until I was between 25 and 30. Anyway, I got beaten, Mark Rowe then fought Ronnie Smith and got beaten so Ronnie then went on to get beaten by Pat Dwyer in the NABC finals.

****

My fight against Mark was my last amateur bout. Selling out

the Royal Albert Hall as teenagers in what was one of the best amateur battles for a long, long time was a great way to leave that side of my boxing career.

To summarise my career at that point – I won the Schoolboys for Great Britain twice, I was also NABC champion twice, a junior ABA finalist and the North East Divisional champion senior.

I spent the summer healing from my bruises following the Rowe fight and then headed back to the gym at the Duke of Fife in Forest Gate. I started training again but I think subconsciously I was already starting to think about the pro game.

What I didn't know then was I was on the cusp of some amazing opportunities – and a first, real taste of boxing fame.

Round 3

FACING THE GREATEST

"Tell Jimmy he needs to head to White City straight away. He's going to spar with the heavyweight champion of the world, Muhammad Ali!"
–Terry Lawless, boxing trainer, 1966

After my epic battle with Mark Rowe at the Royal Albert Hall, a great number of people started to speculate about whether I would turn pro and if so, who would manage, train and promote me.

After about 80 fights with only six losses as an amateur, I had the confidence to move forward, but I was also very aware that progress would only take place with the right team around me.

I had a number of offers and one of note – and not many

people know this – is that the Kray twins wanted to manage me. In addition to be being huge boxing fans, Ronnie and Reggie had also boxed professionally themselves, each having had six fights. They were known for doing everything together and apart from their first pro bout, they boxed on the same bills for their remaining five fights.

The twins showed promise and it's worth noting that they had their six fights in under five months. Reggie retired undefeated while Ronnie, although losing two fights (one via disqualification), won all of his fights by knockout. Their other brother Charlie also fought pro from 1948-1951 as a welterweight, winning 11 out of his 18 bouts.

This is how my meeting with the Krays unfolded.

An associate of the twins contacted my dad and asked if we could meet with them and my dad in turn mentioned to me that the Krays wanted to see me about turning professional with them.

I didn't have any big offers on the table at the time so we decided there was no harm in hearing what they were willing to propose.

My dad agreed and a few days later we jumped in the car and met them in a pub in Bethnal Green.

As we walked in, we saw Ronnie dressed immaculately in a tailored suit, standing at the bar with a few friends. Reggie was sitting at a table and walked over, shook mine and my dad's hands and then introduced us to Ronnie and a few of his friends.

Reggie then led us to a table in the corner of the pub, where we sat down and listened to his proposal and what he believed they could offer me as a pro boxer.

I wasn't drinking as I was boxing mad and keeping in peak condition, but my dad joined Reggie for a beer and they toasted to good health.

Reggie explained about the network of contacts he had within the boxing world, both within the UK and abroad. It was very interesting as I didn't know anything about professional boxing at that point, and the twins were notoriously well connected to some of the biggest names in history such as Joe Louis and Sonny Liston.

Although I knew of a great number of professional boxers, I had no idea of how I would move up from being an amateur and the hurdles which would present themselves during this move.

I had sparred in a number of professional gyms when I was an amateur, but that was about the extent of my knowledge.

Aged 18, I didn't know much about who the Kray twins were or what they were 'doing'.

They weren't really in the media at the time and certainly not in the way they were after they went to prison and in fact, ever since they died.

It seems like a million and one accounts of their life stories and specific anecdotes have surfaced and mine is another to add to the list!

From my episode, they were very nice to me. We listened to their offer and then went away to mull it over.

My dad went to see one of his friends who knew everyone in London, and he said "You want to think about what you're doing Jim. There's plenty of other people who could also make a good offer."

So we decided not to accept the proposal straight away and went in search of other potential managers to benchmark the Krays' proposal.

While looking for a boxing manager, I was unaware that somebody had actually been scouting me for a while from the shadows.

When I sparred with Brian Bissmire at the age of 15 at the Duke of Fife, Terry Lawless was starting to take note of my boxing ability.

As I became older and more physically developed, I started sparring with all the middleweights and it was at this point he had recognised my talent as a potential future professional.

I distinctly remember the moment when I decided to take the leap.

After finishing a workout, I was sitting down taking my hand wraps off, when Terry Lawless came over and said, "I'll give you a sum of money to turn pro with me."

I won't mention how much, but it was a respectable amount. I said, "I'll think about it."

I went home and spoke with my dad who said, "Tell Terry to give you twice as much." We knew Terry's reputation for looking after his fighters and also knew of the people he was working with, such as Mickey Duff and boxing promoters Mike Barrett and Harry Levene.

It would be a prudent move. I slept on the offer and went back the following evening and asked Terry to double the amount. He did and we shook hands!

The next night, me and my dad met with Mickey and Terry at the Green Man pub in Plashet Grove. My dad wanted to buy in to half of the contract, but they refused and said "Leave this to us Jim; we'd prefer to be in control." My dad laughed and said "No problem."

Terry pulled out the papers from a briefcase and I signed them.

Job done. Simple as that.

I was now a professional boxer.

Soon after, my dad went and met with Reggie Kray, but without me this time.

Reg really respected the fact that my dad went down in person to meet with him and explain the situation and Reg respected dad's decision 100 percent.

My dad's only concern was that Terry and Mickey would take care of me. And take care they did. Don't get me wrong, mistakes were made along the way, like matching me against guys who were much bigger than me, but those mistakes happen.

To be honest, I probably would have made identical errors if I was in their shoes.

Everybody thought I was going to be much bigger than I turned out to be. When I turned I pro, I weighed 11 stone 11 pounds. With my dad at that point being a little over 6ft 3in, 17 stone of muscle with massive hands and my mum standing at around 5ft 10in, everybody thought I was going to be following in his footsteps and growing into a natural heavyweight.

My brothers were also big guys, so who would have bet

against me following the pattern? Everybody used to talk so much about me growing into a heavyweight that after a while I almost believed it myself!

I never did get any bigger and although I was able to beat guys much bigger than me, as I stepped up in class I realised that I was naturally a 12-stone fighter. Super middleweight didn't exist back in those days, so I embarked on my professional career as a light heavyweight.

Thankfully my boxing style needed little adjustment from the amateur game.

In fact, I did most of the changes myself. Mickey Duff and Terry Lawless were good business people, but on the training front I would say I took care of myself. Making that leap from amateur to pro was as much a mental adjustment as it was physical.

To most people, going to the gym is something that keeps them fit. It can act as a social meeting place and the discipline is available, but not forced on them.

A professional boxing gym is a totally different place. Discipline is what makes champions and from the second you walk in, the differences you will notice are the smells, the work rate, the sharp sounds of punches making contact on bags and pads, and the sounds of boxers breathing heavily after they have finished a session.

This is not about boot camp or getting a personal training session, this is a way of life that every professional boxer signs up to and I knew that if I wanted to make it to the top, I had to be willing to live the tough life and make those sacrifices.

It's certainly not for everybody.

All this said, because I'd been sparring with the pros since I was 15, I quickly got to grips with the regime. The main differences an amateur has to deal with are usually around planting your feet more, increasing your power and slowing the plan down overall. The point system at amateur level focuses more on 'in and out' strategies, whereas the pro game certainly has more focus on power.

Don't get me wrong, I didn't know everything as a pro.

As you go along, you learn to relax while in the ring. When you're relaxed, you're saving energy and your mind is alert.

Thankfully I was already blessed with the ability to punch hard. With a few adjustments, I was able to work on that foundation and build up a number of combinations, and also work on my defence for what would potentially be harder incoming attacks.

****

A new exciting chapter in my life had just started. My debut had now been agreed. I would be fighting on February 22, 1966, against Eddie Lennon, who had fought 14 times at pro level, half of which he had won.

We didn't have access to video footage in those days and the internet was decades away in terms of being able to cruise the likes of YouTube to research who you would be sharing a ring with.

What we did have was Mickey Duff.

Mickey's knowledge in boxing was unbelievable. He knew

what your opponent had for breakfast, lunch and dinner a year before. He was better than YouTube! I knew all I needed to know about Mr Lennon, and all my opponents in fact, thanks to Mickey.

The fight was set for the Royal Albert Hall, the venue of my last battle against Mark Rowe, and it would be a six-rounder. I was hungrier than I had ever been in my life.

I wanted to get into that ring and bring my opponent to their destruction. It was nothing personal towards Eddie Lennon, I didn't even know the guy. It was just a fact that the man who stepped through those ropes would be the person on the receiving end of a fighter who had a great deal of energy to release.

The fact that I lost my last fight at the same venue was a reason why I needed to make my next opponent pay. Not having an amateur or professional fight in over a year was getting on my nerves and was another reason why I couldn't wait to step through the ropes.

With boxing now providing me with a salary, the person in front of me in that ring was also a threat to my wages so there was no shortage of motivation or reasons to fuel the fire burning inside me.

At the time, I was living with my dad's brother, my uncle Bogey and his wife, my aunt Annie, and their children, my cousins. They used to look after me like I was their own son. His daughter Jane even made me a red under gown which I wore for the ring entrance. The scene was set, the props were in place – I was ready for action.

By the night of the fight I was focused, calm, fit and ready to take on anybody. Eddie Lennon was 32, while I was only 19. Boy versus man? No chance. One hour before the fight, I was in my changing room loosening up and they were putting the Vaseline on me. They don't allow you to use Vaseline all over the body now because it blocks the pores but in those days they used to smother you in it!

I did a bit of shadow boxing, then waited for my name to be called out. I had a little bit of nerves, but nothing too bad. Terry Lawless wrapped my hands and then they started getting me mentally in the zone. "Relax Jim. Get that jab going."

As the house fighter I entered the ring second and received a great round of applause. My first applause as a pro! Terry had his hand on my shoulder as the referee was reading out the instructions – I was buzzing. I had won a number of amateur championships, but this was as exciting as fighting in the ABA finals for me.

Although walking into the ring nearer to the middleweight limit than the light heavy, I felt very confident. Taking Terry's advice into the ring, I moved around, sticking my jab solidly into Eddie's face, whilst still having a look at him and working out his weaknesses. I landed some big body shots which I could see put Lennon in trouble. I didn't have to analyse too long thankfully, as I knocked him out in the second round.

Let's not get carried away though. Lennon was a journeyman. I hadn't just fought Carlos Monzon.

This was one of the most exciting times of my young life. I remember we went back to a pub in Stratford afterwards, purely family and friends, I wasn't drinking, but we all had a great night and I thought to myself, 'You've done the right thing turning pro Jim, and gone with the right people'. There were some good fighters on the bill, including Ralph Charles and Brian Curvis and the media was great to pick up on the latest scoops.

Peter Wilson from the *Daily Mirror* was present that evening.

A boxing journalist of the highest calibre before he died in 1981, Peter had covered some of the most iconic fights in boxing history, ranging from Max Schmeling against Joe Louis in the 1930s to Ali versus Joe Frazier in New York in 1971.

So you can imagine how thrilled I was when I got a mention in his write-up the day after, talking about a young kid named Jimmy Tibbs, who was an up-and-coming prospect. It was the icing on the cake.

My next fight, only seven days later, would be against Joe Sommerville. I was 1-0 and was relishing the opportunity to jump straight back into the ring but after my second round knockout first time out, I tried to go for it again and I started getting extremely frustrated because I couldn't catch him clean.

As a veteran of 67 bouts, I think he sensed my impatience and started messing me about, pulling me around and making it difficult for me to land clean shots.

I won the fight as a clear winner on points and the experience of going the distance was certainly a valuable outing.

Having Terry Lawless as a matchmaker was also a godsend

as he was fuelling my hunger for this sport and provided me with two more outings in April against Billy Thompson and Tommy Woods, both of which I won by knockout in the second and first rounds respectively.

Billy and Tommy fought most of their boxing careers as fully fledged heavyweights, so I was certainly happy with the venom in my punch power so early on in my career.

****

Life was fantastic. I was 19, not even three months into my professional boxing career and I was looking at extending my record to 5-0.

But then life got even better.

At the time, the big fight on the horizon for all boxing fans around the world was the rematch between Henry Cooper and Muhammad Ali. I had seen Ali fight on the television and was very impressed with how he was able to predict what round he would knock his opponent out in.

He had been a relatively unrecognised boxer in Britain until he had had his first fight with Henry Cooper in 1963. I remember Ali, or Cassius Clay as he was then, winning the light heavyweight gold medal at the 1960 Olympics. However, compared to Terry Spinks, he was not a big name – certainly not around Canning Town!

His first fight with Henry didn't do him any favours as he got caught with a jaw-crunching left hook at the end of the fourth round and the bell pretty much saved Ali that night.

If it had happened early in the round he may well have

lost the fight. The vulnerability of one of boxing's biggest personalities had been exposed and although he clinically finished Henry Cooper off in the next round, Ali – or Clay! – was the heavy underdog going into his next fight with Sonny Liston.

I remember watching the Ali versus Liston fight on a black and white TV with a snowy reception and it was at that moment I realised this guy was something special as he challenged for the world heavyweight title.

I was about 16 at the time. It was on about 3am, I'd just come back from a mate's house and I watched the fight with my old man in front of the TV.

Ali was fantastic.

I've since watched the fight again and it looks even better now because as I've matured, I've learnt to appreciate in finer detail what he managed to achieve that night.

The way he dismantled Liston, the 60s equivalent of Mike Tyson, was amazing.

At 15 stone, Clay's speed was unrivalled, and although he didn't possess one punch knockout power, he proved that he would get you with the next one, and the one after that.

After confirming to the world by beating Liston the second time, albeit in controversial fashion, that he was no fluke, he changed his name to Muhammad Ali, and the rest as they say is history.

Ali was meant to be great and he was great. A boxing idol of the highest order.

I had never, ever thought that a kid of my age was going to meet THAT man, let alone spar with him.

Not any heavyweight champion of the world, but THE heavyweight champion of the world.

But that is what happened. And it is something I've never forgotten.

It came about like this.

I was helping put up a fence for a mate of my dad's at a scrapyard in Stratford when my cousin's husband drove over and said, "Jim, I've got your gear in the bag, Terry Lawless has called up, you've got to go to White City to spar with Muhammad Ali." I said, "Lovely!"

Although this was just a bit of light exercise for Ali, Mickey Duff wanted to make sure that I wouldn't come out of that ring black and blue.

I followed Mickey as we walked over and met the legendary trainer Angelo Dundee. Mickey said, "Angelo – just so you know, Jimmy only weighs 166 pounds." Ali was about 210 at the time. Angelo said, "Mickey. Don't worry. Everything is going to be ok!"

With my head guard firmly strapped on and Jimmy Ellis's cup in place – someone had forgotten to pack mine so I borrowed Jimmy's – I touched gloves with Ali and started the sparring session.

I threw a few jabs and can't have been in the ring for more than a couple minutes when all of a sudden, down he went!

I'd hardly touched him.

All the photographers were scrambling like mad to take the shot.

Click, click, click! A picture and a dramatic feature talking about the 'knockdown' made it to the *New York Times* sports pages and was published on May 12, 1966:

'Clay's Flop Makes a Hit in London.
'Feigned Knockdown Delights Fans at Training Drill.'

"Cassius Clay, in training for his heavyweight title defence against Henry Cooper May 21, was knocked down twice by a 19-year-old sparring partner today. But it was only a part of Clay's act.

"An enthusiastic crowd of about 300 turned out to see the champion at work. After three brisk rounds with his usual sparring partner, Jimmy Ellis, Clay stepped into the ring with Jimmy Tibbs of London, who had turned professional in January.

"Tibbs, a light heavyweight, was obviously in awe of the champion. At one point Clay held the young boxer by the shoulders and allowed him to throw punches at his stomach for 30 seconds."

This article made history as I was the first British fighter to ever be featured on the front page of the prestigious *New York Times*.

Ali was playing around, but the attention I received was incredible, and I momentarily had a taste of what it would be like to be a world champ under the spotlight.

I didn't really chat much with Ali on the day.

He was deep into training, but he didn't try to embarrass me or take any liberties, which was handy as he was a big heavyweight and I was a super middleweight really. The whole episode was incredible but it wasn't until years passed and he became a boxing legend that I appreciated the experience that much more and the boxing fraternity refer to it now as a proud piece of British boxing history.

****

Surely my life couldn't get any better than this?

A few days after sparring with Muhammad Ali, Terry gave me a call and told me I would be fighting a guy called Tom Calderwood. I was thrilled as I'd only fought a couple of weeks before. Then there was a gap of silence as Terry then said, "You will be fighting Calderwood on the undercard of Ali v Cooper at Highbury!"

To say I was delighted was an understatement. I would be showcasing my boxing skills in front of an audience that most people could only dream of.

Boxing promoter Harry Levene had taken on a tall order to sell out a football stadium, but he had achieved his goal and then some.

The tickets for the evening had sold out. Ringside seats were about £11 each – approximately the cost of a boxing programme these days!

The weigh-in was in Leicester Square at the Odeon on the morning of the fight. Henry Cooper and Ali weighed in first and then I was up a short while after. There were thousands of people there to see the champ. The atmosphere was crazy and we hadn't even seen a ring yet!

On the day of mine and Ali's respective fights, I remember Terry and Mickey Duff taking me to see Henry before he was going out.

As much as I really wanted to see Henry, I actually didn't

want to go into his changing room because I didn't want to bother him. He was laying down when I walked in but he then sat up, we had a chat about that night's fights and we wished each other luck. He was a very, very polite man, a real gentleman.

My time was rapidly approaching and although this was not a title fight, the fact that I was fighting on the world heavyweight champion's undercard meant it was not far off in my eyes.

There was loads of pressure on me to perform as a great number of eyes were looking at me and I was searching for any advantage I could get before stepping through the ropes.

The changing rooms at Arsenal Football Club were very long and I remember before the fight, sitting there watching Johnny Pritchett fighting against Johnny Kramer through the wooden slats at the end of the room.

It had been drizzling with rain most of the evening and I noticed the canvas was extremely slippery and both fighters were all over the place trying to get a grip. Back in those days we used leather boots with hard soles. So I got a pair of scissors and cut up the soles so I could get extra grip. As I was doing this, the boxing promoter Harry Levene came into the changing room. As he came near to me I put my boots down, stood up to shake hands and he said to me, "Sit down son, you're gonna be a star."

I can't describe how much that pumped me up, but I was ready to take on anybody at that point. It's not as if that evening and the build up had not been big enough as it stood, but to get that comment from Harry made me feel totally indestructible.

The moment had arrived for me to make my way to the ring. Terry Lawless and my cornerman George Wicks were walking with me, when all of a sudden we heard a big roar from thousands of people in the crowds. Me, Terry and George all stopped and looked over our shoulders and then all around us, thinking to ourselves, 'Maybe we mistimed our entrance and Ali or one of the big names had just walked out'.

Then we all realised.

No mistiming – the applause was for me! I had built up a loyal fanbase over the years, but it wasn't until this evening that I was aware of just how large it had become and more to the point, how enthusiastic! I felt the hairs on the back of my neck standing on end, and I looked down to see goose pimples on my arms.

Knowing it was certainly not cold, I realised it was excitement running through my body and I felt like I was gliding into the ring. This was a once in a lifetime experience.

As I stepped through the ropes, I had a brief glimpse at the sea of people in attendance. Initially I was concerned about the state of the canvas but thankfully it wasn't as bad as it had looked when Kramer and Pritchett fought. Although I was intensely focused, I couldn't help take in a few key faces.

The people at ringside resembled an audition for the next Hollywood blockbuster. The likes of Elizabeth Taylor, Richard Burton, Sean Connery, Diana Dors, Eric Sykes, Rocky Marciano and Ingmar Johansson were just a few of the people who were only a few feet away from me.

What an honour for me to fight in front of such a distinguished audience.

As I stepped through the ropes of the open air ring, I saw Calderwood in the corner waiting for me. From good fighting stock, Tom's brother Chic Calderwood was also a talented boxer.

Chic had won the British and Commonwealth titles and later that year challenged Jose Torres for the WBC and WBA world titles. Sadly he died at the young age of 29 in a car accident a month after fighting Torres. Very tragic.

After dancing around the ring to get a feel for the size and to also make sure I was comfortable with the grip on my shoes, we were called to the centre.

The ring announcer gave all the formal introductions and then the referee gave us our instructions. I walked back to my corner and in those days they gave you a big lump of resin, which was placed into a tray in your corner and you would tread it into your boots for extra grip. Away we go.

As the bell sounded, I made my way to the centre of the ring. Next thing I know, I'm on the canvas! The knockdown was half-punch, half-slip, but certainly of no concern to me.

I looked at my corner and let them know I was alright, then got straight up. Just as I've come to terms with coming off the canvas, Calderwood puts me straight back on it again, this time with a valid punch and a more convincing knockdown. I was shocked but not hurt. Certainly not an ideal start, especially in front of this type of audience.

As I came out of the corner for round two, with a couple of knockdowns against me on the scorecards, I knew I had to turn this fight around. I decided to use a tactic which I would pass on to many of my fighters in years to come (Nigel Benn being a great example).

I laid back on the ropes and threw a couple of jabs. Giving the impression that I might be a little fragile after the first round, he went to open up on me with some hard hitting hooks. A great friend of mine, Frankie Simms, used to say, "When Jim's back hit the ropes, it was like he received an electric shock." My intention was to never get hit while on the ropes, but entice the fighter over so that I could move side to side and then use their power to counter them.

Calderwood was obviously very confident after the previous round and must have thought this was the opportunity to finish me off. I had led him into a false sense of security and just as he started to unload I hit him straight through the middle, whack, whack, whack and BANG. Job done.

I never forget Mickey Duff saying, "That's good Jim. When you get knocked down and come back and knock them out, that's even better!"

A few years later Ali would use a similar tactic against George Foreman. I think he might have learnt that from me. (Joke!)

After digesting my win I was very fortunate to then watch Cooper take on Ali and although Henry tried and tried he couldn't get near Ali and that meant he couldn't get his left hook (also known as 'Henry's Hammer') to work this time.

Ali was dancing around and punching at will. He was the quickest, most skilful boxer on the planet. He was simply too good.

No disrespect to Henry, as one of the greatest heavy-weights this country has ever produced, but Ali was in different league. It was like Henry was shaking hands with a ghost.

Ali would go on to shock the boxing world the year after. Unfortunately, not for his incredible skills in the ring, but for refusing to fight in the Vietnam War and consequently not signing up for the draft.

His penalty was a three-and-a-half year exile from boxing at his peak and he would not fight again until October, 1970 when he returned to the ring for his famous bouts against the likes of Joe Frazier and George Foreman.

On the Jimmy Tibbs front, my life was pretty much perfect.

On June 26, 1966, little over a month after the Calderwood fight, I got married to my childhood sweetheart. I first met Claudette when I was 14. We grew up together, only a couple of roads apart. I lived in Tarling Road and she lived in Morgan Street. Funnily enough, with all the urban regeneration that has gone on in the local area, both of our houses still exist.

It's a well-known fact that I don't major on being soppy, but dare I say, on seeing Claudette, it was love at first sight. For me anyway! She left me hanging for a couple of weeks after we first met. We used to go to this little club called St Margaret's. It was just next door to a big block of flats in Canning Town and was a hub for me and my mates to hang out. Everybody used to dance – except me that is! After a few weeks of my 'sit-down on a chair' dance style, somehow we got chatting and started officially seeing each other.

We got married in St Margaret's church on the Barking Road in Canning Town. There was a good turnout including Mickey Duff, Terry Lawless, and our friends and families. Yet just two days later I was back in the ring.

****

1966 was a good time to be a sportsman and especially one in England. While I was extending my unbeaten record to 6-0, the English football team managed to win their first (and only!) World Cup.

I wasn't as mad on football as some of my mates because boxing was my main passion but the win and the atmosphere of 1966 captured the attention of a whole nation, for lovers and non-lovers of football.

It was beautiful to be in the East End after the victory as English flags hung out from most windows and loads of street parties took place as the area made sure the victory was celebrated to its full potential.

Boxing was always my first sport but during this amazing period, I did once have the honour of meeting one of the best English players of all time.

I was training at the Royal Oak gym a few weeks after the final, when Terry Lawless told me he was going to introduce me to a legend.

I thought to myself, 'I've already met Muhammad Ali'. Well, it was at this point I realised there actually be can be more than one legend living at any one time. Terry took me down to Upton Park and I had my photo taken with Bobby Moore. Sir Bobby, as he would become known a few years later, was a true gentleman.

The photo made it into the local newspaper and I was still having to pinch myself as I looked over my shoulder to check that the events of Jimmy Tibbs and 1966 were actually real.

My next fight saw me beat Hugh Lynch at the Empire Pool in Wembley. Although Lynch was a tricky southpaw and with a crouching stance, I had no problems overcoming his style.

I was in peak condition for that fight, and by the time I reached rounds five and six I was just starting to warm up. Catching him with some corking uppercuts and working strong behind the jab, I controlled the fight as I wanted to.

The BBC television commentator made it sound much better than it was though, declaring, "Tibbs is something like an octopus the way he covers up and smothers when his opponent comes in close."

As the referee held up my hand after the final bell of the Lynch bout, I felt content with my performance and was already looking forward to my next outing.

1966 ended with two further fights – and wins – as I fought and beat Ernie Field and Chris Cox, two impressive fighters who I respected a lot.

I was now 9-0 and felt fantastic.

But boxing has a way of humbling any man and I was no different as I tasted my first pro defeat next time out.

It arrived against Johnny Ould, on January 17, 1967, at the

Royal Albert Hall. Everybody thought I would be all over him and possibly even knock him out.

Johnny was a natural light heavyweight and was twice the size of me on that day. I just couldn't get to him and although the scorecards showed it was close, I'm the first person to say he beat me fair and square.

It hurt.

Whilst trying to digest the narrow defeat in the changing room, an up-and-coming film star who had been watching the fight knocked on my door and said, "Just checking that you are alright? You fought a great fight this evening." I replied politely, "Yes, and thank you." I recognised him. He was tall, wearing a sharp suit and had a distinctive voice.

He seemed familiar, but I genuinely didn't know who he was.

The penny soon dropped afterwards. It was none other than 007, Sean Connery! As far as compliments go, that one will be one of my lifetime best, if not the most memorable.

One of the downsides to boxing in those days was that the correct support for fighters after they lost never seemed to be in place.

The changing room after a fight can become a very lonely place. I was lucky to have a great family to console me but my father simply didn't know anything about the emotions involved in losing. He couldn't understand why I got beaten.

This is where I could have done with somebody to say, "Jim. Don't worry. That's only one fight. You'll bounce back. Besides, you're a natural middleweight, not a light heavy. Come on. Let's get you down to weight and you are going to get back in that ring and back to your winning ways."

I had nobody to say things like that then, but that's a big part of what I would offer to my boxers as a trainer, in years to come.

Don't get me wrong, Mickey Duff was trying to be nice by saying, "Don't worry, you'll be ok", but he was a very busy businessman and had to concentrate on his next three or four promotions he had coming up. I'm not having a go at Mickey or Terry, but that's how it was done in those days. The managers and promoters had their jobs to do and part of their role was not consoling their fighters.

As years passed, I would witness more and more trainers concentrating on ensuring their fighters were not left in limbo after a loss. In my opinion, this part of boxing strategy is as important, if not more important, than all the hard work and preparation in the gym. If a fighter finishes a fight with a bad taste in their mouth and a weaker state of mind going into their next fight, it is as bad as carrying an injury.

****

Terry and Mickey Duff didn't give me a great deal of time to reflect on the Ould loss. In their eyes it was a learning experience and I certainly didn't take any punishment during the fight.

Within no time, Terry had organised my next bout for March, 1967, and I would be fighting at the Royal Albert Hall again. I was determined to get back to my winning ways and show everybody I was the real deal.

Terry however, was not intent on giving me an easy ride! They brought over this guy from Italy called Gianfranco Macchia. He was like a little Rocky Marciano, and went on to win the Italian light heavyweight title twice over, a few years after our encounter.

I had him wobbled in the first round and was going to work on him in the corner, but I just couldn't finish him off as he was still alert.

Then there was a clash of heads in the second round and I was cut badly over my left eye, which caused problems as the blood was running into my vision. That clash left me with a visible scar which I carry to this day. I realised at that point that I could not take the risk of allowing this cut to jeopardise my chances of not finishing the fight so I turned up the pressure another notch. Jab jab, right hand left hook, jab jab, walk round him.

As I came out for the sixth round, the referee stepped in and gave Terry one more round to stop the bleeding. I realised what needed doing and threw the jab followed by an uppercut, which landed flush. It rocked him straight away. I thought, 'I've got him here!'

So I got in again, jab jab and another big uppercut and rocked him again. I didn't think he would be able to stand for another one. Jab jab jab and BANG another big uppercut. He went crashing into the ropes and I ran to the neutral corner and I thought to myself, 'PLEASE stay down. I'm begging ya!' But he got up again!

I tore into him one last time and the referee jumped in and stopped it as Macchia collapsed. The crowds were going wild for what had been a truly epic tear up.

That was the first loss on Gianfranco's record and in his next 20 outings he would only lose one more fight. Years later, in the capacity of a boxing trainer, while taking out one of my fighters (Pat Clinton) for a European title fight, I bumped into Macchia's promoter.

He didn't realise who I was at first, but when I told him my name, he instantly remembered the fight and was delighted to have had the chance encounter. We struck up a bit of a friendship and I met with him on my next two visits to Italy soon after.

My next outing was against a French lad called Daniel Leullier, who I drew against on April 17, 1967. It was the first and only draw on my record. I suffered a broken nose early in the fight. It was the first time I had suffered a broken nose and I can confirm it's not a pleasant experience!

Despite that, I was soon back in the ring against a tough Tunisian called Mahmout Le Noir who I managed to put away in the fourth round.

That win was the best medicine for my nose and I went into my next fight with Guinea Roger in September, 1967, in good spirits.

However, I then suffered my first ever knockout from a good left hook in the second round. Again, boxing will put you in your place, every chance it gets.

****

My corner should have made the decision a long time before

this fight, but in my mind, this loss highlighted that I was fighting in a division above my natural weight.

I therefore decided to drop down to middleweight on my next fight against Clive Tranter and I soon got the better of him in the third round, a win that boosted my self-esteem after coming off the knockout loss to Roger.

I was then back in the ring against a tough Nigerian, Joe Nwansi, in February, 1968, only 14 days after beating Tranter.

After dropping down a weight division I had certainly not lost the strength and if anything, the drop had improved my speed.

As a light heavyweight who fought most of his time around the 11 stone 11 pounds mark, I felt very comfortable making the 11 stone 8 pounds limit for non-title weight. 11 stone 6 pounds was title weight and Terry was happy with me coming in a couple of pounds over. I only had to cook down a few pounds from my natural weight, and keep an eye on my diet.

Well – what we thought was a diet! Looking back on the food we fuelled ourselves with in those days, it was suicide. We didn't have energy drinks or protein shakes, or anybody to advise the best time to feed or take on fluids.

I would eat meat, greens and water, and that was that. I guess I should have had the odd potato here and there, but I didn't have a clue what carbs or protein were in those days.

I boxed Joe in Shoreditch and suffered a broken jaw in the first round from a right hand – the only right hand he probably connected with in the whole fight!

At that point I didn't know I had a broken jaw, but I distinctly remember the second it connected, because the crowd went completely silent, wondering if I was going to fall. I'd already been knocked out once before in Shoreditch, so I'm sure the crowd was wondering if lighting was striking twice.

Thankfully all the punch did was shake me up a bit, and I got through the round.

Terry Lawless gave me clear instructions in between rounds one and two, in terms of how to wear him down. I listened intently and I got to work on him for the next seven rounds. I found it hard to get my reach with this guy, but then in the eighth I pinned him into my corner and unloaded on him.

Double hooks, right hands, uppercuts, you name it. The ref had seen enough and stepped in.

I didn't feel that much discomfort during the fight, but when I woke up the next morning, the jaw was severely swollen.

Claudette made me some eggs and bacon, but I just couldn't bite anything. I tried eating some porridge, but even found that difficult. I called Terry up and he took me round to the hospital. I remember my jaw swelling badly when I got to hospital and later that evening my dad came round to visit me with a mate of his.

I never forget that moment, because the second he saw my face, he became emotional.

They gave me 16 injections to numb the pain, and then kept me in for a week as they went to work on repairing the damage.

The jaw was then wired up, and stayed that way for the next couple of months, which ensured I would not be boxing for a while.

All I could do was suck soup through a straw for about a month. I soon got tired of this diet so thankfully, my dad being a resourceful guy, managed to find a way to adjust the wire holding my jaw together, so I could eat some Chinese food!

After a month of soup, that meal tasted delicious and it also cheered me up to be able to eat something different!

Although I never thought about retiring, I did on a few occasions think to myself, 'Is it all worth it?'

I suppose I was just down in the dumps and, again, that's when I could have done with the consolation from somebody who knew boxing, who could have told me that it was not the end of the world and how we would move forward and continue to be winners.

Following the Joe Nwansi fight, I spent until the autumn of 1968 recovering from a broken jaw and getting back into shape.

I was looking in good condition and I felt ready to get back in the ring. After careful discussion with Terry and Mickey Duff, I got back into full-time training again and was scheduled to fight at the American Sporting Club in January, 1969, against an unconfirmed opponent.

So what happened?

Why did that fight never take place?

Well, the Tibbs family were about to enter into a long running feud with a family called the Nicholls. And the conflict would involve violence at levels I had never before witnessed or could ever have thought possible.

Round 4

TROUBLED TIMES

"There was never a bad peace, or a good war."
– Benjamin Franklin, 1783

There's an old expression, "actions speak louder than words." And so do their consequences – as I would later find out. The irony is that words are usually always the root of any actions.

On December 7, 1968, my uncle Bogey was having a drink in the Steamship pub in Poplar with a few mates when he ended up getting into an argument with a man called Albert Nicholls.

Albert made a derogatory remark about myself which my uncle responded to and consequently got a punch in the face for his troubles.

After being hit, my uncle said, "Is that the best you can do?

If my nephew Jimmy was here, he'd flatten you." And with that Albert responded by laying into my uncle.

He suffered two black eyes and lost a couple of teeth. The man was in his early 20s and my uncle was 65 – it was an unfair fight.

Even if Bogey was not a relation, I would've stepped in to what was a liberty being taken by a younger, fitter and stronger man.

This episode would turn out to be the start of a sad series of events which would eventually land me behind bars.

Soon after, I was told of what had happened and wanted to pay Albert a visit, to let him know he could not get away with this.

It was the early hours of a cold December morning and me and two friends drove over to the minicab office in Poplar where Albert worked.

I had a shotgun in my hand as we entered the office.

The reason for bringing the gun was to put the frighteners on the bloke.

Not to shoot him.

To be honest, I didn't even know if the gun was loaded or not. I soon found out though, as I took the butt and hit Albert in the face with it.

On contact, the shotgun went off, which sent everyone into a panic.

I checked to see if anybody in the room had been shot. Thankfully we were all unharmed. A struggle then occurred, where Albert tried to take the gun of me and unfortunately it accidentally went off again and he suffered injuries to his leg this time. I didn't want Albert dead, but I certainly wasn't sorry that he had suffered an injury.

We left him on the floor in pain, but not with life threatening injuries, and walked out quickly.

As we were walking back home, a police car screeched up at high speed beside us and four officers jumped out and said, "Don't move. Put your hands behind your head." We were nicked. I'm guessing somebody must have instantly called the police on hearing the gunfire.

The whole episode happened incredible quickly.

Within minutes another three cars had arrived, one for each of us.

They wanted to make sure we did not communicate with each other and fabricate a different series of events. They didn't need to, because when we arrived at the station, we confessed straightaway.

We had nothing to hide, as we had not started the first attack. Aware of what we had done, we were willing to take the consequences of our actions.

This was the first time we had been arrested in our lives and didn't want to get into further trouble if we could help it.

We were arrested on the Friday and spent the next three nights in a police cell, before appearing in the magistrates' court on the Monday.

The van which took us from the police station to the court-house had separate cages inside and was like of a battery hen pen on wheels. We didn't say a word for the whole journey.

We were then remanded in custody and spent the next nine months in Brixton prison. It felt like a lifetime.

Although we had not been sentenced, it was the first time I'd ever experienced something like this and at the age of 22 was hoping it would also be the last.

Finally, our court hearing arrived and we were assuming the outcome was not going to be good. Mr Justice Lyell at the Old Bailey said:

"You have been guilty apart from anything else of the most appalling folly. I sympathise with your feelings but at the same time, living in the part of London where you live [there] is a great deal too much violence."
(James Morton, 'East End Gangland')

At this point we thought the judge was leading up to the line of, "You've been sentenced to..." but the tide was thankfully about to turn in our favour.

The prosecution had discussed our case with the defence panel and had taken into account that we had never previously had a brush with the law and decided to give us a plea bargain.

A plea bargain is when the defendant agrees to plead guilty in return for some form of concession from the prosecutor. We were acquitted of attempted murder, but sentenced to two years imprisonment, which was suspended for three years.

Our legal brief then turned to us and said, "Would you like to go home now?" We looked at each other a little confused and said, "What?" He then said, "You are free to go home." We looked at each other again, smiled, and then started laughing and said, "Thank you!"

We would have agreed to anything at that point to get home. As with many stages of my life, the boxing fraternity were there to support me before, during and after this episode. Terry Lawless and Mickey Duff came to the Old Bailey and a number of other well respected boxing names such as Denny Mancini also showed up.

Their support was much appreciated and showed their friendship extended past a boxing ring.

As I walked out of the courthouse, Albert Nicholls wanted to shake hands with me. I refused, walked away, headed home, and looked at embracing my second chance in life. I had committed a stupid revenge attack and a big lesson had been learnt.

Or so I thought.

****

It was almost two years before I stepped into the ring again. Terry and Mickey wanted me to get back in the gym immediately but I wasn't keen so soon after being released, simply because I was a little shaken up and not in the best frame of mind.

Thankfully with their persistence and belief, they eventually got me back in training a few months later.

My friend Frankie Simms helped get me back into shape by picking me up at the crack of dawn most days and then driving me to Wanstead Flats where I would run about six miles. He was so dedicated to that commitment and he would often come straight out of a nightclub at four or five in the morning, jump in his Mini (car that is, not skirt!) and take me for my run.

My first fight of 1970 would be against a journeyman called Ray Hassan at the Royal Albert Hall on January 20. The bill was packed with some great names.

The headliner was a rematch of Mark Rowe and Pat Dwyer. Mark repaid the favour to Pat, knocking him out in the fourth.

Joe Bugner then beat Johnny Prescott on points and future world champ John H Stracey knocked out Tommy Carson, in his fifth pro fight.

I was also back to my explosive winning ways.

On my return to the ring, as a strong middleweight, I knocked out Ray Hassan in four rounds and then three weeks later knocked out Billy Deasy on February 10, in the second round.

A fortnight later, I took on a seasoned boxer by the name of Johnny Kramer. Although Johnny was nearing the end of his career, he used to hold the Southern Area belt, and at 29 still had a lot to give.

We were both Canning Town fighters, so the prospect of a derby on East London's doorstep at the York Hall helped to sell the place out.

In those days we used thumbless gloves which basically meant there was no padding over the thumb. He caught me accidentally with his thumb and I couldn't see out of one eye for three rounds so I spent most of the time during those rounds bobbing and weaving. He caught me with a couple of strong right hands bang smack in the middle of my forehead, but he never moved me.

Once the eye had cleared, I went to work on him. The decision was close, but I was confident I had done enough to win, and thankfully the referee saw it that way also. I stayed in contact with Johnny and in fact we are still good friends today.

****

My very last professional fight was a rematch with Ray Hassan, who I'd fought two months earlier. It was March 24, 1970.

It turned out I would be having two battles that evening. One in the ring, and one inside myself. I remember being in the dressing room and not feeling up to the task. I didn't say anything, but Terry Lawless could tell I wasn't 100 percent and brought the doctor in. They all stared at me.

Terry and the doctor had a chat and then told me everything was ok, and to have my fight with Ray. I did the business and stopped him in five rounds.

It wasn't until after the fight Terry Lawless said to me "You've got shingles Jim." I didn't even know what shingles was at that point, but soon found out it was connected to being run down.

Looking back on it, I probably should have had a bigger gap after the Kramer fight. I trained very hard for that one and it took a lot out of me.

It made sense though, as I felt exhausted, having one fight on top of another. After the Nwansi contest I had been tempted by a break from boxing after feeling that I was not being properly looked after and the shingles episode had helped further make my decision to retire.

Putting all that hard work in the gym and not giving myself a break had finally caught up with me.

Taking all this on board, I decided the risk versus return was not worth my health and I decided to hang the gloves up on May 8, 1970.

It was then that life really took a turn for the worse.

****

After having earlier served my time on remand for the shotgun incident, I had no intention of ever seeing the inside of a cell again and I just wanted to get back into my boxing – plain and simple.

And when writing my book, I was actually quite happy to skip over this part of my life at speed.

However, I have decided to put pen to paper and share what happened in order to put the record straight on a few fronts.

There are a number of books which have given accounts of the violent episodes in my life and unfortunately many are factually incorrect.

Over the years I have become sick and tired of reading what other people assumed happened in my life, who was involved and worst of all, trying to glamorise the violent content. I know what happened in my life. I was there!

Soon after retiring from boxing, a nasty series of events started to unfold, which started to mould a very dark part of my future.

On a cold misty Saturday night in November, 1970, while sitting at home watching the TV, somebody knocked on my front door to let me know that one of my brothers had been attacked at the Rose of Denmark pub in Canning Town. Somebody had come up behind him, cut his throat and left him for dead.

I drove down to the pub with a great deal of bewilderment, not anger. I didn't know the full story and those left at the pub didn't want to get involved, and kept their mouths shut. This person had left the scene of the crime and my brother had been taken to hospital.

That was a relief in itself, because if my brother had still been at the pub when we arrived, it probably would have meant he was dead.

I went straight to the hospital from the pub. He was half-conscious, having just come out of emergency surgery to stitch up his throat, and looked a real mess. It was a harsh shock and a sight which no family member should ever have to see.

The doctor said he was lucky to be alive. Another millimetre deeper and the knife would have ruptured his vital arteries and certainly killed him.

There are a number of stories floating out there about how the incident regarding my brother's throat being cut actually happened.

Each book gives their suspicions but none of them give a definite name of who committed the crime. I was not at the scene of the crime, and was passed the information by a secondary source, so I'm only going on who 'allegedly' carried out this act of violence.

Can you believe nobody ever got arrested for this crime? It didn't even go to trial.

After my brother's throat was cut, attacks started to happen constantly on both sides and unfortunately there seemed to be no clear solution to break the cycle.

I would have loved nothing better than for somebody to have stood up and say, "Let's stop", but it never happened.

As the rally of violence continued to and fro, I was involved in an attack against a man called Lenny Kersey and I want to set the record straight on a few fronts.

A number of sources imply that this episode started as a result of the Tibbs family being labelled "dirty pikey bastards." Apart from the fact that we were not pikeys, we were not about to engage in an act of violence of this level, simply in reaction to three words.

The Kersey attack I got involved in was part of the ongoing two-way violence which was occurring, as opposed to a number of sources which almost make out that I just woke up one morning and fancied cutting him to pieces.

Here's what happened.

A group of us set upon him in a blind rage and he was severely cut, bruised and left in a bad way. He needed a huge number of stitches and time in hospital afterwards.

There are a number of sources which imply that when we

carried out the attack on Kersey we were aware that his wife had been watching from the outset and – even worse – that a friend who was with her was holding a baby.

This is untrue.

We would have never carried out the attack if at any moment we had seen women and children present.

The fact that his wife had to witness the end of the attack, and the fact that her friend dropped her baby on the pavement in horror, makes me feel sick as a dog.

Many people started branding me and my family as gangsters for this and other similar episodes which took place during these years.

This is not the movies.

I was not one of those people who celebrated after inflicting pain on somebody.

Gangsters like notoriety, but I was absolutely nothing like that.

I was admittedly now a criminal, but there is a big difference. I was not out committing crimes to climb the ladder of the gangster hall of fame. The violent acts I took part in during these years were 100 percent down to revenge for the similar pain and horror inflicted on my own family members.

Lenny Kersey, Albert Nicholls and Terry Nicholls got what they deserved, and at that time I did not regret what I had done.

I stress "*at that time.*"

Who did they think they were?

Did they believe that they could bully, cut and shoot me

and my family and we would simply roll over? That was never going to be the case.

****

The level of violence continued to get increasingly worse. Fist fights had been replaced by knives and now, only a matter of months later, I had a gun pointed in my face.

This involved the Nicholls again. Me and a couple of others got involved in a punch up with them outside the Rose of Denmark pub. During the fight a gun was taken out which I then removed from the person's hand to avoid somebody being killed.

I'm not saying who the gun belonged to, but for the record, it wasn't mine.

After further punches were thrown, I jumped into my car and drove off.

The second I drove round the corner I thought, 'Shit. My fingerprints are on that gun'. I drove back, but by this stage the place was swarming with police so I put my foot down to get out of there as quickly as possible.

This episode has been scripted wrong by every book out there.

All those memoirs state that I returned to run Albert and Terry Nicholls over in my car.

But think about it.

The whole place is covered with coppers and I want to run these two guys over in front of them? I was in enough trouble as it was! I might have been stupid to have left my prints on a gun, but implying I would have gone back to run these guys over in front of the police would classify me as dumb and insane.

After the incident, I laid low for about a week, trying to stay out of the way at a mate's house, before I then got the biggest shock of my life.

I thought the violence could not get much worse but the bar was about to be raised to a disgusting, all-time high.

I had been out with my wife and sons at a fair in Wanstead on a Sunday afternoon and later that evening I parked my van up outside my uncle Bogey's greengrocers, just round the corner in Nelson Street.

The bonnet on my Ford Thames van used to open facing the windscreen, the opposite to most cars. However, my van had the added bonus that the bonnet never closed properly. I used to clip it down just before driving it, but after a few miles, it would always unclip and open again.

When parking up, I would push it down to make sure nobody could see it was open. For some unknown reason, I decided not to close it on that evening.

This forgetful action would later contribute to saving mine and my son's lives.

The morning after, I was taking my son to nursery in East Ham. We both got in the car, with my son sitting up front with me. We didn't have seatbelts on as it wasn't the law back then and the majority of people didn't wear them anyway. I popped the key into the ignition and as I turned it, BANG.

A deafeningly loud explosion.

A split second later, as a pillar of smoke came out of the

engine block and people started to spill out of their front doors in shock and terror, it became obvious it was as a result of a bomb which had been placed at the front of the engine, just by the radiator.

First thing I did was to check my son was alright. He was in total shock. He didn't understand what was going on and why. I was also shaken, but the adrenaline helped me to focus and realise that I needed to get my son out of the car. I told him to mind his legs where the metal of the car by his feet had blown inwards and was sticking out razor sharp.

I pushed the door open and he got out and ran back to our house round the corner to my wife. If that bomb had been placed a foot further into the engine block, we would have certainly been dead.

I stayed with the van for a minute – totally stunned – trying to take in what had just happened. It was like being in a living nightmare. People around me were trying to check if I was ok, but between the numb feeling I was experiencing and the ringing in my ears from the blast, I couldn't tell you what people were saying, what they looked like or what time of the day it was.

My emotions were scrambled and I was disorientated on a number of fronts.

Thankfully, with the bonnet not securely closed, the majority of the blast went upwards and out of the engine block, leaving the bonnet lid firmly prized open with a continuous stream of smoke coming out of it.

Although a great deal of debris came off the explosion, me and my son were lucky that we didn't have a scratch on us, never mind having our heads blown off.

The blast shattered my uncle Bogey's shop windows and a number of nearby properties. The street was now starting to fill up with families emptying from their houses and within minutes the police turned up from East Ham, swiftly followed by a forensic team.

I was told not to touch the van and I became just another spectator to the scene. By the end of the day, the police towed it away to Woolwich Arsenal. They kept it there for evidence to see if they could find any clues, although they were never able to recover or uncover anything.

They were only able to confirm it was a bomb which had caused the blast. I could have told them that!

The reality of what had just happened was starting to set in.

Anger was now starting to build up inside of me and thoughts were entering my head at a million miles an hour as I tried to understand the logic of the people who had planted the bomb.

If they had been following my movements, they must have realised I took my son to nursery five days a week. Had the person who had planted the bomb intended to kill me and my son, or were they plain stupid and had simply not thought their actions through?

I would never find out who planted the bomb and consequently never found out the answers to these questions. Either way, somebody had taken a huge and reckless liberty at my family's expense.

I can't speak for the people we were at war with but me

and my dad were certainly sick of what was happening and wanted it all to stop.

It was messing with our lives, our living and most worryingly, our families. It was far too hectic and there was no possibility for anybody to call a halt. I wished there could have been, but that opportunity never became available. It was a case of everybody stopped or nobody stopped.

****

Commander Bert Wickstead had been following the violence for some time in the shadows and the bomb episode was the deciding factor which made him intervene.

Born and bred in the East End, Wickstead was head of Scotland Yard's Serious Crime Squad during the 1970s and was the man responsible for cleaning up a great deal of major crime over a number of decades in London.

In fact, some of the cases he worked on have gone on to be blockbuster movies. His levels of research, detail and contact on the ground were thorough – but not always accurate.

Wickstead was aware that what had started as a few punches in a pub a couple of years earlier had rapidly got out of control.

It was a matter of time before somebody ended up dead. Someone had obviously intended for me to be the first with that bomb. Everybody has a mother and father and no parent needs to be put through the grief of attending the funeral of their child.

On the flip side, a wife and young kids should be spared

the experience of attending the funeral of a young father or husband.

Whatever I may say about Wickstead, I cannot argue with the bottom line he was trying to achieve. He wanted to stop the madness and all the violence and the best way of doing that was by sending out a strong message to anybody else thinking about plotting a similar murder.

If this meant the life of an innocent four-year-old child would be saved then any time served in prison by those involved with these events would be worth every minute.

It is only now, over 40 years later, after reading a number of accounts from various authors, that I am able to piece together how the moment of our arrest was plotted and who was involved.

According to his own memoirs, Bert Wickstead met up with a man and convinced him to grass on my family. I am the first to put my hands up to say that I deserved to pay for the violent crimes I had committed during these troubled times.

However, it has also now become obvious that my family, to an extent, had been used as scapegoats to send a stern message to everybody else in the East End of London who had been involved in gangland violence.

The sickening part was that many who had committed parallel crimes during this period did not only get off scot free, but some ended up being principal witnesses against us in court. I'm not sure how that can be quantified as equal justice.

Quoting Wickstead from his own memoirs 'Gangbuster'

when referring to plotting the Tibbs family arrest:

"I believed that there was only one way in which this could be done. We would have to persuade their enemies, the Nicholls, the Kerseys, Michael Fawcett and others, to witness against them. You can accuse me, if you wish, of taking sides – of using one band of villains to break another band. And I wouldn't deny it for a moment. In the twilight world of the gangster, archbishops are thin on the ground. You have to use what you can find – and inevitably that means fellow criminals.

"The man I most wanted to talk to was Michael Fawcett, because I had a hunch he could prove to be the key figure in all of this.

"In the days that followed I saw a lot of Michael Fawcett and found him to be a very likeable man. However, it soon became clear that if we were really going to bring down the Tibbs, he would have to change his role from that of informer to that of witness."

Correct me if I'm wrong, but I believe Wickstead was priming Fawcett to be what is commonly known as a 'grass' of the highest degree.

With all this going on at the time, there were also allegations that I broke Chazzer Chapman's jaw for not letting me train at West Ham Amateur Boxing Club due to the professional versus amateur boundaries of where I could or couldn't train.

This is one lie I cannot let slide and want to categorically say that this episode never happened.

If you look at my history of violence, it has always come as a result of defending my family for major wrongdoings against them.

I have never initiated a violent episode and I certainly wouldn't hit someone over something as trivial as being told I couldn't train at an amateur boxing club.

What has been implied here is that I was prepared to use bully-like tactics to get my way but Chazzer was my matchmaker when I trained as a senior amateur at West Ham Amateur Boxing Club and I have nothing but good things to say about him and everything he ever did for me.

This episode is complete fiction and if I had asked Chazzer to train at the club and he'd refused, I would've had no problem whatsoever.

In fact I probably would've asked him if he fancied grabbing a pint down the pub once he'd finished that day!

I travelled all round Europe with him during my amateur days, which gave me the opportunity to experience so many diverse cultures and he ensured no harm came to me while I was under his wing.

So again – why would I have ever wanted to threaten such a positive and influential person in my life?

Also, I'm very good friends with Chazzer Chapman's son, Joey. I remember him as a young kid training when I was a senior. He's one of the top trainers at Newham Boxing Club and has been running the place for the last 20 years. I'm sure Joey would be the first to support my story and would also be amazed at the accusation in the first place.

Anybody who knows me, knows that I have spent a great deal of my life sticking up for people who have been bullied. I detest bullies.

I deeply resented reading the episode, so hopefully, for

those of you who know me and knew Chazzer, this has put that episode to sleep.

After the bombing, me and my family attempted to get back to our normal lives and get back to earning a living. However, with Wickstead's wheels in motion, we were living in the lull before the storm.

Not only was I fighting for my family's life but I also made the decision, in March, 1972, to make a comeback to professional boxing.

I could see everything was getting out of hand with the gang violence and needed to refocus my life. The best discipline I knew was boxing and if the possibility was available, I had decided I would try to get my licence back. I spoke with my manager Terry Lawless and after a few days he told me that he had managed to sort it.

I was only 25 and I was mentally and physically getting stronger every day. A fight had been set for April against a boxer called Maurice Thomas, and I would be headlining at the London Hilton Hotel.

Unfortunately, a couple of weeks before fight night, my world was shattered.

And this time there would be no walking away from the courtroom as a free man.

Round 5

10 YEARS

"Mr James Edward Patrick Tibbs, I hereby sentence you to 10 years imprisonment."
– Mr Justice Lawton, 1973

While people were getting shot, stabbed and blown up, I was attempting to make my comeback to professional boxing ring and I was in deep training for an eight rounder after an 18-month rest.

I was even sporting a 30-inch waist! I was delighted to be getting back to something I was genuinely good at and had a great deal of passion for.

During my lay-off, Terry had been building up his stable with some great fighters which certainly helped me when sparring for my comeback fight. The more I trained, the more the gang violence moved further away from the forefront of my mind.

I genuinely thought I might be finally seeing the light at the end of the tunnel.

How wrong I was.

****

BANG BANG BANG. On April 4, 1972, in the early hours of the morning, I was awoken by a series of very hard knocks on my front door.

The police made it obvious that this was a big thing for them. Outside was Bert Wickstead's squad, assisted by a large number of officers from the Special Patrol Group, along with dogs and a number of cars all parked up in front of the house with lights flashing.

I was nicked.

They came in pretty heavy, and to be totally honest I was pretty shaken up. My two young boys and my wife were very scared and nervous, and I knew I was not going to be given the time to comfort them or explain anything. At this point, unless you have been in this position yourself, you can never understand the emotion of what I was going through. As I tell this story, it's the first time in 40 years that I'm going into this level of detail and I'd be a liar if I didn't say that I'm writing this chapter with a tear in my eye and regret in my heart.

As they confronted me, one of the coppers said, "You can do this the hard way, or come with us the easy way." I told him, "Let's do this the easy way." This was traumatic enough as it was and I didn't want to make the mental scars of my loved ones even greater by causing a bigger scene. I asked one of the officers if he would mind not handcuffing me in front of me kids.

He said, "Alright," and did it out front, before shoving me into a police car which was specifically earmarked for me. They drove me to a police station somewhere in Shoreditch and I was placed in a cell. I knew at this point I was in plenty of trouble. I felt numb and helpless and kept thinking, 'How long will I be here and what's going to happen in court.'

In the meantime, the police were arresting other Tibbs family members, making sure they left no stone unturned.

After they took my fingerprints and mugshots, I was interviewed by Wickstead and a number of other high ranking policemen over two whole days and nights without a break. It felt like I was in there for a month.

It was interrogation at its best and life at its worst. Bert told me you've done this and done that, and I told him my side of the story, but he was not interested in it. So I decided to keep my mouth shut and say nothing.

Next thing I knew, we were all in Brixton prison on remand. As we were sitting in reception, there was another guy sitting there with a bemused look on his face.

He was the owner of the local pub I used to drink in with my mates. I turned to him and said, "What are you doing here?" He replied, "I don't know?!" He had nothing to do with our family troubles, so I didn't know what to say to him. Rumour was that the police had raided his pub just because we used to drink there.

The cops had told him nothing and I didn't want to start

filling him in on our situation. From his side it was just a bizarre experience, which he had no grasp of. The police were hoping he was going to say something about the Tibbs family, or provide some evidence against us, but he knew nothing. We literally only used to drink there. Later on the police found a couple of shotguns at the pub but he had licences for them.

After a week or so of holding this guy in Brixton, they released him, realising they had made a mistake.

Soon after the police had finished with their interrogation, we were sent to Brixton prison on remand for 10 months, but thankfully all in the same wing.

We tried to make light of the situation by watching television, playing chess and not discussing the ensuing trial. After a couple of months, a few of my mates (not connected to our case) arrived, which again helped to take the edge off the prison environment.

As nice as it was to have friends and family around me, I knew this was short term.

There's nothing worse than going to trial when you know you don't stand a chance.

The future had already been decided so it didn't matter who was going to give evidence for us, we were going down. I had a feeling of emptiness and the reality was that my future lay in the hands of the judge and jury.

The 10 months of limbo felt like an eternity. As much as I tried to block the outside world from my mind, I would get stark reminders of the downside of serving time in prison. One time while in Brixton, my wife brought one of my sons with her, who was about three years old.

There was a glass partition between us and my boy broke down screaming and crying, "I WANT MY DAD. I WANT MY DAD." It was tough keeping a front for them both and even worse when they left, because all I kept thinking to myself was, 'What have I done here? Look at the mess I've got myself into and look at how much my loved ones are now suffering'.

I hadn't thought that far forward while all the trouble was going on. I just wanted revenge.

****

In January, 1973, the trial was heard by Mr Justice Lawton at the Old Bailey, which consequently led to seven people being jailed.

It was a joke.

I still have an official copy of the entire script, which states who said what, who retracted which statements, who grassed against us and who stood by us through thick and thin.

Those who knew the Tibbs family knew that the levels of discipline being dished out were not proportional to the crimes we had committed. Wickstead was intentionally making an example of us, and there was nothing we could do.

On that fateful Friday at the Old Bailey, the jury pronounced us guilty. However, we were left hanging until the Monday, at which point the length of our sentences would be revealed. You can't imagine how we felt.

Although we all tried to make light of the situation, inside it was eating away at me.

Robin Simpson was representing me at the time, he knew I was guilty and he also knew I had no way of talking myself out of it.

I told my story, and he did his best to help me, but it was too late.

Nobody could help me.

Nobody could help any of us.

We knew we were on the verge of being locked up for a long time. I would find out many years later that Robin was on the British Boxing Board of Control.

He was a very nice man, and thankfully I had the opportunity to thank him in person on being released.

It was bad enough that I was about to have my sentence confirmed, but awaiting the sentences of my dad and my brothers was torture.

The court treated me like another East End gangland criminal but the thought kept going through my head that I was just trying to defend the honour of my family and protect those closest to me.

We were being used as scapegoats to set an example to anybody involved in gangland warfare in the East End of London, or for anybody who was contemplating getting involved. None of our enemies were convicted.

If two people, or groups of people, commit a violent act, or repeated acts, should there not be two groups or at least two individuals from either side being prosecuted? Not in this trial. One side went to prison and the other side kept their freedom. How does that work?

After being found guilty, we were taken up one at a time on the Monday morning. First up was my dad. He was sentenced to 15 years. That was a massive shock. I remember saying to my dad before going into the court that they were probably going to give him a five or seven-year sentence, tops.

My dad said, "What do you mean a five or seven? I haven't done anything!" Then his massive sentence was pronounced which was far, far worse than any of us had ever expected.

I don't want to talk about the trial because that won't change the past and what's happened has happened. However, on that day, the definition of justice was certainly not textbook.

My mind started racing away at a hundred miles an hour as I thought to myself, 'What am I gonna get then?' Standing there, if they had just sentenced my dad to 15 years, I was certain I would be looking at 20.

I was able to accept the sentences me and my brothers had coming, but I just couldn't digest the fact that my dad had been served a 15-year sentence. That really upset me. I was absolutely gutted for him.

When I went up in front of the judge I remember him saying, "Tibbs, you have a good side to you like your father, but unfortunately you also have a bad side."

He then went on to give me two sentences. Seven years for attempted manslaughter and three years for attempted murder. The sentences were pronounced to run consecutively as a 10-year stretch.

Don't get me wrong, the news of 10 years tore me in half,

but it made no sense in relation to my dad's sentence. It was a joke. My mum collapsed on hearing the verdict and needed to be taken to hospital.

My emotions were running high but I can't even begin to imagine how a person would take in the news of being told their children and husband were being sentenced to prison for a long stretch.

She'd just lost her family behind bars. I had put myself into a situation which I deserved, but my family hadn't.

It didn't help that at the time the film 'The Godfather' had just been released. Wickstead even referred to my dad as the 'Godfather of the East End' in his own book. I didn't fight the decision, but gangsters we were not.

I had taken the law into my own hands but I pleaded not guilty because I didn't feel that I should be going to prison. I was only reacting to my brother having his throat cut and my four-year-old son almost dying from a car bomb.

I was never the person who started the problems, I was always the person reacting to them. The whole trial was very harsh and biased against anything Tibbs related.

After the sentence had been passed, I stepped off the dock and was taken downstairs into a big cell, where we were all reunited for the next hour. We spent that time discussing our sentences and although we were all trying to take it on the chin, we were very aware of how serious the situation was.

With our one hour credit expired, the prison guard proceeded to take us to a big van and started to drop us off at our respective prisons. Not the best of memories. My dad and one of my brothers went to Wandsworth and I was sent to Wormwood Scrubs.

I was pleased that my brother went with my dad so at least I knew there was somebody who could keep an eye on him. My dad was only 46 at the time, so he wasn't an old man, but he was still my dad.

I was the first to be dropped off. As I passed my dad I said, "Keep your chin up." I was absolutely gutted. I just wanted to cuddle him. Writing this episode over 40 years later still stirs up deep emotions.

****

Throughout the drive to the Scrubs, I was numb. I couldn't tell you how long it took or any noises or smells during the journey – nothing.

I remember being lead out of the van and next thing I knew I was at the reception.

As the van arrived at the prison, the reality now hit me. I was no longer a free man. With all the media publicity plastered on the TV and the papers, everybody was waiting for Jimmy Tibbs – not me, but the fictional character the press had created.

I'm sure the screws and the cons were expecting to see a 6ft 6in gangster with jet black hair, talking with an Italian accent stepping out of the van. After people met me, they realised I was just an ordinary fella.

After getting over the initial shock that I was not Al Capone's twin brother, the screws issued me with a couple of towels, a tube of toothpaste and my prison clothes.

My civvies were placed in a box and I would not see them again until I walked out of the prison gates. I was then issued with my prison number – 108161. A number that would be ingrained in my memory for life.

Everything I was given behind bars belonged to that prison. The fact that they gave me a number stressed that I was owned by the prison system now. Although I had clothes on, I felt naked in terms of my value.

The cell was about 12ft x 9ft. Thankfully, I didn't have to share the cell, which was a good thing just based on the size of the room alone.

The smell in that cell was just like the rest of the prison – almost indescribable. Simply not representative of anything you would smell as a free man. The contrast, especially after coming out of a nice home, made it worse.

There was a bed on the floor, no toilet, and a small window high up which barely allowed natural sunlight to shine through. There was also a small table with a jug of water, so you could drown yourself. Jokes apart, it was the bare minimum for a human being to survive on.

I realised there was nothing I could do apart from accept it and make the best of the time and the lavish surroundings. Although I was gutted, I soon realised it was going to do me no good sitting on the bed sulking.

No one is a man if they don't admit to being gutted while in prison. I will openly say that I shed a few tears in private, thinking about my family.

After a short while, I started to get a little disheartened

being locked up. Same old routines, same old food, same old clothes. Same old everything. Thankfully, and unbeknownst to myself, there were some good people looking out for me. After a few weeks of settling in, I started to walk and exercise with a couple of mates, who knew me and my family and not only had sympathy with my situation, but had empathy as they were serving their own bit of bird.

I never asked them for any help, or even shared too many problems with them, simply because I didn't want to burden them, but they could see I was a young kid and wanted to make me feel a little more at ease.

One day a screw came over and said, "This package is from one of your mates." He had sent me over a couple of shirts, some soap and toothpaste. Right at that very moment things started to change a little bit. The atmosphere seemed different.

I also noticed that I was never bullied in there by anyone, and the screws never got on my back either. I'm not suggesting for one minute that my mate had instructed people to steer clear of me, and perhaps it was my imagination, but it just felt like he was a guardian angel in there.

He was a good support and spoke logic in a place which was seemingly not very logical.

Just so we are clear – prison is not a holiday camp. Thankfully I never witnessed anybody being raped in prison, but it did happen. The only time I witnessed anything getting out of control was when a mini-riot broke out between the cons and the screws in the Scrubs. It was all over in seconds and I didn't need to get involved. The reality is that riots do happen in prison and if a screw was going to try to inflict harm on me or one of my friends or family, I would have had to defend myself and no doubt retaliate.

Thankfully I was never put into this compromising situation, but the thought of having my sentence extended for defending myself was always a worry. Defending myself and my family is what got me into this mess in the first place.

When you lock up a large number of men, deny them constant access to their friends, family and freedom, it's inevitable that violence will occur. That's why so many cons get involved in sport as a good way to release their built up frustration.

Standard procedure is to get all prisoners to graft. After a very short time, they put me in a sewing machine shop to make kites. I thought to myself, 'This ain't for me'.

So I turned round to the screw and said, "I don't think I can work this machine." He said, "What do ya mean? A little baby could work that." I said I was worried about my fingers, but the truth is I just didn't want to do it. I didn't fancy sitting there all day sewing. The other cons in the room were laughing at my obvious antics.

The screw said, "Sit down and give it go and see how you get on." I sat down and he showed me how to use the machine, as I gave the impression that I was concentrating intensely. When it came to me having a go, I intentionally kept messing it up and showing I was scared of my hands being caught up in the machine. After doing this about half a dozen times, he said, "Give him a broom and sweeper."

And that was the end of my career as a seamstress! Don't

get me wrong, I wasn't about to win the award for sweeper of the year, but it certainly beat the sewing.

I didn't realise at the time but this episode was a godsend. I was as thin as a rake, and doing nothing but stressing, thinking about my family on both sides of the prison fence. That little episode took my mind off everything that was going on and I did something I hadn't done in a while – laughed.

Just as I thought I was starting to build up an inner strength, I had a brief episode which took the wind out of my sails. My wife visited me as regularly as she could, and in every nick I served in.

On one occasion she turned up with a patch over her eye. My heart dropped. All kinds of sinister thoughts ran through my head at 100 miles an hour. Had somebody hit her? Has she lost the sight in her eye?

I asked what she had done to herself and she explained a bit of cigarette ash had gone into her eye. Although it was a relatively small thing, I panicked because I was not able to help.

****

After nine months at Wormwood Scrubs, the governor called me up to see him and informed me I was going to Chelmsford. I was actually glad to hear the news, as I had a couple of mates at this prison.

As the car stopped outside the prison gates and the driver opened his window, I noticed straight away that the air was far fresher. Chelmsford is on the verge of the English countryside and it was a distinct contrast to smoggy West London.

However, the second I walked into reception and then proceeded to my cell, that same old indescribable smell was back.

I didn't know many people in prison until I got to Chelmsford. Thankfully, I had a number of friends in there and they had been given a heads up that I was on my way.

When you arrive in any prison, you go down the block for three days before being allocated your cell. Days "down the block" are intended to help you acclimatise. The first night I was there a good mate of mine who was serving a five-year stretch asked the governor if I could come up and have a meal with him and his mates. The governor agreed and we all sat down to a nice roast dinner. My mate said, "Don't worry Jim. I'll get some meat on you." It was like a different world compared to Wormwood Scrubs. Don't get me wrong, it wasn't a holiday. You never for a second forget about your wife and kids, but the contrast certainly helped me pick up my self-esteem.

After my three days, I made my way from the block towards my cell. As I walked inside, I could see it had been freshly painted – again, organised by my mate. It was nice to smell the fresh paint, as it almost sterilised the room.

When my mate was released before me, he continued to do everything he could to make me feel comfortable in a prison environment. On arriving home, he even got his wife to make me curtains and a quilt for my cell!

Having just left Wormwood Scrubs, I couldn't believe

what was going on. Freshly painted cell and roast dinners? I had to make out it was all normal. It didn't stop there either. There was a guy who had a full bar in his cell. He used to serve you wearing a shirt and cufflinks!

I remember having a few drinks one night and the morning after I won the three-mile race in the exercise compound. The booze had given me extra energy!

Although freedom was not yet in my grasp, Chelmsford was a great contrast in terms of restrictions, certainly in comparison to Scrubs. I would wake up at 7:30am, have my breakfast, which was mainly porridge – no pun intended – and I would then move on to my place of work, before having lunch.

I would then lay down for an hour, with the cell doors left open and I didn't need to be back inside before 9pm. Effectively, I was out of my cell all day.

Another major difference on moving to this prison was the staff.

The governor, Mickey Selby, and the chief security officer treated me with respect. I will always remember, at a later stage when I was in Chelmsford and my dad was in Maidstone and got ghosted to the Isle of Wight, (Parkhurst). I was very upset.

The governor came out one day and realised I wasn't playing rugby and said, "Where's Tibbs?" One of the cons explained that I was upset about my dad being ghosted. When the game was over, the governor sent for me. I put my jacket on and saw him. He asked me about my dad and I explained that my mother would have to travel a great deal to see her sons and husband and it was too much for her. He said, "Would you like to speak to him now?" I said, "Yes." He made the call to Parkhurst, but he turned to me and said, "They won't let you speak to him right now Jim".

Although the guys in Parkhurst had refused my call, the fact that he was willing to try on my behalf meant something. He was a fair man.

The prison was made up of little groups. Within our group we formed what was known as a 'food boat'. This basically meant we would all get together at meal times and one of us would cook.

It certainly beat the regular prison offering, and with one of my mates working in the kitchen, we always had access to quality ingredients.

In addition, I was also very lucky to have my uncle Bogey who would take me round a lovely curry!

My quality of life inside moved up another notch when one day the screws called me up and asked, "How would you like to work in the canteen?"

Bearing in mind this is one of the top jobs in the nick, I said, "I'll think about it." The screw then said, "Do what Tibbs?" I repeated myself, "I'll think about it." This must have been the first time anybody had ever refused such a great opportunity. The screw was in shock! I walked over to my prison wing and spoke with a mate of mine, who quickly convinced me that it was a fantastic job with benefits so I went back and accepted.

I kept my head down in the canteen and then landed an even better position as the gym orderly. Responsibilities included looking after the equipment, making sure the weights were out for when the lads came down to use them and keeping everything tidy.

I was not in charge of keeping the cons in order, that was still down to the screws. Little would I know that years later my next taste of running a gym would be at a completely different level.

I was delighted to get this position. Probably more so than the canteen, which to many would have seemed strange. I wasn't allowed to exercise a great deal when I was on remand in Brixton or when I was sent to the Scrubs.

However, Chelmsford was my allocated prison for my long-term stretch and I used to do a lot of running, gym work, sit-ups, push-ups and some weights. Having been in and out of gyms since the age of 11, I felt somewhat more at ease in this environment.

Not at home, but at ease.

Boxing was always at the forefront of my mind, despite everything that had happened. I used to think of the various bouts I had fought and the level of detail that would run through my head was very vivid. Upsettingly vivid.

I was able to remember what I did well and what I could've improved on. I could almost hear the sound of the crowd applauding, but each time I daydreamed, I would always get hit with the reality of being inside. I was still a young man, so it would anger me to think that I could have perhaps been a champion at that point with a completely different lifestyle and outlook.

Boxing was not allowed in the prison, so it was kept alive

in my head during those years. I never even shadow boxed in the gym or the yard. The cons and screws knew I was an ex-fighter and I didn't want to look like I was trying to show off, so I used to do my exercise with other cons at the gym. We would have routines, which were enjoyable, but it was certainly a damp replacement for training at the Royal Oak or West Ham Amateur Boxing Club.

Thankfully, I had good friends on the outside who kept me in touch with the boxing scene as much as they could and I also had the *Boxing News* sent to me.

Some things had not changed – Muhammad Ali was still champion and was still shocking the world and on one occasion, I opened a copy of *Boxing News* and saw a six-year-old kid in a photo with world champ John H Stracey. I looked a bit closer and then realised it was my son!

A friend of mine had taken him to Repton to train and John was there to have a look around his old gym, which he had trained at many years previous. John then asked who the little lad was. My mate said "That's Jimmy Tibbs' son", and John asked to have a photo taken with him and next thing it's in the paper. At a time of my life where not a second went by without thinking about the welfare of my family, it was quite an emotional episode to have seen that not only was my son happy, but that he was being looked after.

****

Just as I was starting to get comfortable with the sounds and smells of Chelmsford, one morning, I received a knock on my door. The governor wanted to see me.

And the news couldn't have been much worse. I was off to Wandsworth.

I hadn't been there yet, but Wandsworth had gained the reputation as 'The Hate Factory'.

It was the hardest prison in England at that time. I asked why I had to go and the governor just said, "Someone has been on the phone and you have to be transferred. Me personally, I'd love to keep you here."

I was about to be ghosted at a rapid pace. Let me explain what 'ghosting' means. It's when a prisoner is shuttled from one prison to another, usually at night time, so that you disappear without causing too much chaos, or attract too much attention from the other cons.

The theory behind ghosting is to reduce the potential disruption caused by certain individuals. It was obvious that the governor and chief security officer didn't feel that I was a threat of any kind, hence wanting to move me out in broad daylight as opposed to sending me down the block and then making me disappear. This order had come from somebody above them.

Someone who was most likely involved with the trial. Either way it was unjust.

I found out later that there was a rumour going round that I was looking to escape. This was the furthest thought from my mind. As a married man with two children, I wanted to serve my time and get out as quickly as possible, especially half way through my sentence.

The governor didn't want to make an example of me, or

make me feel like an outcast. When the ghosting process starts, they usually send over the 'burglars' to your cell.

A burglar is a prison officer who comes and gets all your gear and they pack it for you. But instead they told me to go and pack all my own gear. Again, the governor wanted me to just get on with it, without any fuss or unnecessary attention.

After getting my belongings together, I was packed into the back seat of a car with a couple of screws and we started with the journey to Wandsworth. I can distinctly remember we drove past a hardware shop which Terry Lawless owned in Leytonstone and also drove past streets which I used to walk around as a free man a few years earlier.

It was quite an emotional experience, as I was handcuffed with two screws sitting either side of me, reminding me that freedom was not on the agenda for this journey either.

On arriving at reception, I was handed over to two new screws.

Wandsworth was the only place I had to wear the set uniform all the time and that was grey trousers and blue shirt. The colour was like everything else in that place – dull and lifeless. The other prisons gave you options instead of the standard uniform. Don't get me wrong, I couldn't wear what I liked and come out in a tux for a walk around the exercise area, but I spent most of my time in the other places and out of my cell in either jeans and a shirt or shorts and a training tops when it was summertime. Wandsworth was different.

I'm not sure what it's like at Wandsworth these days, but

back then the screws were dogs. I thought to myself, 'If I ever see any of you outside, I'll smash you to pieces'.

I probably wouldn't even recognise them now and they are most likely dead, but the way they used to treat me and everybody in there was a disgrace.

Boredom was a huge factor, not just in Wandsworth, but in all the prisons. I guess Wandsworth highlighted this more because I was at my unhappiest in there. Many people got depressed, some would crack up and some would go the other way and become violent.

There are not many success stories to report behind bars. There's not the opportunity for success to develop when you are inside. That happens when you get out and it's down to the individual to make it happen.

While in Wandsworth, I wrote a letter to my mum explaining how things were, how much I missed my family and how gutted I was by the overall situation. A few days later, I was in a workshop and a screw came over and said, "You've got a visit Tibbs."

I asked who it was and he said, '"It's your mother." I said, "All due respects, but I haven't got a visit organised with my mum, my wife and kids have all my visits." He replied, "So what you're saying is you don't want to see your mother?" I said, "I'd love to see me mum, but I ain't got a visit sorted for her."

He then said "I'll tell her you don't want to see her then." I said "Tell her what you like." I had a feeling my mum would not accept what the screw was about to say, especially after the letter I had sent. She had a fiery temper and could usually get her own way.

Next thing I know, the screw came back pretty quickly and said, "You can have this visit on me!" She was there with my brother, who had been given a 15 month sentence, and had served about six. When I walked into the visiting room she started screaming at the screws like a raving lunatic. "WHAT HAVE YOU DONE TO MY SON?"

I was extremely skinny and she was going to make sure somebody was going to be held responsible. She was going so mad I had to leave! That wasn't the end of the visit for her though. She wasn't leaving until she had seen the governor.

The screws kept telling her the governor wasn't here but she shouted, "I ain't moving and you ain't gonna move me." Within a week I was off to Maidstone! Good old mum. If it wasn't for her I probably would have been in Wandsworth for the rest of my sentence.

****

With the Maidstone transfer confirmed, I packed my bag and a couple of screws walked me to a van which contained a number of other cons. I was glad to see the back of Wandsworth, but was even happier to be heading to Maidstone as my other brother was already there and the governor had arranged for us to be on the same wing.

After deciding that working in the carpenter's shop wasn't for me, I decided to meet up with the governor and asked if I could get a place working in the gym.

I explained that I'd been a boxer since the age of 11 and

an active athlete, and as opposed to putting me in the paint shop or the carpenters, I could be of far greater value to the prison as a gym orderly.

He picked up a clipboard and showed me the long list of cons waiting to work in the gym and asked why I thought I was special. I looked at the list and said, "All of those guys are doing short stretches. Put me to the top of the list!" Within a fortnight I was working in the gym.

Soon after starting my new post as gym orderly, I came close to jeopardising the terms of my sentence by unintentionally getting involved in a comical riot episode. I was in charge of getting the football pitch ready for a match of two prison wings. In essence, cons versus cons. With both teams out on the pitch and the whistle blown, I stood on the sidelines spectating a fairly good match.

However, as the game progressed, I could see that the tackles started turning into fouls and handshakes started to turn into shoves. As the game gradually became more heated, an argument broke out between two cons from opposing sides and I thought to myself, 'It's about to go off here any minute'. My concern was that a couple of my mates were playing in one of the teams and if it did kick off I didn't want to get nicked.

Next thing I knew, the inevitable happened, a fight broke out and everybody started throwing punches. Within seconds of it all kicking off, I ended up getting cracked on the chin, but with my boxer's instinct, I responded by landing a straight right, knocking this guy out!

Before I knew it, my shirt had been ripped off and every-

Start them young: I'm on the second to back row, (third from left), sporting a shiner, aged 14, at St Bonaventure's School

Early glory: The Marquess of Milford Haven presents me with my Schoolboys Champions trophy, 1961

My mates: Me (fourth from right), hanging around the Ground Rent Tavern, Canning Town, aged 19

A bloody business: Tussling with Italian great Gianfranco Macchia, 1967

Pain: I finally overcame Macchia after six gruelling rounds

The end: My last pro fight against Ray Hassan, 1970

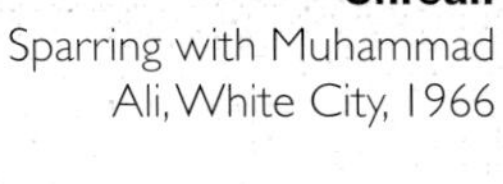

Unreal:
Sparring with Muhammad Ali, White City, 1966

Taking a tumble:
Ali entertains the watching crowds with a mock fall during our sparring session

The Greatest vs Our 'Enry: Henry Cooper, left, fought Muhammad Ali at Highbury, 1966. I was on the undercard that night and got a real taste of the Swinging Sixties

ANOTHER £100 TO BE WON. See page 6

BOXING NEWS

World's Premier Fight Weekly

Vol. 23 No. 9 58th Year

PRICE ONE SHILLING

MARCH 3, 1967

YOSHIICHI TSUGANEZAWA

ALAN RUDKIN

HIROSHI SHOJI

All these boxers will be appearing at the Royal Albert Hall next Tuesday (see page 7)

JIMMY TIBBS

JIMMY ANDERSON

MARK ROWE

Closer to home: I used to feature in *Boxing News* (front left) on a regular basis

Love at first sight: Claudette and me on our wedding day, 1966

My two nans: Claudette and me with my nans, Rose and Kate, on the big day

Active behind bars: Me (third from back) playing rugby in HMP Chelmsford, 1975

Frank and Charlie: Frank Bruno gives Charlie Magri a lift, 1983

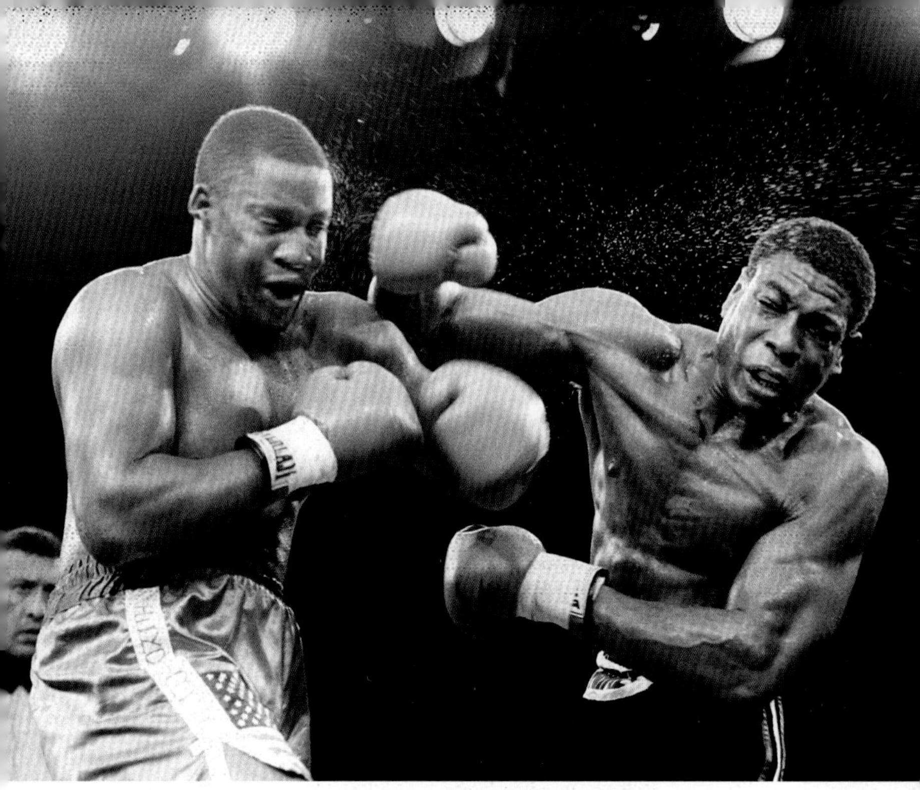

A sweaty business: Frank Bruno and Tim Witherspoon exchange some serious power, 1986

The stable: Barry McGuigan (centre with left to right) Charlie Magri, Lloyd Honeyghan and Jim McDonnell. I had the privilege of coaching all these fighters at some point in their careers

Barry McGuigan
NO.1 FOR BOXING

Sports Wire

Edvald speeds to desert win

Newton: I've been a dope

Tibbs has opened up a whole new world for Mitchell

TURN YOUR OLD PHONES INTO CASH TODAY WITH MIRRORCASH4PHONES!

Why not recycle your old phone and sell it to us? It only takes a few minutes of your time, so go to www.Mirrorcash4phones.co.uk

YOU CAN GET UP TO £180 FOR YOUR OLD MOBILE!

Recycling enables all of us to have a brighter future.

By recycling with The Mirror we can offer you the following:

- A completely free process from start to finish; we'll send you a welcome pack - simply put your mobile phone in the bag and send it to us using our freepost service.
- Sell 4 or more phones and you'll qualify for a free courier service, we can even collect your phones from work if that's easier!
- On-line tracking of you mobile phone's trading progress through our 'My Account' area online.

As soon as we receive your mobile phone and validate that it meets our terms and conditions we'll get your payment out to you in three days.

It's as easy as 1, 2, 3...

1. Simply find your mobile phone online...
2. We'll send you a freepost padded envelope...
3. Post it back and wait for your money!

£114.09 £21.03 £117.03 £50.76

www.Mirrorcash4phones.co.uk

The reason we do it: Carrying Barry McGuigan around the ring after his victory over Francisco Tomas Da Cruz, 1988

Returning the favour: The Clones Cyclone saying some positive things about me in his second career as a successful pundit body was fighting on the pitch. It was like an audition for the sequel to 'Mean Machine' with Vinnie Jones – loads of little fights going on all over the pitch, arms swinging wildly and missing most of the time and a few people out cold on the floor! I didn't want to get into deep trouble so I stopped throwing punches soon after and without any particular reason, everybody else stopped also. Just like that!

I then proceeded to carry on with my duties and walked over to the nets and took them down. In the meantime, the cons drifted away and a screw came up to me and said, "Why did you get involved Jim?" I replied, "I got chinned and simply threw a punch back!"

A few hours went by and I found out that a few cons from each wing had been nicked, and if truth be told, I was involved more than anybody. So I walked over to the screw at the gym and said I needed to have a word with him.

We walked down to the changing rooms and I explained that he had nicked this person and that person but he hadn't nicked me. I said, "I can't afford to get a bad name. I don't want anybody saying I didn't get nicked because I was friendly with the screws."

I told him straight, "You've got to nick me." He didn't think I was serious. He said, "Stay there a second Jim," and he came back with a piece of paper which had a prison officer's report from the afternoon's events. "Look at that," he said. I read it, and it said "If it wasn't for Tibbs, there would have been a full scale riot!"

What could I do? The screws thought I was a hero and I wanted to be nicked. In the end, I went over to the guys down the block who had been nicked from both sides and explained that they didn't want to nick me and they burst out laughing! We all shook hands and everything was fine.

Apart from that episode, I was well behaved. Don't get me wrong, I wasn't a goody goody in prison. I had a drink, smoked a bit of dope, but I kept my head down and got on and did my time.

****

After 18 months in Maidstone, they decided to move me back to Chelmsford. By this stage, I had been behind bars for a few years and was able to reflect on prison life.

What made it so tough? I don't mean this in an arrogant way, but nothing scared me behind bars. I used to hang around with my crew and I kept myself to myself. I was never bothered once and I never bothered anybody.

Although I might have been different to some cons who did experience bullying and violence against them and those who didn't have access to decent food, the one thing we all had in common was the lack of freedom.

Whatever highs you have during the day, you're always brought back down to earth when you go to sleep or have a visit from a loved one, reminding you that you have no other option but to return to that same cell every night at a fixed time. Choices of where to go, who to see, how to live and not being able to help anybody on the outside are pretty much taken out of your hands.

That's far worse than being beaten up behind bars, or not

having a slap-up meal. You learn to get over those things pretty quickly. Having your freedom taken away is what prison is there for and you never forget that for every minute you are inside.

I can only imagine it's like having one of your senses of sight or sound temporarily removed – you only notice how much you miss them every day once you are without them. Very frustrating and simply nothing you can do to change that situation.

My stint this time round in Chelmsford was on a different block and I felt more relaxed with this transfer than my previous ones.

Maybe it was because I had become used to the constant ferrying over the last three years, or perhaps it was because Chelmsford still had the same governor and chief security guard. Truth be told, there was one major piece of icing on this cake – my dad was in Chelmsford.

He was my mentor and my rock as a kid and should never have been stitched up the way he was. From the time we all received our sentences, right the way through the time we spent at this prison, and the years after we were released, he never moaned once.

He never said to me, "Jim. I'm innocent. I shouldn't be here." He never once muttered a word about revenge, or even talked about those mugs who had put us behind bars in the first place.

All he wanted to see was his family get out and no harm come to his kids while they were inside. He was the last of our family to come out of prison – a few years after I did.

Everybody involved with giving evidence and passing judgement on my father's sentence has had to live with that their whole life whereas he walked out of jail with a clear conscience.

Round 6

SECOND CHANCE

"Training at the Royal Oak was hard work in a very busy environment. Everybody was trying to work harder than the person next to them. It was buzzing. Everyone was dedicated to getting ahead in the fight game and when Jimmy came on board he pushed our ability and ambition to another level."
– Mark Kaylor, 2013

Finally, after four years and four months of being locked up, the news came that I had been praying for.

I was getting paroled. I was obviously delighted with the news, but I wish they had only given me a few days' notice instead of a four-month wait. That time dragged badly and it's not as if I needed to call in the removal people to clear out my cell.

The night before the release, my mind was working overtime preparing me for what I might face after walking out of those gates. I lay on my bed all night just staring at the ceiling. There was no way I was getting any sleep.

What would the initial reactions of my wife and my boys be on seeing me walk through the door? How would I adjust to society? How would I react to people asking me questions about my time inside or the episodes that led to my arrest? I was up early and had a mixture of emotions.

I was both happy and sad, but the overriding factor was excitement, as I was looking forward to getting back to East Ham where I lived.

The screws came to my cell about 7am. I don't even remember if I had breakfast or not. The minor details of that morning are a blur. I went to the reception and changed into my civvies, which fitted me perfectly as I came into the prison at my fighting weight and was pretty much the same on my exit.

After signing a few forms, I was escorted by a guard to the gates. From the moment I walked out of my cell, to the moment I stepped out of the prison and inhaled my first breath of freedom, I never once looked over my shoulder.

As the gate clunked closed behind me, the first thought in my mind was, 'Thank fuck I've done that – I'm out of here!'

One of my brothers was waiting for me. It wasn't a Hollywood style emotional encounter, as we had served in the same nick together and he had only been released nine months before me.

However, it was certainly great to see him on the other

side of the wall. He had a nice shiny Audi waiting for me as I stepped out onto the pavement. I thought, 'Brilliant!' Although, 24 hours later the big end bearings went!

I was released at 9am and was home by about 11am. I drove up to the house, parked my car and went indoors, where my wife and kids were waiting.

I was very happy to be home, but it took me a fair while to settle down and for my wife and kids to get used to me being a regular around the home again.

It wasn't as if they hadn't seen me in months or years as they would visit every couple of weeks. However, to be getting that first embrace with all of them, in my house, in my clothes was priceless. Claudette had kept the place spotless. It was literally sparkling and for some reason it's one of the strongest memories I have of walking through my front door. I don't know if it was a contrast to the dull tones I had been surrounded by in a prison cell for nearly five years, but everything looked vibrant and smelled fresh.

Each time I inhaled the air and looked around, I would have another 20 reminders of how prison had torn away my freedom and enough reasons as to why I would make sure I would never go back in.

Intent on keeping myself busy, I drove the replacement car my brother had organised for me and headed down to the scrapyard and before I could think of which trade to turn my hands to, I was back in the family business, seven days a week.

With all three of us out of prison, still young and with plenty of drive, the Tibbs brothers started to rebuild the scrapyard again from scratch.

Good friends surfaced to get us on our feet by giving us expensive machinery which enabled us to get the business running in a very short space of time. The list of people who helped us was a long one and as with many episodes in my life, please accept my apologies if I have not mentioned you by name. The main thing is, you know you were there for me at my time in need and you will never be forgotten.

We were all provided with a good living and the intensity of the work helped me not to chew too much on flashbacks of my time in jail and the events that had put me there.

However, I wasn't in the happiest place in my life at that point and I can't imagine I was that easy to get on with. Wondering what the next question would be from somebody and how I would answer it would become a big hang up of mine. Thankfully the scrap business picked up very quickly and we just kept on going and going, seven days a week.

****

Within a couple of years, the scrap business was doing very well, so we moved from East Ham to Seven Kings in Ilford. I was able to buy luxuries for my wife and children and I was becoming ambitious again.

Watching the business grow increased my self-esteem and although there were times I would get resentful about everything that had happened, I was slowly rebuilding my life and was embracing everything positive.

My friends and social life were something I often dreamt

about when I was inside, however, when the first opportunity came to mingle with my friends at my local pub, I was very apprehensive.

My mate had a pub in Canning Town and soon after coming out he told me that he had organised drinks in honour of me coming home. I told him I didn't want to go at first, but I didn't want to be rude, so me and my wife went down there and had a few drinks. To tell the truth, more than a few, as the hangover in the morning reminded me. The timing wasn't exactly great, as I had to check in with the probation officer later that morning!

Hanging out with my mates again proved to be very helpful in terms of getting my self-confidence back.

My true friends wanted to meet with 'me', Jimmy Tibbs, and not meet the person who was supposedly a gangster. After my mate's party, I used to meet with the boys on a Friday at the Golden Lion pub, and although initially I was a little bit quiet, they never gave up on me and made sure I was involved in all the conversations. After a short while, I started having a bit of a joke and a laugh and this paved the way for great times ahead.

However, I also need to come clean and admit that I used to take liberties after coming out of prison. I probably went out far too much with the boys, drinking and partying and yet through all of that, especially after standing by me in prison, my wife Claudette is still by me today.

She often jokes that she deserves the George Cross for putting up with me!

To be honest, I don't think there's a lady on the

planet who could have put up with me back then – I'm a very lucky man.

****

Despite me finding my feet on the outside, a day never passed without thinking about my dad still being in prison – the man who had received the longest stretch. We made sure my mother never went without anything while my dad was inside. We would take her to see him whenever she wanted to and made sure she had everything she needed.

Knowing myself how important it would be to dad thinking how his family was on the outside, we did our best to give him peace of mind.

Thankfully he was released after eight and a half years. It was a big concern to me while he was inside. When I came out of prison aged 31, he was in his early 50s and still had about four years to go. He was in Leyhill towards the end, which thankfully was an open prison. Although it wasn't ideal, we were far less worried about him being in an open system as the quality of life he had was far better. We realised we couldn't get him out of there any quicker so we put all our efforts into building the scrap business up.

When my dad did eventually come out, he stayed in the industry for a while and then worked in the pub game for a number of years before retiring.

With the Tibbs family out of prison, money in our pockets and ambition in our lives, we were all able to smile together again. I was happy with my life and there was nothing that could energise me more at that point. Oscar Wilde once said, "Every saint has a past and every sinner has a future."

Little did I know, but my future was able to take another wild turn.

****

Whilst in prison, I remember watching Alan Minter fighting the legendary Emile Griffith on television and thought, 'I might have fought this guy'. In fact, Alan Minter's professional debut was against Maurice Thomas, the guy I was supposed to be fighting for my intended comeback in 1972.

At the time he fought Griffith, Minter already held the European crown and three years later would be the undisputed middleweight champion of the world. On watching the fight against Emile, I found myself stepping away from the action and asking myself, 'Could I have been that good?'

How would I have progressed as a professional boxer? Would I have become a title holder? I was still young, so maybe I would have grown into a natural light heavyweight? Many of my friends and family would often say I could have achieved this or that, maybe have become a champion and fought this person and that person, but I would never get to chance to try and answer any of these questions in a boxing ring ever again.

The fact that prison had taken the answer to this debate out of my hands was a very jagged pill to swallow and was unbelievably frustrating.

The initial stages of readjusting into mainstream life after my release certainly came with their testing moments. Lying in bed in our two bedroom house in Park Avenue, I would sometimes wake up in tears, dreaming that I had been in a training camp for an up-and-coming fight. I would open my eyes and the dream had disappeared.

I kept pondering, 'Should I apply for my boxing licence again?' but the same feeling would always stop me – embarrassment.

I didn't want the British Boxing Board of Control turning to me and say, "Sorry Jim, we can't grant you your licence, because you're a convicted criminal."

It would turn out to be one of my biggest regrets, especially as Terry Lawless, a few years later, told me that I probably would have got my licence back.

But a second chance with boxing was on its way and I was about to take it with open hands.

****

By 1981, prison was four years behind me and I was delighted with the direction my life had taken. Working alongside my brothers, we had built up the scrapyard business to two sites. It was hard graft, but looking back these were happy times, with a lot of laughs.

However, out of nowhere a curveball was thrown our way.

The Greater London Council (GLC), approached me and my brothers with a compulsory purchase order. They needed to build a road straight through the middle of our primary scrapyard and were willing to pay us a generous settlement for the inconvenience. After discussions with my brothers and with no real chance of opposing the decision, we accepted the compensation offer.

Growing up as a child, the scrap business had provided the financial backbone to my family. I had witnessed my father grow his yard into a successful operation, which had enabled his family to experience a good quality of life.

But now, at the age of 35, with money in my pocket and without sounding ungrateful, I came to terms with the fact that I'd had enough of the scrap game.

The offer from the GLC had given me the time and space to consider other options. Admittedly though, I didn't have a Plan B and was left scratching my head thinking, 'What are you going to do with yourself now Jim?' I've always been a very driven person, in need of dynamic goals and I was lacking direction as to where my next 'real' challenge would come from.

Opportunities in the East End had also shifted and I had been blind to how the docks had faded. The hive of activity and opportunity that shone in the 1950s was halted by the introduction of containers for transporting cargo. Unfortunately, the East End docks were not large enough to accommodate the bigger ships which were needed for the containers and the likes of Tilbury and Felixstowe became the new docking hubs.

Right at that moment, a part of the East End died. For some reason, the scrap trade benefitted from this, but unfortunately we were not destined for the long haul. Well, myself at least!

While in limbo and for no particular reason, I decided to take a walk to the Royal Oak gym, which was literally just round the corner from the scrapyard. This unplanned visit was about to mould the rest of my future.

****

My old trainer and manager Terry Lawless was still running the show and had an incredible stable of boxers. As I walked in, the likes of Frank Bruno, Charlie Magri, Lloyd Honeyghan, Mark Kaylor and many others were pounding the bags, skipping rope and sparring.

The atmosphere was intensely focused, the smell was intoxicating and as I started to catch people's eyes, they gave me a nod of recognition. As corny as this may sound, it felt like home.

Funny thing is, it hadn't changed much from 20 years ago either. It wasn't run down, but the place hadn't been renovated either! It was just how I had remembered it.

I spotted Terry and walked over to him. With a big smile on his face, he stood up, gave me a warm handshake and asked me to sit down for a chat and a cup of tea. I explained the situation with the scrapyard and that I was on the lookout for a new challenge.

Delighted that I'd made a success at the yard, he swiftly moved on to ask if I could do him a favour. I asked, "What favour Terry?" He said, "I'm going to America for a few weeks and was wondering if you could help out Frank Black with training the lads whilst I'm away?"

At the time, I was helping a little bit at West Ham Amateur Boxing Club, but this was totally different in so much as it was a bit of fun, and certainly not with professionals. I asked him to check with Frank Black to make sure he was happy with this arrangement, which he was, and within a matter of days I was back in the Royal Oak, but for the first time, on the outside of the ropes looking in.

The day after, Terry left for the US and I turned up to the gym to be greeted by dozens of hungry eyes. I was not fazed one bit as I picked up a pair of pads and started coaching Charlie Magri, who at the time was the European flyweight champion.

I started to call out the punches, "Jab, right cross, left uppercut. Again, but faster this time Charlie.' With a little more venom in my voice, I then shouted out, 'JAB, RIGHT CROSS, LEFT UPPERCUT AND THROW THE RIGHT OVER THE TOP TO FINISH. HARDER AND FASTER THIS TIME CHARLIE."

Out of the corner of my eye, I could see that some of the boxers had stopped their routines to see me and Charlie working the pads at a vicious pace.

Each punch was making a lovely banging noise which was echoing throughout the gym and with me shouting commands and Charlie growling with his punches, we now had the attention of the Royal Oak.

As we took a breather, Frank Bruno walked over and said in his polite deep tone, "Can I be next Jim?" I replied, "No problem Frank. Just let me wrap up with Charlie and we can get to work."

Same happened with Mark Kaylor soon after and by the end of the day, I had given the entire stable of boxers a crack at the pads with me! I soon ended up creating a rota and placed it on the wall so everybody could get a bit of Jimmy Tibbs.

Within a matter of days, my ethics were being respected and I was officially being recognised as a person who knew how to coach boxers.

Teaching is not about telling a boxer what to do, it's about telling them why you want them to do it and being able to answer their questions or challenges with confidence. While Frank Black was working with the lads on the groundwork and fitness, I was having the time of my life with some of the best fighters Britain had to offer.

I was however very conscious to not get overly excited, as I realised I was, in effect, a temp covering for a few weeks while Terry sorted out his business in the US.

On the day Terry was coming home from America, I decided not to turn up to the gym as I had assumed he would want to get back in the driving seat. As he walked through the doors, before he could get to his office, Charlie Magri walked up to Terry and asked, "Terry, I'd like Jimmy Tibbs to be my trainer. Is this possible?"

Before Terry could respond, a group of other fighters followed suit. Charlie had also presented Terry with a letter for the British Boxing Board of Control, again fully endorsed by the rest of the stable, requesting that I be granted a boxing trainer's licence. Terry was taken aback, but not half as much as I was about to be.

Next day, he gave me a call asking if I could come to the gym as he needed to discuss something with me. As I walked in, he looked me in the eyes and said, "What would be your response if I'd ask you to train the lads for the next six months?' I remained calm and said, 'I'd love to have that opportunity Terry! Thank you."

He then went on to explain the lengths Charlie Magri and the other boxers had gone to in order to keep me at the Royal Oak. I was excited and humbled all in one. There was no way I was going to let these lads down and I would make sure I showed them the same confidence they had shown me.

With the offer on the table, I thought to myself, 'Why not. Let's give this a crack'. I had never dreamt that an opportunity of this size within boxing would ever come my way again, but was also very aware that there was a great deal of pressure on me.

I would either be highly regarded as a trainer after six months or be the laughing stock of boxing.

The intention was to train the fighters over this period, at which time we would apply for my boxing trainer's licence. In the meantime, although I was fully involved with the boxers preparations, on fight night I would not be allowed anywhere near the corner.

Those six months were very intense. This was different to doing Terry a favour while he was on holiday for a few weeks. I was on the payroll and under the spotlight. It wouldn't have been so bad if I was starting out with one unknown fighter who was having a pro debut, based in a small village in the middle of the countryside but this was the total opposite. I was training a stable of very good fighters, many of whom were already champions and many more who would go on to pick up championship honours.

With the majority of the boxers under my wings being in the media spotlight, there was no hiding place for me and I certainly couldn't afford any margin of error. This was a chance to rebrand myself and remind people that Jimmy Tibbs was a boxing man, first and foremost.

I needed to learn – and I needed to learn quickly – and my university was the Royal Oak gym.

It wasn't like there was a diploma in boxing tuition, with a specialism of wrapping hands and cuts management available in evening classes. Watching Frank and Terry was my schooling and I was assigned a level of responsibility which Terry felt I could handle.

My benchmark for success was seeing the belief in the fighters' faces. There's an old expression, "You can't kid a kidder." In this case, "You can't kid a fighter." In addition to telling a boxer what I wanted them to do, it was essential for me to explain 'why' I wanted them to do it. Everything I did had logic behind it and it was essential each boxer understood the rationale behind each and every move I told them to do.

Within a matter of weeks, Terry turned to me and pointed to one of the fighters and said, "Jim. Wrap his hands." I had been watching Terry and Frank up to point, but this would be my first time wrapping hands myself.

As I confidently walked over to the boxer, a million and

one different things started running through my head, with the main thought of, "What makes a good hand wrap?" being at the forefront!

I started to think to myself, 'What if he's got brittle hands? What do I do? Shall I wrap heavily around the knuckles or the thumbs? Tight or loose wraps?' As I started to apply the fabric, everything fell into place.

Wrapping a fighter's hands is as individual as their signature – they all have their own preference. I had a fundamental area to cover on the hand which was dictated by the British Boxing Board of Control, but after that the fighter would let you know their exact needs.

The same went for cuts. I used to watch Terry and Frank go to work on them and had a fairly good idea of how to tackle the various scenarios. When I was assigned responsibility for my first cut, I realised that I simply needed to have confidence in myself and my ability. It is all about faith and ensuring the boxer that you will do your very best in the time available to try and lessen the damage.

I've never had a cut I was unsure about. My ethic was and still is, 'If I can't treat the cut, the fight has to be stopped.'

There's 60 seconds between each round. By the time the fighter sits down and is cleaned up, the actual amount of time I can dedicate to a cut is going to be between 30-35 seconds, tops.

I don't have time to do plastic surgery in the corner or give 15 stitches. It's all about trying to stabilise and stop the cut from becoming worse.

My on the job experience was teaching me this and many

other gems of knowledge and as the clock ticked on, my confidence and self-esteem were rising to new heights.

****

After an intense six months at the Royal Oak, the day had come to try and get my trainer's licence. I travelled up with Terry to the British Boxing Board of Control's headquarters and they cross examined me as if I was in court.

One of them was going through my records and said, "You got nicked for GBH didn't you?" I said, "No. I got nicked for attempted murder!"

There was a small silence before they all started firing questions at me from every direction. In the end I decided to say my bit.

I explained my passion for the sport and how I regretted what had happened in the past, but unfortunately I couldn't turn back the hands of time. It was now time to look to the future.

I explained that I had a great deal to offer the world of boxing but if they didn't accept me for my ability as opposed to my past, this would never work.

The tone of the discussions and the mood in the room was negative and tense. I was holding little hope for any success and was pretty much ready to walk out of there. As I was halfway through my justifications as to why I would make a good trainer, Terry interrupted me and addressed the board bluntly with a raised voice and said, "I TRUST THIS MAN WITH MY LIFE."

Everyone in the room went silent. The board members looked at each other, followed by some nods of approval and lo and behold, I was granted my licence!

The impossible had happened.

I would never have thought I would be given a second chance to enter the world of boxing, a sport I had fallen in love with at the age of 11.

And I was more determined than ever that this time, no matter what, I would make the most of my experience and skills to become the very best I could.

Round 7

MARK AND LLOYD

"I won't be long mate. Be ready to jump in the ring soon!"
– Mark Kaylor to Jim McDonnell as he's leaving the changing room to fight Errol Christie, 1985

As I embarked on my career as a professional boxing trainer, I felt fairly confident of my ability.

The truth was, my learning was only just beginning. I was starting to realise that there was big difference between listening to instructions and giving them. Thankfully, I could continue to learn from Terry Lawless over the years.

He had techniques which I observed over time, which proved to be priceless. For example – I remember watching him getting a swollen eye down with a bit of grease on his thumb. You won't find that in any textbooks!

Terry's greatest asset was his time involved in the game.

He knew what to say and when to say it on fight night. For example – an inexperienced trainer (such as myself at the time) would have screamed out in a rage something like, "OI REF. WATCH HIS HEAD!", when they are concerned about their fighter's opponent.

Terry would instead shout out to his boxer, "Watch his head John", (or whoever the fighter was called), so in that way the referee could hear the comment and take note of it, without feeling like he's being told how to do his job. Terry acted as a great mentor in those early days.

****

As a fully fledged trainer who was now not only allowed to train his fighters but be present in their corners on fight night, I embarked on a number of journeys with some great characters.

Mark Kaylor was one of the first.

I'd known Mark from when I trained at the Ruskin pub gym shortly after being released from prison.

He walked in one day and I knew who he was because I'd already heard all about him.

He had a reputation for being a very good amateur but I hadn't seen him in action up to that point. One of the guys with Mark turned to me and said, "Jim. Do me a favour. Could you spar with Mark for a couple of rounds?" I said, "No problem." Mark was about 17 and was very fiery and enthusiastic, while I was 32.

Mark starting wildly swinging punches in my direction, but

I was dodging them easily by simply moving my top half.

In between his looping blows, I would calmly throw out a jab, which landed every time. This went on for a couple of minutes – slip, bang, slip bang.

In the end, Mark was so frustrated that he spat out his gum shield out and shouted, "I CAN'T HIT HIM!" I picked up his gumshield and told somebody to wash it. I turned to him and said, "Mark. You never want to do that. Never show your opponent any emotion." He listened to every word intently and then nodded his head. We then sparred for a couple more rounds and left it there.

About two years later, our paths crossed again. I was punching the heavy bag, when the same guy from two years before asked again if I could spar with Mark for three rounds. I looked over and thought, 'Bloody hell, he's got big!'

He was now training for the 1980 Olympics in Moscow, which he subsequently qualified for. I replied, "Of course." He was a completely different person this time round. First round, he was keeping me at a distance with his jab and it was me who was now struggling. I was bobbing and weaving his punches and when I got in close I was working his body – when I had the rare opportunity!

Second round was slightly better, but I was still struggling to tag him clean. As we were about to start the third round, Mark's mate shouted out, "Thanks Jim. That's enough!" I replied, "Are you sure?", and he said, "Yeah. That's fine Jim." Who would have guessed a year later I would be training Mark as a professional?

After becoming the ABA middleweight champion and reaching the third round of the Olympics in 1980, Mark turned professional later that year with Terry Lawless.

The first fight I trained him for in 1981 was against a boxer called George Danahar who had lasted the eight round distance with Herol Graham three fights prior.

From the very first moment I spoke with him in that ring in 1978, it was obvious Mark was a very good listener. It only took me a few days to realise he was an equally good worker and in fact an excellent overall student. I asked him how far he wanted to go and he said, "As far as possible Jim." That's all I needed to hear.

Mark had already turned pro before I had joined Terry, so I didn't need to iron out the amateur traits from him. He was a very brave fighter. I taught him to keep his chin down, smarten his jab up and not get caught up in a scrap if there was no need.

He already possessed a good right hand and left hook and his fitness was fantastic. With the likes of Lloyd Honeyghan, Chris Pyatt and Tony Wilson to spar with, George Danahar was in trouble!

Inevitably Mark stopped Danahar in three rounds and within three years of turning professional, Mark was unbeaten and had already racked up 20 stoppages in his 23 outings.

His following was getting bigger and bigger, and whenever he fought, East London was empty. Fresh off a fifth-round stoppage of Bobby West, we were handed the opportunity to fight against Roy Gumbs for the British and Commonwealth middleweight titles, in September, 1983. At this point, Gumbs had held the British belt for a couple of years and successfully defended it on a number of occasions.

He had a reputation for being a destructive puncher, but he was also known for leaving himself open while on the attack. Mark was certainly the underdog entering this fight.

After having squeezed out of our tiny changing room, we made our way to the ring and before we knew it, I was climbing out of the ropes and leaving Mark to get on with business. Within seconds of the bell ringing, Mark stuck the jab in his face. Once, twice, three times, then the left hook to the body. Gumbs responded with his own assault, sending Mark into the ropes. Both fighters continued to exchange vicious assaults for the rest of the round and it was already obvious that if they continued to throw punches at this rate and with this amount of force, the fight would not be going the distance. Hooks were followed by uppercuts and uppercuts followed by more hooks.

A high octane, relentless first round – and the fight got even better as it continued.

Mark dictated rounds two and three behind a beautiful jab but he took his eye off the ball for a moment in the fourth and that was enough for Gumbs to knock him down for an eight count.

Fully recovered, Mark came back hard in the fifth and with about a minute to go he unloaded a massive assault on Gumbs, landing successfully with every punch thrown. Left jab, big straight right, jab, right hand, left hook to the body, left hook to the head – Gumbs was down!

Not able to make the count, Mark at the age of 22 was now the new middleweight British and Commonwealth champion. I flew through the ropes and went over and hugged him and we all ended up collapsing on the canvas as the celebrations took over.

Mark's next fight was against an American fighter called Tony Cerda.

Unfortunately, Mark was not able to unleash his full potential on the evening, as the bout was stopped from a low blow from Mark in the ninth round, resulting in a stoppage by way of disqualification. This was the first blemish on his previously unbeaten record and in all honesty could have been avoided.

Moving on from the Cerda loss, two months later he went on to beat Ralph Moncrief by a fifth round stoppage and a couple of months after that beat Randy Smith on points, before facing Buster Drayton in May, 1984.

I had a bad feeling about this fight during the latter stages of our training camp. For some reason, Mark was struggling to make weight. Two days before the fight, I went for a nice, slow walk with him, just round the corner from where he lived and while having a chat, he started to mention that his legs were aching.

Mark was very big for a middleweight and I'm pretty sure this was as a direct consequence of cooking down to make the weight. Either way, he wasn't 100 percent.

When we went for the weigh-in, Buster Drayton looked great. Better than I'd ever seen him before. Weight issues aside, the truth is, the better man won on the evening.

When Mark was knocked down he should have taken the full eight count, but being as brave as he was, he didn't want to show he was hurt.

At one point I was literally running round the ring telling him to stay down and take the count! After a number of knockdowns, the referee did the right thing and stopped the fight.

Soon after the Drayton loss, we were approached to put Mark's Commonwealth and British titles on the line against European champion Tony Sibson, for a winner-takes-all titles contest.

Mark's training camp for this fight went extremely well and despite his recent defeats, he oozed confidence again.

However, after 12 rounds, Tony was awarded a close unanimous decision, with each judge having him ahead by two points. Sibson was always going to be the favourite, having fought the higher calibre of boxers at that point in his career. Mark boxed really well, but Sibson was just a little bit too ring crafty for him.

Five months after the Sibson loss, Mark knocked out American Richard Beranek in three one-sided rounds, before winning a points decision against Dwight Walker in June, 1985.

Next up, we would be fighting Errol Christie on Bonfire Night, November, 1985. Although we didn't realise it at the time, this fight was about to become an iconic part of British boxing history.

The scheduled fight between Mark and Errol was a final eliminator for the British middleweight belt. Christie had won an ABA title in 1981 and with the exception of one loss, had earned himself a fierce reputation as a hard puncher, by winning all but one of his pro 18 victories by knockout at that point in time.

He had an outstanding amateur record to boot and had been trained at the legendary Kronk gym.

Little did we know, but the hype for this fight was about to resemble that of a world title contest. The irony later would be that neither fighter actually got the opportunity to fight for the British title.

Many had Christie odds-on favourite to win and the press had sold the fight to the public as one fighter who was trying to regain his title status versus another who was using the fight as a stepping stone to possible world title contention.

Racial tension had started to build up around the edges of the publicity and when the two exchanged words and fists, followed by a comical tumble in a fountain at a press conference at the Stakis Regency Casino a few weeks before the fight, it didn't take long for the National Front and opposing equivalents to rear their heads and build up a following.

Christie claimed that Mark called him an "ugly black bastard", whereas Mark claims he called him "an ugly bastard", and still maintains that to this day. Either way, it's water under the bridge as neither fighter was a racist but this episode proved to be the start of a massive pre-fight build up for one of the biggest grudge matches in British boxing history.

On the day of the fight, Mark and Errol came face to face for the weigh-in. At the time, everybody was expecting

Christie to come in heavy and possibly struggle to make the weight. However, on the day of the fight Christie came in light and I instantly knew we had an advantage.

With all the pre-fight activity indicating that there could possibly be crowd trouble, it was obvious on the evening that the level of security had been increased. The number of policemen visible inside and outside the venue was immense, including about four times the number of officers you would normally have ringside.

As we stepped into the ring, it was obvious that we were carrying the flag for West Ham. Mark was sporting claret and blue shorts, and Terry Lawless, Frank Black and myself all had matching coloured cloaks.

To top it off, the boxing ring was also claret and blue! As Mark was introduced to the audience, the response was deafening, with short and sharp chants of "KAY-LOR, KAY-LOR, KAY-LOR."

There was no doubt that his following was massive, but his focus was firmly fixed on Errol across the ring, and although he was appreciative of the support, he just wanted to tear into his opponent.

After the referee had given both fighters their instructions and we were walking back to our corner, I gave him his final piece of advice. "Mark – after the bell sounds, get straight into the centre of that ring and make Christie dance around. Keep him moving."

As the bell sounded for round one, Mark instantly landed the jab followed by a right cross. Christie started throwing out the jab and Mark threw a ramrod of a right hand which not only cut him over the left eye, but put Christie on the seat of his shorts taking an eight count! I thought to myself, 'Lovely! Could be an early night!' As he started to stand up, it was obvious he was seriously hurt and he staggered with wobbly legs to the ropes, trying to clear his head. The referee waved them to fight on and Christie held on for about 10 seconds before showing that his head had cleared and then fired back shots of his own.

With all this happening, a firework exploded in the crowd. Can you believe this was all in the first 60 seconds of the opening round??

As the second minute unfolded, they started to work well behind their respective jabs, but with Mark looking for the knockout punch to finish off the job from the previous minute, he left himself exposed and Christie caught him with a clubbing right hand of his own, which put Mark on one knee looking very dazed. Coming up at the count of eight, it took Mark about 30 seconds to regain his senses and despite getting tagged with another right hand seconds before the bell, he made it through the round.

In fact, he had enough energy to throw a cheeky little punch in Christie's face after the bell, which earned him a warning from referee Harry Gibbs!

As we got back into the corner, I reminded Mark that he was the better fighter and that he needed to take the centre of the ring and not back up. "The combination I want to see is the jab, right hand and a left hook over the top," I told him. He nodded confidently.

Thankfully, the only fireworks involved for the rest of the

fight took place inside the ring as a tense, close battle turned into a classic.

However, in the eighth round, Mark threw the jab followed by the trademark straight right which dropped Christie and despite a brave attempt to walk to the corner on his knees, Christie never made it to his feet before the count of 10.

Mark had won the grudge match of the decade!

The second the referee declared Mark the winner, he sprinted over into the corner, jumped up on the ropes and screamed out in joy to the crowd. Despite the fact that we were all delighted, I was still aware that there was a lot of tension in the arena, so I pulled him off pretty quickly and tried to keep our reactions calm until we got back to the changing room.

Animosity apart – one of the first things that Mark did was walk over to Errol's corner, check he was ok and thank him for the fight.

As Errol was getting ready to leave the ring he started to get a bad reception from the crowd. I wasn't having any of it, so me and Terry did something very simple which flipped the situation around in a matter of seconds. We walked over to the loser's corner and stood there applauding, hands above our heads, and the jeers soon turned to cheers.

Bout finished, war over.

Mark's next fight was a rematch against Tony Cerda – the man who had put Mark's first blemish on his record three years earlier. Mark left no doubt who was the better fighter this time round and beat Cerda up until the fight was stopped in the sixth round.

Mark then made four more attempts to try and capture the European title against top opponents such as Herol Graham and future world champion Mauro Galvano, but as time progressed, his peak days were moving further behind him.

Mark's last fight against James Cook for the European title was memorable for a number of reasons. Cook was a regular in Terry's gym and had sparred a fair bit with Mark a few years prior – lovely chap and a good fighter.

Through discussions with promoter Harry Holland, the fight happened in June, 1991, at the York Hall.

It was always going to be a tough fight and as the bell rung for the first round, James started to throw out the jab faultlessly.

Every time it hit Mark's head, it jolted back and the old reflexes from years gone were simply not there anymore. As James became more confident between rounds two and four, the jabs were followed up by heavy right hands over the top.

Mark was more than a fighter to me, he was and still is a dear friend and friends don't allow other friends to take unnecessary punishment.

As the final seconds approached of round five, knowing this was his last fight, I had a plan.

I turned to Dean Powell and said, "I'm not going to stop the fight at the end of the round, because I know Mark will go mad. I'm going to wait until he's touched gloves and started boxing for the sixth and then I'm going to throw in the towel and walk in the ring and stop the fight."

Round six started and after a short while I could see Mark was taking a bit of a belting and I didn't want to see anymore. I stepped through the ropes, apologised to the referee straight away and walked Mark back to the corner. As I walked him back, he growled at me, "What did you do that for Jim?"

In the meantime, I was on the receiving end of a large number of angry Kaylor fans, calling me every name under the sun and starting a number of scuffles in the crowd.

At the time, I had my two sons ringside, the Rowland brothers and a string of good fighters supporting Mark's efforts. As all this is going on, a couple of minutes later, Mark turned to me and said, "Sorry about that Jim. You did me a right favour. I was shot. Thank you." I said, "I know mate. Don't worry about it. I was just looking out for ya."

For some unknown reason, we were then asked to do an interview for a French TV channel! Neither of us spoke French, but thankfully the interviewer spoke English. We sat on the canvas, on the outside of the ring by the corner and just as we are about to start, a guy from the crowd shouts over, "TIBBS. YOU'RE A NO GOOD CUNT!"

Before I could even take in what the guy had said, one of my sons picked up a chair and cracked it over this guy's head. My other son jumped in to back his brother up and was knocking people out left, right and centre. I thought to myself, 'I've got to stop this!' I stood on top of a chair and shouted, "STOOOOOOOOOOP!"

And within seconds, everybody did as they were told. It was as if I was directing a fight scene in a movie, as people holding chairs just froze, people ready to throw their next punches dropped their hands and looked over, and my sons tried to make out they were innocent by doing their ties up and tidying their shirts and jackets with that, 'I didn't start it' look on their faces. The day after, the story made it into the *News of The World*, with me apparently stopping a full scale riot!

The James Cook fight was Mark's last as a professional boxer. He retired with a fantastic record of 48 fights, seven losses and 34 stoppages. I was fortunate to have trained him for 44 of those bouts.

After Mark retired from boxing, our families remained very close. He now lives on the West coast of the USA and looking over my shoulder, I can honestly say it was a pleasure to have worked with one of the East End's best ever exports, especially during his peak years.

****

The Ragamuffin Man – AKA, Lloyd Honeyghan – was probably one of the most naturally talented fighters I ever trained. An outspoken character with dynamite in his fists, I trained him for 11 fights over a two-and-a-half year period, in which time he won three titles.

Before training Lloyd I didn't know a huge amount about him, or his pedigree and the fact that he lived in South London also meant that he wasn't somebody who was talked about that much in the East End.

The first time I started working with him in 1981, I knew,

with dedication, this kid was going to go all the way. He was very hard to hit, he could duck, dive, bob and weave and had a knockout punch in either hand. He also possessed good stamina and as an all-round fighter he could spar with anybody – and I mean 'anybody'. He could spar with Chris Pyatt (light middle) for four rounds, Mark Kaylor (middle) for four, and Tony Wilson (light heavy) for a further four and he would still be in great condition.

Although I had worked with Lloyd from 1981, it wasn't until 1983 that I officially took on the role as his trainer, preparing him to take on Lloyd Hibbert for an eliminator of the British welterweight title. The fight took place at the Royal Albert Hall in January, 1983, and Lloyd beat Hibbert comfortably, without having to exert himself to his full potential. He won the fight behind his jab, solid hooks and some beautiful combinations, many of which we hadn't even rehearsed in the gym. His trademark punch was his left hook, but he showed in this fight that he was an all rounder who had plenty of boxing ability. Hibbert would go on to win the light middleweight British and Commonwealth titles a few years after.

Six weeks later, in his 15th fight, Lloyd knocked out Sid Smith in four rounds to become the Southern Area champion. We were both delighted, but with this fight being a final eliminator for the British title, our sights were already set on the next fight. We didn't have to wait long as Lloyd was back in the ring challenging Cliff Gilpin for the British title just a month later.

Gilpin had Lloyd in all sorts of problems early in the fight, pinning him up against the ropes and tagging him with a flurry of hooks which finally sent Lloyd to the canvas. He made it through the last few seconds of the round, but he walked back on wobbly legs. Not the ideal start to a British title fight! Rounds three and four were fairly even and round five had a freak moment where both fighters landed at exactly the same time, almost knocking each other out!

Rounds six to 12 proved to be a real tear-up, but Lloyd was simply too much for him, winning by a wide points margin over the distance. Watching the fight again recently, I had to appreciate just how talented Lloyd already was at that stage of his career.

At one point, Gilpin had him up against the ropes and was in the power position, but Lloyd was the one dictating the fight, rolling and slipping punches, while landing vicious counter hooks to the head and the body. Harry Carpenter was commentating on the fight and said, "He came off those ropes having done more work than the man who was pressing him against them, and Gilpin had to give way in the end." After clocking up two more wins, we gave Gilpin a rematch which would be Lloyd's first defence of his British title. This time was more one-sided than before, with Lloyd winning by an even wider margin.

With only one fight in 1984 due to sustaining a badly cut eye and a broken thumb while taking a points victory against Roberto Mendez, we were given the opportunity to take on the European welterweight champion, Gianfranco Rosi, in his own backyard of Perugia, Italy, in January, 1985.

The training camp was at the Royal Oak, simply because

I knew there was always plenty of sparring guaranteed. Up to about 10 days before the fight I had Lloyd sparring with decent boxers, but in the remaining days I just needed somebody to go through the motions with him and someone who wasn't going to cut him or cause him any injuries.

The truth is I didn't have any suitable boxers in the gym for him to spar with – then in walks Dave Dent. Dave was an ex-ABA champion but he was certainly not renowned for his punch power.

As he walked in I called him over and asked if he would mind sparring with Lloyd. He said, "No problem." I then had a word with Lloyd and asked him to take it easy as it was his last week of light sparring before tapering down to fight night.

Dave jumped into the ring with Lloyd and they started to move around while I was looking through the ropes and while Terry Lawless was in the office.

The sparring was very fluid, with Lloyd going through the motions of what he was going to do with Rosi, by way of cutting off the ring space and keeping busy in front of him. After about three rounds, Dave was backed onto the ropes and had nowhere to go, so he threw a right hand at Lloyd which knocked him spark out! Lloyd – if you are reading this, I'm only including this story to show what a great fighter you are and how quickly you bounced back and turned the tables a few days later – I'm not having a pop at you!

I turned him into the recovery position and as I took his gumshield out a load of phlegm came out of his mouth and nose. It was obvious he had a cold of some sort, but had done well to disguise it.

In the meantime, Terry had obviously heard the sound of about 11 stone hitting the floor and popped his head out of his office door and said, "Everything ok Jim?" I replied, calmly without trying to highlight the situation, "Yes Tel. All good over here mate!" Lloyd was 100 percent fine after a few minutes and three days later we went out to Italy to fight for the European title.

From my experience of taking boxers abroad, you are rarely done any favours by the judges so our intention was to dominate from the outset.

However, after the first three minutes it was obvious that Rosi had not turned up to lose his crown and after the first round it was about even, which in my eyes meant that the judges would probably edge the round to the champion. Round two I had to give to the Italian.

Although Lloyd was hunting him down, he wasn't able to execute his jab the way he wanted to and Rosi's experience showed, with some effective right hand counters and generally a slightly more effective use of the ring.

As Lloyd came back to the corner, I told him to keep the jab going but to also unload more with the right hand. About 15 seconds before the start of round three I told him to get to the centre of the ring before Rosi, to let him know who the boss was.

As the bell sounded, Lloyd started to pump out the jab to the body. Single shots at first, then doubles followed by the right hand over the top which landed successfully, forcing Rosi to pedal backwards. This was Lloyd at his absolute best and it was a pleasure to see such a master in action.

As they started to circle the ring, with Lloyd in control flicking out a light jab and with no punches having been landed from either fighter for about 10 seconds, Lloyd threw an overhand right which landed immaculately.

The well travelled punch landed so hard to the side of Rosi's left jaw that it spun him around and sent him face down between the last two ropes of the ring. As Rosi lay motionless for about seven seconds, the referee started one of the slowest counts I've ever witnessed, during which time Rosi had just about managed to get on all fours, with a bit of help from the officials at ringside.

In the meantime, Terry Lawless, Frank Black and myself were screaming and shouting, disgusted with what was going on.

As it became obvious that Rosi was not going to make it to his feet for the count of 50, never mind 10, his corner jumped into the ring and Lloyd was the new welterweight European champion! The fight was regarded by many, including myself, as one of Lloyd's best ever finishes.

Rosi would later win the WBC and IBF light middleweight world titles, making over 10 successful defences. This was a great scalp for Lloyd and showed just how talented he was.

Immediately after the fight I went to see Rosi in the medical room. It took him about 20 minutes to completely clear his head and when I went over to offer my thanks for giving us the chance to challenge for the title, and also to check if he was ok, he said, "C'est la vie!"

A true professional and as I said, one who bounced back

to have a great career in boxing. Eager to stay busy, Lloyd was back in the ring one month later and fought against RW Smith. Smith was a last minute replacement and although he put up a very brave attempt, he was behind on the scorecards before being retired with a suspected broken hand in the sixth round.

I've known the Smith family most of my life and only have good things to say about them. Robert now sits on the British Boxing Board of Control and his dad Andy used to manage Joe Bugner.

****

My last fight with Lloyd was against another American called Danny Paul. This time we crossed the big pond to fight in their backyard in August, 1985, in Atlantic City, New Jersey. Mickey Duff and George Francis were already out there, so Lloyd, Terry Lawless and myself travelled out and met up with them.

Danny was not meant to cause Lloyd much bother and in all honesty he didn't. All three judges gave the decision to Lloyd and our mission to get him recognised in the USA and on the world scene was accomplished. Although this was my last fight with Lloyd, I was absolutely delighted when he went on to beat Don Curry for the WBC, WBA and IBF world titles one year later.

Mark and Lloyd were both brilliant fighters and great men.

And they were by no means the only world class boxers I would get the honour of working with...

Round 8

BRUNO

"Jimmy's one of the best British trainers of all time. Whether it's a six rounder or a 12 rounder, he's equally as passionate and committed to his fighters and treats them all like world champions, inside and outside of the ring."
– Frank Bruno, 2013

Within four years of walking into the Royal Oak gym, I had trained Area, British and Commonwealth champions, but I never dreamt that I would then be training boxers to win their first European and World titles so early on.

I'd seen Franklin Roy Bruno in the late 1970s, fighting in the amateurs and it came as no surprise whatsoever that he went on to win the senior ABA heavyweight championship in 1980. He abandoned an impressive amateur career of 21 fights, with only one loss, to turn pro in 1982.

Although Frank had not become a British boxing icon at this stage, he was already a popular guy for a few reasons – he was very polite, he was always immaculately dressed, he was a big strong man with a distinctively low voice and he could hit – very hard.

At that point, my honest opinion was that he wasn't the best in the world but he most certainly wasn't the worst either. I felt there was a lot I could do with him, especially because of Frank's willingness to learn and his ability to deliver from what he was taught.

I officially started training Frank for his fourth fight against Ronald Gibbs in May, 1982. He had already blasted his previous three opponents in the seven weeks before, with only one of them making it as far as round two, so I certainly didn't need to concentrate on getting rid of his amateur traits by looking for methods and techniques to anchor him down and increase his power.

If anything we were looking to do the opposite. Work on his movement and get him to be a more elusive fighter with far more lateral movement.

Frank was very rigid when we first started working together, which was a concern to me, simply in terms of the long haul. When you are very rigid and tense, your body gets worn out far quicker than when you are relaxed.

Although this was very early days, I was already starting to sense that he'd end up fighting for the world title, so I knew this was not a short-term strategy we needed to adopt into the training camps.

For his first fight under my wing, my aim was to get him to

relax, move his top half and hook off the jab. Pleased with the new moves and techniques I was throwing Frank's way, he very kindly coined a new phrase to sum up the impact I had made on him – "The Tibbs Touch"!

In 1982, Frank was very fortunate to have some great sparring partners training under the same roof. For his early fights he was part of an elite sparring group made up from Adrian Elliot (1982 ABA super heavyweight champion), Gary Mason (future British heavyweight champion), and Horace Notice (future British and Commonwealth heavyweight champion).

Over time, we had to split the four of them up, simply due to the fact that they were all improving at a rapid rate and we didn't want them getting hurt between themselves. By the mid-1980s, Terry Lawless had to call over a group of American sparring partners – who, for the record, never used to last long once Frank got to work on them!

In addition to having great sparring partners at the Royal Oak, Frank was also fortunate to have some of the most dedicated fitness fanatics on the planet based in the gym, which complemented his love of training.

Running, sparring, pad work, he loved it all. He was a great runner and I remember joining Frank, Mark Kaylor and Mo Hussein for a run through the woods in Hainault one time.

I remember Mo saying to me, "Keep up Jim, not long to go. Just another couple of corners and a few straights and we will be done." Frank was whistling and hardly breaking sweat and Mark Kaylor was deep in concentration.

What they didn't realise, was that I was holding back on purpose and giving them the impression that I was a knackered old man. I was in my late 30s at the time, and was in great shape! We went on a bit further and Mo said, "Just round this bend, up the hill and we are finished Jim." I turned around to them and said, "Brilliant. See ya later", and sprinted off, beating them all to the finishing line as they all shouted and screamed behind me, calling me all the names under the sun!

Anyway – back to May, 1982, and Mr Ronald Gibbs. Inevitably, Frank smashed him in four rounds, but credit to Gibbs for hanging in there so long, because (with the exception of one five rounder), Frank went on to stop his next 14 opponents over the next 17 months in four rounds and under. He was now 18-0, with twelve of his wins coming within the first two rounds. Frank was no doubt a concussive puncher but up to this point he had not been in the ring with somebody who could match his power and could also box.

That was until he crossed paths with Floyd 'Jumbo' Cummings in October, 1983, at the Royal Albert Hall.

Floyd's previous opponents included Tim Witherspoon, Mitch Green and Renaldo Snipes. He had also pulled off a draw against a faded Joe Frazier, who had decided to come back after a five-year lay-off.

Thankfully Joe retired after that fight. In brief – Cummings had shared the ring with a much higher calibre of opponent than Frank at that point in their respective careers. That said, around this time, Terry Lawless sent Frank over to the US for a few weeks to share the ring with an up-and-coming kid who was looking for tough sparring partners.

The kid's name was Mike Tyson.

Aware that Jumbo would not be a walkover, we hired a ring veteran by way of an American called Leroy Caldwell to spar with Frank for three weeks. Leroy had fought an extremely long and impressive list of world ranked fighters including the likes of George Foreman, Ron Lyle, Joe Bugner, Oscar Bonavena, Trevor Berbick and many others. If anybody could push Frank to his limits and also advise him from within the ropes, it was him.

During the weeks they shared the ring, Leroy educated Frank on how to attack his opponent while on the ropes and gave him some advice on moving to the side and countering when an opponent throws a punch, as opposed to walking back in a straight line. In the words of Leroy at the time, "The guy is very strong and trains like a mad dog!" Frank came away a more complete boxer three weeks later and I felt overall preparations had been near on perfect.

The atmosphere on fight night was immense. Frank had unintentionally worked his way into the British sporting public's hearts and the number of people supporting him inside and outside of the hall was unbelievable.

Back then and possibly even today, you could ask any 'non-boxing' individuals if they knew who Frank Bruno was and there is an 99 percent chance the answer would be "yes". Ask them who Larry Holmes or Joe Frazier are, and you could be waiting a long time.

Frank had cemented his place in British history and had not even won a title yet. His relationship with Harry

Carpenter provided the extra icing on the cake outside of the ring, with his famous phrase, "You know what I mean 'Arry!" People wanted Frank to win because he was a very good boxer, a genuinely lovely guy who never trashed talked and who was in the news headlines for the right reasons.

Despite the long list of boxing greats who Cummings had fought against, he had only been stopped once. There was even talk that he could be the first man to stop Frank in his tracks. Although 33 at the time, Cummings was relatively fresh, having started boxing professionally at the age of 29, due to earlier serving a 12-year prison stretch for murder, which is where he learnt to box.

In fact, at the time of the fight he was on parole.

As the bell sounded for round one, the crowd died down and Frank spent the next two minutes and 58 seconds controlling Cummings behind the jab. Literally just before the bell, Jumbo hit Frank with a big right hand which had his entire body weight behind it and almost caved in the left side of Frank's face.

At that point he should have been walking back to the corner, but the impact of the blow had anchored his feet to the canvas and it was a miracle he was not horizontal. He was badly shaken up. If there had been another 15 seconds left in the round, Cummings would have only needed to tap Frank and the fight would have been over.

After forcing him onto the stool, Terry Lawless took a cold sponge to Frank's face, while I removed his gumshield, poured some water over his head and started to give him his instructions for the next round. For every second that passed Frank was clearing his head and starting to nod to everything I was telling him.

With about 10 seconds to go I looked over at Jumbo and reminded Frank that he had the better boxing ability and power, not Jumbo. I then said, "Frank – he's gonna come after you in this round." He leaned over, took a look at Jumbo, leaned back and gave me the nod.

As the bell sounded for round two, he headed off to the centre of the ring to meet Cummings. As predicted, Jumbo was looking to finish where he left off and unloaded with a semi-successful heavy assault on Frank. Thankfully two things happened which saved the fight for Frank – his boxer's instinct of holding on and tying up Jumbo at close quarters and secondly, Jumbo had blown his engine!

Halfway through the round it was Jumbo who was now holding on and for no other reason than being absolutely exhausted. With rapid chants of "BRU-NO, BRU-NO, BRU-NO" bouncing around the hall, Frank brought the fight back to the centre of the ring and started firing the jab confidently. The last minute was 50/50 and it was clear that Frank needed a complete recharge before going out for round three.

As the bell sounded for the third, Frank threw out about half a dozen jabs and then landed with a heavy right hand, which had Jumbo holding on. Right at that very moment, the tide had turned. Frank continued to throw out his piston-like jab for the next three rounds, landing occasionally with a left uppercut or the big straight right hand.

Cummings' face was starting to swell up heavily and he

was almost breathing through his ears trying to take in as much oxygen as possible to keep him on his feet.

About two minutes into the seventh, Frank unloaded a perfect right hand to the left side of Cummings' face, making up for the right he himself had been on the receiving end of in the first round.

After trying to hold on desperately, the referee split them up and Frank threw out a couple of teaser jabs, before unloading a beautiful right hand cross which left Cummings tangled between the ropes, incapable of getting to his feet. The fight was over and so was any anxiety which had had us all concerned in the first round.

I was extremely proud of how Frank had flipped the fight around while on the verge of defeat. He stuck to the game plan of working behind the jab and unloading when Cummings was on the ropes, but he also exposed how open he was to the big right hand – a weakness other fighters would exploit in future bouts.

Vulnerabilities aside – Frank proved he was capable of lasting more than four rounds with durable opponents and we all felt he deserved a shot at a major title in the near future.

On catching up with Frank recently, he made an open confession to me about that first round with Jumbo. "Jim – I got knocked down in the first round and thought it was over. Whatever it was you said in that corner motivated me as I was completely gone."

The blows Frank received in that fight certainly didn't affect him in the long term because two months later he disposed of Walter Santemore in four rounds and three months after that victory, in March, 1984, he smashed the Argentinean heavyweight champ in under a round before taking on an unexpectedly tough adversary in May, by way of an American called James 'Bonecrusher' Smith.

Although Smith was the bigger of the two fighters, I knew Frank's power was far superior and by round five I wanted him to open up, but Terry had made it clear that he wanted Frank to work behind the jab all night and take the opportunity of the haymaker as and when it came.

I'm convinced Frank would have overwhelmed him if he had unloaded in the early rounds. I was so convinced, I was almost having visions of the referee stopping the fight. Frank had way too much for him on every level. Smith was only landing with the jab and for the first half of the fight he was struggling to land that on target.

Unfortunately, in the later rounds, as a result of using the 'non-stop jab' strategy, Frank was suffering from the medical term known as 'being knackered'. He was so tired, he could barely hold his left arm up.

Although he had won all nine going into the tenth and final round and had rocked Smith throughout the fight, after being caught with a couple of left hooks, Frank simply didn't have the energy to hold up his hands and was consequently dropped.

Frank was unable to make the count and when he finally did manage to stand up, he collapsed into my arms and I had to hold him tight whilst walking him to the corner to sit down. He was exhausted.

I feel that I need to clarify something. My opinion versus Terry's is purely a personal perspective and it's always easier looking back to make comments about how Frank should have fought.

Based on the way Frank was landing his punches in the early rounds, combined with the fact that Smith was shying away, I still believe he should have opened up early, as his power was simply too much for him to take.

Nine rounds into the fight I guess you could say Terry's strategy was winning the day, as Frank hadn't lost a single round, but I think when you can unleash right hands with concussive power against a scared opponent, why lead with a jab all night and last the dangerous distance?

In the days which followed, I paid Frank a visit. While playing a game of chess, I asked him if he wanted to discuss the fight. He had accepted the loss and was happy to discuss, but he wanted my honest opinion of whether he could bounce back from defeat.

I put down the chess piece from my hand, which was a bonus as Frank was beating me and told him exactly how I felt overall. I explained that we didn't need to change anything about his boxing game and that it was the tactics which failed him on this occasion, not his ability.

I didn't need to say any more than that. He smiled, we shook hands and he went on to execute a few lethal moves on the chess board.

I actually used to play chess with Frank a fair bit but one occasion does stand out. We were travelling up to Scotland on the plane with Terry and we decided to pull out the table on the back of the chair in front of us and get the chessboard out. Within no time Frank was beating me proper!

Next thing we had a bit of turbulence and the plane went from left to right and up and down and the chess pieces went all over the place. Frank was furious because he knew he was on his way to winning. Seconds later, all three of us cracked up laughing out loud. Good memories.

****

With valuable lessons learned from the Cummings and Smith fights, Frank was more determined than ever before to get straight back into the ring and prove he was not just another domestic heavyweight struggling to make his mark beyond the British shores.

Four months after the Smith defeat, Frank smashed Ken Lakusta, Jeff Jordan and Philipp Brown within a two month span and had the European heavyweight title in his sights. His only hurdle was a warm-up fight against the former European champion, Lucien Rodriguez, and he turned out to be little more than a brief sparring session as Frank blasted him to the canvas in two and a half minutes.

No disrespect to Rodriguez intended, as this was the first time he had been stopped in six years, but Frank was operating with world level power and deserved to be in the ring with higher calibre opponents. Frank's rapid win over the Frenchman was starting to get the likes of Don King paying attention and we knew that it would only be a matter of time before we challenged for a world title.

With Rodriguez etched onto Frank's record as his 25th victory, he then challenged a huge Swede by the name of Anders Eklund for his European heavyweight title. I had seen Eklund fight on a number of occasions and knew the way to beat him was to get in close, work the body, unload with the uppercuts and generally not allow him the space or time to breath.

Aware that this was his first title fight, Frank's hunger and desire to be in peak condition was very evident. Too evident in fact. Frank, like Jim McDonnell, had a bad habit of wanting to do that little bit extra in training, so I had to pull him back. I always used to say to him, "You need to have trust in your trainer. Do you trust me Frank?"

He would always reply, "Yes Jim", with that deep gentle tone and a smile on his face. I would tell him when I thought he was ready and you could instantly see he was more relaxed. Getting a person prepared means mentally and physically, and he was good on both fronts.

The support for Frank that night at Wembley was very memorable.

They were supporting Frank Bruno, the boxer, the person and the icon. As the bell sounded for round one, Frank threw out his long hard jab in sets of twos and threes. Every time a blow landed, the crowd would cheer him like a matador and on that particular evening, he was missing with hardly anything, so it was a nonstop cheer for three minutes of each round.

Within the first 30 seconds Frank had already smacked out the confidence out of the champion and was now starting to enjoy himself. Landing left hooks at will, slipping the jabs and countering with right hands, Frank was the best I'd ever seen him at that point of his career.

Coming out for round two, Frank continued to top up his damage, as he threw out the faultless jab again, causing Eckland's nose to bleed. It wasn't major damage, but it was enough to boost Frank's confidence, yet enough to provoke the champion to launch his own assault of straight rights which resulted in partial success, leaving Frank with a slight swelling over his left eye.

I wasn't too concerned but the second the round was over I had a shout at Frank, telling him to keep his hands high and not take unnecessary risks because this fight was all his for the taking. I also told him to unload with the uppercuts as we had practiced on the pads.

Round three was very relaxed up to the last 30 seconds, at which point Frank let loose with a heavy right hand behind his jab, followed by another right hand, which had Eckland hanging on for dear life.

The bell saved him and it was clear that he would need every second of that break to regain his senses. The instructions to Frank were very clear as he sat down on his stool. "He's done Frank. Unload the second that bell goes!"

Even if Eckland had come out with a clear head, the attack Frank brought his way in under five seconds of the fourth round was too much for him. Frank threw a stiff jab followed by a crunching right hook, cocked back the right arm and threw an uppercut followed by another two right hooks. It was like a perfectly executed combination on the pads. Eckland was forced to collapse on all fours onto the canvas. Unable to make the count, Frank became the new European heavyweight champion at the age of 23.

Terry, Frank Black and myself were going crazy, the crowd was going crazy and the world was now taking him very seriously.

Forget the loss to Smith – Frank had been forgiven, redeemed and resurrected all in one swoop. I was absolutely overjoyed. Although he never fully admitted how gutted he was after the Smith loss, I could tell that this fight partially made up for that defeat and his smile reflected that.

Two months after the Eklund fight, in December, 1985, Frank gave himself an early Christmas present and knocked out American Larry Frazier in two rounds. He was certainly no relation to his namesake Joe.

However, next up was a tough South African, by the name of Gerrie Coetzee, who went by the nickname of 'The Bionic Hand.' Gerrie had held the WBA world title crown two years before, beating Michael Dokes and had beaten enough recognised names to make us take him seriously.

A victory over Gerrie would certainly put Frank into the mandatory challenger's position for a world title shot for the WBA crown.

Before Frank could even think about strategy, with a massive crowd behind him at the Wembley Arena, he threw a massive straight right and knocked out Coetzee cold in one minute and 50 seconds. Job done! Many boxers have often said, "You don't get paid for overtime in this sport." Frank certainly paid tribute to the phrase on that night.

The last fight I trained Frank for was against the WBA heavyweight champion of the world, 'Terrible' Tim Witherspoon.

Statistically, at 28-1 versus Witherspoon's 24-2, Frank was in with a chance, However, you must remember that Tim was a two-time heavyweight world champion and had already defeated the likes of Greg Page and Tony Tubbs, suffering his two losses at the hands of Larry Holmes and Pinklon Thomas by very close split decisions.

For the first six rounds, Frank was boxing beautifully. He was trading in close quarters to the head and the body, and blocking a great deal of what Tim was throwing.

As the seventh started, it became obvious that Tim simply had a bit too much for Frank to cope with and although suffering from a badly swollen face as a result of Frank's punches, his ring craft and looping right hands were starting to wear Frank down both mentally and physically.

As with the Smith fight, Frank was still in the game up to the 11th round, but once he was tagged with the first punch of a relentless set of punches, we knew it was time to throw in the towel.

I don't think there's a single fighter I have worked with who had more support, before, during and after a fight, especially once beaten, than Frank Bruno.

In the words of Don King straight after, "Bruno fought one hell of a fight."

Although the Witherspoon fight was my last with Frank, we parted on good terms. I followed his career with great interest and nobody was more delighted than me when

Frank went on to achieve his goal by beating Oliver McCall for the WBC world heavyweight title in 1995.

I was working with Chris Pyatt on the undercard that evening and was lucky enough to be a part of the celebrations, which were like the World Cup final, 100 metres Olympic final and a Lotto win all in one.

Fireworks, confetti, music, lights and big Frank standing in the middle of the ring in tears, with the WBC strap around his waist.

If there was ever a man who had earned the right to fight and win that title, it was Frank.

Another tribute I feel I need to give to him is the fact that he was the very first person to hurt Mike Tyson. Up to that point in 1989, Mike Tyson was 35-0, at his peak and was verging on being classified as immortal.

At the end of the first round, he caught Tyson with a left hook that had him holding on for dear life right the way up to the bell.

I remember listening to the fight on the radio and hearing Harry Carpenter saying, "Go on Frank! You've got him!" I was jumping up and down shouting at the radio, "COME ON FRANK!"

Perhaps if he'd hit Tyson earlier in the round the fight might have been over, but Frank can always say he was the first person to stun Iron Mike as a professional boxer. It's also worth taking the time to stand back and look at just how impressive his record stands.

Of his 45 fights, his five losses came at the hands of James Smith, Tim Witherspoon, Mike Tyson and Lennox Lewis.

Some of the best heavyweights to ever walk the planet. Of his 40 wins, 38 didn't last the distance. That's a 95 percent stoppage rate.

Take time to think for a minute – who has the heavyweight stats to compare to that?

Round 9

CHARLIE AND CHRIS

"There's a lot more to training fighters than just training them. Jimmy understands fighters and fighting. There's a big difference, as close as that sounds. We have the same principles. A lot of trust. You have to trust the people in charge of your welfare."
– Chris Pyatt, 2013

Frank Bruno was part of a very good stable of fighters that I trained back in the early 1980s at the Royal Oak gym, alongside Mark Kaylor and a number of others, all of who deserve recognition for the skill and dedication they brought to their profession.

Perhaps the most recognised champion I started to train around this time was a flyweight called Charlie Magri. Originally born in Tunisia, but training out of the heart of the East End, Charlie had a very highly decorated amateur career and turned professional in 1977.

Two months later in only his third fight, he won the British belt. A big achievement by any standards.

My first fight with Charlie, with my official 'trainers' cap on, was for a defence of his European belt against a Spanish guy called Enrique Rodriguez Cal, in a cattle market in Aviles, Spain.

Charlie had just come off a loss against a tough American called Jose Torres, but I was not too worried about Enrique as Charlie had stopped him in two rounds the year before.

My main concern at that point was the journey across Northern Spain, travelling through the Basque Country in a hire car, on the wrong side of the road, at night time!

We were lucky to get there alive. Truth be told, I didn't fancy driving, simply because I didn't have a great deal of experience abroad and that particular route was notoriously bad. So I asked Frank Black if he could drive and he agreed. Before we got the tickets for the plane, I said to him, "Make sure you bring your driver's licence Frank." He replied, "No problem Jim." I popped mine in my pocket just in case...

The flight was nice and smooth and I thought this was a good omen ahead of the last leg of our route. Terry Lawless was already with Charlie at the training camp, so it was myself, Frank and Jim 'The Biscuit' who made our way over to the car hire stand. It was at that moment that Frank very calmly and casually said, "Jimmy – I've forgot me licence." I said, "Forgot your licence! I knew this would happen!" So I now became the nominated driver. I wasn't happy!

I have no idea how we made it there in one piece. Driving in the dark in a foreign country on the other side of the road, in a crappy hire car, especially when you are not used to it, was not my idea of enjoying Spain. We must have had an angel looking after us all the way, because there were no street lamps and 1,000ft cliff edge drops with hardly any barriers to stop you coming off the road! Somehow we arrived at the training camp and by this stage I was fuming. I parked the car in the middle of the road, pulled my case out and while walking away said to Frank and Jim, "I AIN'T DRIVING THAT BACK!"

The less dramatic part of our visit to Aviles happened when Charlie repeated his previous performance against Enrique, stopping him in two rounds.

Charlie beat Jose Torres in his next fight – a really tough opponent – before WBC flyweight champion, Eleoncio Mercedes, gave him a crack at his title in March, 1983.

It had hardly been two years since Terry Lawless had asked me to look after his fighters for a few weeks while he went to the USA and here I was training one of those for a world title fight.

The pressure was intense and surreal, but not overwhelming enough to take my focus away from the task in hand.

The atmosphere on the night of the fight was something else. Charlie was a very popular guy and had sold loads of tickets, and when he came out of the tunnel he received an unbelievable reception.

It was a classic, edgy fight that could have gone either way but as soon as the bell sounded for round seven, Charlie came out of his corner and threw every punch he could. Just over a minute into the round, referee Ray Solis called over the doctor, who quickly waved his hands. Charlie was the new WBC flyweight champion of the world – the first person from the British Isles in 16 years to have held the title since Walter McGowan.

That night Charlie was unstoppable.

Although the fight was stopped on cuts, he was always in charge and was ahead on the scorecards at that point anyway. Charlie had won the world title and I had guided my first boxer to a world title. A very memorable day on many fronts.

Six months later, Charlie was challenged by a tall rangy southpaw from the Philippines called Frank Cedeno. Although he was the big underdog and right up to the sixth round was behind on the scorecards, Cedeno pulled off the upset, throwing a well-timed left uppercut, followed by a number of punches from every angle, resulting in Charlie being floored three times.

Britain had lost its only world champion and Charlie had lost the crown he had spent his whole life working towards.

After the Cedeno fight, Charlie took almost a year out but decided that retirement was not for him just yet. I was happy with his decision, because although he had just over 30 fights at that point, he was still fresh and was certainly still good enough to compete at world level.

So in August, 1984, he took on the Italian flyweight champion, Franco Cherchi, for the vacant European title, in his own backyard of Sardinia, Italy.

After a long training camp and a two-hour plane journey, the fight was stopped in the first round on an accidental clash of heads, in which Cherchi suffered a bad cut over his right eye.

Charlie won the fight, but nobody walked away from the fight with any contentment.

After that, Charlie had to relinquish his title due to injury but 18 months later, fighting fit again, he had his last attempt to regain a world title by challenging the WBC champion and ex-Thai boxing master, Sot Chitalada. The fight took place at the Alexandra Palace in London, in February, 1985.

This was a boxer who was a genuine threat. Chitalada walked into the ring with two samurai swords and a rather interestingly dressed entourage. They wouldn't have made it past the changing room in this day and age without being nicked by the police for carrying a deadly weapon!

Swords apart, Chitalada had won the WBC belt in only his eighth fight, but on the night he fought Charlie, they were very evenly matched on all the scorecards, right the way up to the sixth round.

Unfortunately, Charlie suffered a bad cut and Terry Lawless made the decision to pull him out. It was a real shame because the bout was developing into a great fight, but that cut was only ever going to get worse over the course of the evening, so I can't disagree with Terry's decision.

After defending against Charlie, Chitalada would hold the world crown for six years, during which time he only suffered one loss. He was a great opponent and Charlie had nothing to be ashamed of. We were very proud of him.

Eight months later, Charlie stopped Franco Cherchi in two rounds to win the European crown before finally bowing out in May, 1986, with a loss against Duke McKenzie.

Although still a great fighter, Charlie was on the declining end of his career and this test was proof that it was time to bow out. Standing in front of a younger fighter having your head jabbed off all night can make a boxer feel a lot older than they actually are. Charlie had nothing more to prove and had retained his health so the choice to retire was a prudent one. Charlie will go down as one of the hardest hitting flyweights of all time and one of the most popular sporting characters in East London.

****

The same night that Charlie Magri lost his title to Cedeno, I also had a charismatic young lad on his fourth outing, looking to impress the crowds at Wembley.

Hailing from Leicestershire, this boxer had given up his local community to move down to the Costa Del Canning Town, to explore his full potential. His name was Chris Pyatt and I'm so glad he decided to take the leap of faith.

My first impressions of Chris were very good. As a 19-year-old with pretty much every amateur title to his name, he was very quiet, very sensible and very streetwise. The last quality being extremely valuable in Canning Town. On the boxing front, Chris had everything.

He could box, he could punch and his levels of fitness were

incredible – he just needed a little bit of smoothing out and a training plan to make sure he didn't overtrain.

When he first moved to London, he didn't really know anybody, so we invited Chris over to have dinner with us. As a polite and well-mannered lad, it was a genuine pleasure to have had the opportunity to make him feel welcome in the big smoke and also for my family to get to know him so closely.

The first fight me and Chris prepared for, in September, 1983, was against a durable boxer called Darwin Brewster.

Chris beat him and then steamrolled through his next seven opponents before winning a clean cut performance against Brian Anderson for the British light middleweight eliminator.

With the title in sight, Chris beat his next three opponents by stoppage, but unfortunately suffered his first loss against Sabiyala Diavilla, by way of a nasty eyebrow cut. That was a shame because Chris was ahead on points but the cut was so bad that it required stitching inside and out. There's no ideal way to lose a fight, but at least we both knew that Chris was the stronger fighter on that night and neither one of us came away with any mental scars to bear.

Five months later he was back in blistering form and in February, 1986, at the Royal Albert Hall, we challenged Prince Rodney for the British light middleweight title. This was not a guaranteed win by any stretch of the imagination. Rodney had won the title back in 1983 and had already successfully defended it three times, gaining him the coveted Lonsdale Belt.

His intention, as a fighter who had a record of 30-6-1 at that point, was to hold onto the belt for some time to come.

Thankfully, that night, Chris boxed beautifully and scuppered any plans Rodney had for further cementing his place in British boxing history.

In fact, little did he know it, but Rodney would be handing over the baton to Chris, for a long relay of future title successes.

On the night, Chris glided around the ring choosing his shots and landing with venom as and when he wanted. As the fight entered the last minute of the ninth round, Chris knocked Rodney out and had won his first ever title. He was only 23 and I was very proud of him.

The European title soon followed as Chris beat John Van de Elteren but unfortunately he lost it to Gianfranco Rosi on points two fights later.

Chris licked his wounds though and came back stronger, fighting for world title honours against the reigning WBO champion, John David Jackson, in October, 1990.

We knew he was a good smart box fighter and a southpaw, and although Chris hurt him with a big right hand in round five, he just couldn't get a grip of him.

Just before the bell sounded for the final round, I was giving Chris his instructions and as I looked over at Jackson, he stamped his feet up and down and gave me a smile, basically letting me know he had plenty of life left in him to throw Chris's way!

Jackson was a little bit too ringwise at that point and had already been the champ for a couple of years so there was no shame in losing to a fighter of his calibre.

Chris's next fight was on November 5 – that date again –1991, for the vacant Commonwealth title against a very durable opponent, Craig Trotter.

And exactly six years to the day after Mark Kaylor beat Errol Christie to become British champion, Chris beat Trotter over 12 rounds on points and was crowned the new light middleweight Commonwealth champion.

He successfully defended the title a couple of times and then added another belt to his honours cabinet, by way of the WBC International middleweight belt and clocked up a further eight wins. With Chris building up an impressive set of titles, there was only one piece of the jigsaw missing – a world title strap.

After 10 years of boxing as a pro, Chris was handed his second opportunity in 1993.

In order to accept the challenge, he needed to step up to middleweight and face a very respected world level fighter, by way of Sumbu Kalambay. The Congolese born Italian had already beaten the feared Irishman Steve Collins the year before and also Errol Graham – twice.

At the time I had to spend a little bit of time out in Tenerife to set up Nigel Benn's camp for a world title defence and consequently I asked Dean Powell to hold the fort for me for a few days during my absence.

However, about three weeks before the Kalambay fight, Nigel hurt his back, so I came back to the UK to take full control of the camp.

When I arrived, Dean asked if he could come round to my

house and have a chat. I said, "Of course." He said, "Jim – Chris is in a terrible state. He's got the flu, a big cold sore on his lip and looks drained of all energy. I've been taking him round orange juice for the vitamin C, but I'm not sure if he'll be ok for this fight."

I needed to see Chris in person. First thing in the morning, he came round to see me. As I opened the door, I thought to myself, "He looks awful", but we agreed to carry on and see how he progressed.

Over the next couple of weeks we did some very light training, allowing his body to regain some strength. In my opinion, as the day of the fight approached, he was only about 60-70 percent fit, and I said to him, "Chris. Pull out. We can do this again at a later date." He replied, "Jim – we can't do this at a later date. If I don't take this chance now, I might never get another." I said, "Ok mate. I'm with you."

The day finally arrived. May 19, 1993, Granby Halls, Leicester for the vacant WBO middleweight championship of the world.

Kalambay was the taller fighter with a longer reach, so the intention was not to outbox him, but to stay in close, work the body and bob and weave anything Kalambay had to offer.

The first three rounds were Chris all the way. He climbed all over Kalambay, not giving him the chance to breath, but Chris couldn't quite land a haymaker due to Kalambay's slipping and sliding.

In round four, Kalambay hit Chris with a left hook that practically lifted him off his feet. The punch almost made me feel sick, but I never said anything to Chris as he walked back to the corner for round five.

In the meantime, Barry Hearn, who was promoting this fight, came over to the corner screaming, "You're in front Chris. You're in front!" I turned to Chris and said, "Keep on him. Work him!"

In rounds six and seven, Kalambay seemed to be getting stronger while Chris slowed down a little bit, but he was still on track for winning the title at this point.

Round eight was a good round for Kalambay, catching Chris twice with big right hands and at this point most of the scorecards, both official and unofficial, had Chris ahead by one round.

As Chris walked back to the corner, I wiped him down, told him to breathe deeply and then told him to stay close and hook him to the head and the body for the ninth. Following instructions strictly, Chris's attack was nonstop, but by the end of the round he looked exhausted and I was starting to get a little worried that his flu might have perhaps taken away some of his stamina.

You must remember that Chris weighed in under the limit for this fight, as a natural light middleweight, whereas Kalambay probably walked in about 10 pounds heavier on fight night.

With the strategy of staying in close and leaning into Kalambay, Chris's stamina would not only need to be huge but it would need to be better than a larger and more experienced champion.

At the end of the tenth round, I met Chris in the centre of

the ring to walk him back and turned him round and said, "Look at him Chris. LOOK AT HIM!" They were pretty much carrying Kalambay back to his corner. Chris looked at me and smiled.

I knew we had Kalambay at this point.

Fighting at the Granby Halls in Leicester was a great move. Chris was a local hero and as the bell rung for round 11, the cheers and support from the crowd were nonstop, which gave him a boost, as he could sense their pride in their homegrown champion.

Kalambay was having success with the jab, but every time Chris would eat one, it would act as a reminder to get in tight, close his range down and unload the hooks and uppercuts. The strategy also meant that he could hold on if necessary, taking a breather, but also close down any attacks which Kalambay might like to offer at range. Both fighters were desperately tired, but Chris continued to set about him for the remainder of the round and with 30 seconds to go landed a corkscrew left uppercut which proved that not only did he have fuel in the tank, but that he was still the hungrier and more active boxer.

I told Dean Powell to pour some cold water over Chris, whilst getting him to take deep breaths (Chris not Dean that is!) Although both me and Dean probably needed the deep breaths more than Chris at that point. I was aware that the scorecards must have been very close, so going out into the final round, I told him, "Do exactly as you have done for the previous 11. Be brilliant Chris!"

He gave me a wink and as the bell sounded he did exactly

as I asked, keeping on Kalambay's chest, throwing the right hand over Kalambay's jab and not giving him time or space to build up momentum or power.

Again – the nonstop chants for three minutes of "PYYYYYYYYAAATT, PYYYYYYYYAAATT, PYYYYYYYYAAATT," inspired him up to leave everything in the ring and leave no doubt in anybody's mind that the blown up light middleweight who everybody had written off in advance of this fight was the real deal.

With a minute to go, Chris was starting to hold on out of pure exhaustion.

At that moment, Chris's family stood up screaming their support, swiftly followed by his friends and followed by the thousands in attendance! He battled through the fatigue and as the bell sounded for the final time, me, Dean and Barry Hearn flew through the ropes to congratulate Chris on his performance.

Irrespective of the result, Chris had just put on an outstanding show against a seasoned and well respective champion.

As we all waited in anticipation for the results, I stood in front of Chris, ready to embrace him whatever the result. The judges produced their cards very quickly and were all in agreement that the winner had won by two rounds, "... AND NEEEEWW MIDDLEWEIGHT CHAMPION OF THE WORLD... CHRRRRISSSSS PYYYYYAAATT!" He walked straight into my arms and we hugged solidly for about 20 seconds. It's a cliché, but it genuinely couldn't have happened to a nicer person. Chris had achieved the goal every boxer dreams of and he had done it against the odds.

He silenced those doubters who said he wouldn't cope with the champion's pace and strength and he now deserved all the praise that was coming his way while I can't even describe how happy I was!

This also meant I had two world champions under my wing at that moment in time (the other was Nigel Benn – more of him later). I was as proud as a boxing trainer could be and that night goes down as one of the biggest highlights of my professional career.

Four months later, we were back at the Granby Halls as Chris defended his title against the Argentinean middleweight champion, Hugo Antonio Corti. The Argentinean had only lost three times in 29 fights at that point, including a loss to Chris Eubank in 1990.

However, the preparations for this fight couldn't have gone better and Corti was in for an unpleasant surprise.

Chris had had enough time to relax after the Kalambay fight, didn't have a flu to contend with this time and was razor sharp in the gym with both his training and sparring. By December, 1993, he was like a caged animal ready to be released and halfway through the sixth, Chris caught Corti with a peach of a left hook, followed seconds later by a well-travelled right hook which completed a perfect semi circle before crashing into the left hand side of Corti's face. Eight... Nine... 10.

The fight was over!

As the ring announcer gave the official decision of win by

knockout over the microphone, "...AND STILL...", Chris held his arms above his head and I had the task which every trainer loves to do – strapping the world championship belt to their boxer.

Five months later, Chris defended his title with a quick one round destruction of South African Mark Cameron before losing his world crown to the 'Celtic Warrior', Steve Collins, who was just starting to mature into his peak years. No excuses – Steve was simply too big and too strong for him. Chris was a natural light middleweight fighting at middle and Steve was a big super middleweight struggling to cook down to middle.

As with the latter stages of my own boxing career, we decided it would make more sense to step down a division and finish the balance of Chris's fights at light middle – his natural resting weight.

With more than a little something still in the tank to prove that Chris was still very capable of winning a title, he had two warm-up fights before challenging the Australian light middleweight champ, Kevin Kelly, for the Commonwealth belt.

Kelly was a good fighter who went on to become WBU world champ five years later, but in December, 1995, Chris was too much for him and beat him comprehensively over the 12 round distance and became the Commonwealth light middleweight champion again – a title he had won four years earlier.

Two fights later, after beating Maurice Forbes in May, 1997, Chris made the wise decision to retire.

In my opinion, he had achieved every major accolade as an amateur and professional boxer and genuinely had nothing more to prove to anybody, especially himself. Chris is transferring his knowledge to future generations as a trainer himself now.

He has a great deal to offer the boxing community and I look forward to working opposite corners to him at some point in the near future.

Let me leave you with this last little nugget of information about my old mate Chris Pyatt.

Even when I wasn't in the corner for fight night with Chris, or not around for the full training camp, he would always ensure I received full pay.

There were times where we didn't even have the cash between us to pay for a new gas canister to keep the gym warm in the freezing winter months, but he still stuck by me, knowing that there were brighter times ahead. I don't think there's many people like that who exist on this planet, never mind in boxing.

During my time coaching Chris, and others, I had developed from novice coach to a trainer of champions and I felt equipped to take on pretty much anything and anyone.

I was however about to come up against one opponent who I didn't have a strategy, gameplan or contingency for.

This one would catch me completely off guard.

Round 10

FEAR

"You don't know, Mr Tibbs?
"You've got cancer, Mr Tibbs."
– Mr Hackett, cancer consultant, 1985

I was getting well placed to be able to reflect on my rollercoaster life to date.

I had experienced the huge highs of boxing success followed by the devastating lows of prison.

I had then rebuilt the family business and rebuilt my name as a respected boxing trainer. However, another low was around the corner as nature was about to remind me that we are only flesh and blood.

One day, Doctor Ross from the British Boxing Board of Control walked in to the gym to visit Terry Lawless. I was dripping with sweat but wanted his opinion on a blemish on my skin so I walked over to him and asked if he would mind taking a quick look.

He said, "No problem. Lift up your shirt up Jim." I did as he said and revealed a small pink mole on the surface of my stomach.

I then said, "What do you think doc?" He said he couldn't really comment and that it was best that a specialist had a look.

He wrote me a letter there and then and told me to take it to the Outpatients at St Margaret's Hospital in Epping. I was 39 at the time, very active and I felt physically strong.

But I had a gut feeling that all wasn't right.

Two days later, I drove up to the hospital on my own and saw one of the doctors.

After introducing myself, I went to take my shirt off and he told me, "Tell me all about it." I replied, "What do you want me to tell you?" He wanted to know when I first spotted the mole and if I had been to any hot countries. I said "Yes. I was in the USA a couple of months ago."

I had taken Lloyd Honeyghan to Atlantic City, but had also trained out in Florida where it was beaming hot. I also explained that I had gone to Spain for a couple of weeks for a break. Then I said something which made him look more intently at me. I explained to him that I love to lie out in the sun when on holiday and at that point he asked to have a look at the mole.

He got out his magnifying glass out and had a good look, then asked me, "Would you like me to remove it now?" I lay down on the patient bench while he froze it, snipped it off and gave me three stitches. Easy as that. The doctor then sent off a biopsy to the laboratory.

I thought to myself, 'That wasn't so bad,' and went back to the gym the very next day.

A week later, I was sitting at home watching the television, when I received a phone call from the hospital telling me I needed to go there straight away.

I asked the reason for the extreme urgency and the lady on the phone explained that the conversation with the doctor needed to be done in person. The bad gut feeling that I had experienced before now surfaced again, but far stronger this time. I realised that something must be seriously wrong. I was terrified to even mention the word 'cancer' at that point.

I mentioned to Claudette that I was going to hospital, but told her I was having some plastic surgery done. She didn't ask too many questions, but she must have picked up on the tone of my voice that it could potentially be something serious.

I felt I needed to have somebody with me for the visit and picked up a mate on the way. After arriving at the hospital, we went from room to room to room, answering a battery of questions from a number of experts. Throughout the whole process, not one of the many doctors I had spoken with had mentioned the word 'cancer'.

This had actually led me into a false sense of security because I was sure that after meeting with so many people, at least one of them would have mentioned the word or at least implied it might be cancer. As I came out of the last room, before seeing the main doctor, I turned to my mate and put my thumb up as if to say everything was fine.

I then walked into an office, whilst my mate waited outside and a gentleman named Mr Hackett was waiting for me. He had his head down and was going through a file of notes relating to my condition. The anticipation was killing me, so I decided I had to say something. "Excuse me Mr Hackett." He looked up and I said, "What is wrong with me?" He replied, "You don't know Mr Tibbs? You have cancer Mr Tibbs."

I was shocked. I was so shocked I went deaf. I could see his lips moving, but I couldn't hear a thing. All I remember him saying was that I needed to come to hospital. The word I had not asked about or wanted to hear had now become reality, or more accurately a living nightmare. The news told that I was about to serve a 10-year sentence in prison was nothing compared to what I had just been told. These words had sunk me.

I went back home that evening, but stopped off at my dad's first and told him the news. I was very upset and broke down. I asked my dad to look after Claudette and my kids if anything happened to me. He said, "Of course I will Jim. Don't you worry about any of that." He then jumped in the car with me and my mate and we headed home so I could get a bag together. About 10 minutes later, the three of us headed off to the hospital. I was sat up front while my dad drove and my mate sat in the back. We didn't chat very much, as the news had taken the wind from all our sails.

I remember looking out of the window as we were on the way to the hospital, going through the country lanes with green fields all around me and I thought to myself, 'If there is a god, please let me live to see my children grow up'.

The next morning I was sat on the hospital bed when Mr Hackett walked through the door briskly and expressionless. He could see I was deflated and dejected and proceeded to give me a slap on the leg, before saying, "You're not going to die. Not from that!"

I immediately broke down in joy.

Up to this point all I could think about was dying.

When Mr Hackett told me I was going to survive, I can't describe how much I valued life at that particular moment. Being told I had just won millions on the Lotto 10 times over wouldn't have even come close in terms of value.

He explained how the operation would unfold. Due to the cancer being a melanoma, my belly button would have to be removed and he would reconstruct something similar, about an inch higher. Although the blemish was only half the size of a small finger nail, the infected area was much bigger and the surgery would leave a horizontal scar of about 15 inches across my stomach.

The last time I had been cut with a blade was during the troubled times in 1970.

This was the total opposite of that. This time I was actually asking to be cut, to the tune of 15 inches across my stomach albeit by a specialist doctor with a sterilised blade and by a man who didn't want to inflict pain on me.

Within a couple of days of the surgery, the medication was reduced and the tubes were removed. Mr Hackett was delighted with the procedure and told me that I would be out within a couple of days. I had been left with 40 stitches and was reminded again to be very careful with not overly exerting myself in the first few weeks. Not sure if I heard him clearly for that part!

Thankfully I never needed to have chemotherapy or radiotherapy. I wouldn't say the operation was as easy as removing a tooth, but in relation to what many people have to go through when having cancer, I believe I was very lucky indeed. The main reason for the success of this whole episode was that they had discovered the cancer early.

If I had waited a few more weeks or months, I may have not have been writing this book.

Over time, Mr Hackett would end up being a very good friend of mine. He used to love his boxing but after that operation he became far more passionate about it, almost as if he was partly looking at the sport through my eyes.

I used to get him tickets to come and see the fights I was involved in and it was always a pleasure to see him arrive in the crowd. He made sure my aftercare was always immaculate. For my checkups, if he spotted the smallest mole, he would remove it immediately. He always wanted to be one step ahead of the cancer.

A number of years passed and one day, whilst walking into the reception to have my routine quarterly check-up, I noticed that all the nurses were crying. I asked what was going on and they said, "Haven't you heard Mr Tibbs? Mr Hackett has died. He's had a heart attack."

I was shocked, gutted and upset. He was one of the most conscientious and caring men to have walked on this planet. There's no justice when a good man of about 50 passes away, after having saved so many lives.

A Welsh doctor called Mr Jones took over my check-ups and after only a few visits said, "Jim there's no need for you to come anymore. You are in the clear." Your health is wealth and at that precise moment, I felt like a multi-millionaire.

Thirty years later, I've not only got to see my children grow up, but my grandchildren also.

****

Coming out the other end of my cancer episode also allowed me to continue my journey with boxing – apparently my work was not finished just yet! I was now established and recognised as a credible boxing trainer and was setting off on some great adventures with some outstanding talents, one of whom was a 22-year-old lad from Camden, with an unparalleled appetite for training and working at peak performance.

His name – Jim McDonnell.

My biggest challenge on first training Jim was taming him. As an amateur, he would win most of his fights by overwhelming his opponents, simply not giving them the chance to surface for air or give them the space to get their punches off. The second he stepped through those ropes, he became a very aggressive fighter who was always ready for a punch up.

However, I realised during sparring that he was not a concussive puncher so I started to get him to work behind the jab with the intention of converting him into a technical boxer. I had spotted something which many others had overlooked about Jim McDonnell – he could outbox pretty much anyone.

As our relationship developed, I had to introduce a new element into Jim's training regime.

The element was called 'rest'.

Anybody who knows Jim McDonnell will know that very few boxers trained to his extremes. If a fighter was training for six or eight rounds, he would train for 20. When they ran five hills, he would run 20. When they ran three, five or eight miles, he would run 10, 15 or 20. When I first mentioned the benefits of having a day off, or stopping before collapsing, he seemed somewhat confused.

I had to make him understand that resting was as important as training and that he needed to have faith in me as his trainer. Jim stood there scratching his head trying to work out what I was talking about.

After beating a guy called Jeff Roberts we had the task of fighting for a title shot five weeks later.

Requests about taking rest during training now turned into orders. Jim had been in the habit of training up to a couple of days before a fight but I got him used to tapering down about seven days before, making sure his body would fully rest so that he could build up his natural energy.

During that tapering phase for this fight, I remember giving him a day off and the day after we met at the gym. He looked a little tired so I asked him, "Did you run yesterday?" Jim replied, "Of course not Jim. You told me not to." Then

I started to train him on the pads and asked him, "How come you are tired when I gave you a day off yesterday?" There was a short silence then Jim replied cautiously, "Jim. I did have a little run." I went berserk! Turns out he had put in a long run the night before – not ideal.

Our opponent for the European featherweight title, which Barry McGuigan had vacated, was a tough Spanish boxer by the name of Jose Luis Vicho.

As the hours counted down, I could tell Jim was understandably a little nervous. We sat down in the changing room and drank some water before getting ready to battle the 37-fight veteran. I could see a slight bit of doubt in Jim's face, whereas I had all the confidence in the world that he was going to win. I ran through the game plan again, cracked a few jokes and before we knew it, we were standing in the middle of the ring face to face with Vicho.

Vicho was not a big puncher, but he had a very awkward style which meant Jim had to use every piece of ring craft he had to get inside him.

After doing as he wanted with Vicho for three rounds, Jim went on to knock him out just before the end of the fourth with a lovely left hook to the ribs. He was now European champion! We were both ecstatic. All the hard work we had put in, the new training routines and converting the brawler into a boxer, had all paid off.

Jim's next fight was set against a guy from Texas for a world title shot, but unfortunately it never happened. A replacement was put forward for a non-titled bout, against a very tough Colombian called Ruben Dario Palacios, at the Royal Albert Hall. This was without doubt Jim's toughest test.

The first round was a nightmare. Ruben came out like a machine and bullied Jim, inflicting a nasty cut over his eye. As the bell sounded for the end of the round, I realised I had about 45 seconds to get a deflated Jim back in the zone.

The calm gentle approach was not on the agenda. As he sat down on the stool, I grabbed a hold of him and said, "Listen. LISTEN! You have to man up Jim. You want me to pull you out?" I repeated, "DO YOU WANT ME TO PULL YOU OUT? This is where you change from a boy to a man. You know what to do Jim. Wear him down and make him pay."

He listened to every word I said, and with about 10 seconds to go before the bell for round two, I felt like I was unleashing Jake LaMotta on Palacios. Jim went out and did a number on him, stopping him in seven rounds. The turnaround was incredible. He put in an outstanding performance, and although it was not a world title fight, he fought like a world champion. I was very proud. My last fight training Jim was against Salvatore Bottiglieri on the Frank Bruno versus Tim Witherspoon undercard in July, 1986.

In my opinion this marked a run of possibly three of his best performances. Jim beat Bottiglieri comprehensively over the 12 rounds, showing how to outbox, outhit and outwit his opponent. He was double and triple jabbing, throwing the right hook followed by a left hook, then getting out of the way and frustrating Bottiglieri. He retained his European title and was simply brilliant that evening.

Jim looked like Sugar Ray Leonard that night. In fact, Sugar Ray Leonard had actually come down to the Royal Oak in the build up to this fight and mentioned what great condition Jim was in.

When commentating for the television that evening he repeated this comment again. You can't get a better compliment than that. I believe we parted terms on a career best performance for him.

Jim McDonnell now trains a number of good fighters including world title prospect and Olympic gold medallist James DeGale. I wish him all the best with his future. Our past was certainly a pleasure.

****

Throughout the late 1980s I also had the good fortune to work with the likes of Mo Hussein and Terry Dixon; two terrific, disciplined and superbly talented boxers.

Thankfully, I still see a lot of Mo these days, mainly down the TKO gym in Canning Town and we will often work the corner together on fight night. As a former Southern Area, British and Commonwealth champion, he has a great deal to offer the boxing community.

My time spent working with him as a trainer was a sincere pleasure and I can honestly say, hand on heart, Mo never entered the boxing ring unless he was willing to give 110 percent.

Keep an eye out for his son Eddie, who will no doubt follow in his dad's footsteps.

I also used to train Tony Wilson – who was famously involved in one of the most amazing sights ever seen in British boxing.

It was September 21, 1989, and the venue was the Guildhall in Southampton.

Terry Dixon was debuting on the undercard and stopped his opponent in the first round, so he went and took a shower and then joined, Mo, myself and big James Oyebola to watch Tony Wilson.

We were a very tight bunch, like a family really.

The bell sounded for the first round and Tony started using the jab beautifully, taking his time to place his shots and using the ring space to his advantage against Steve McCarthy. The action remained pretty much unchanged for the rest of the round and the next one in fact.

As the bell sounded for the third round, I noticed a number of racists standing ringside, hurling abuse at Tony. At the time I wasn't a Christian and I literally growled and shouted at them in a rage, defending my boxer. While in mid flow, my peripheral vision caught Tony and he was on the canvas. I wasn't worried, because pretty much every time Tony had hit the canvas in his pro career, he came back and knocked his opponents out.

The crowd was going crazy, thinking McCarthy had won, but then Tony picked himself up so Steve rushed over to the corner where I was and started throwing a number of punches, under the impression he could finish Tony there and then. Seeing that Tony was certainly not even rattled, I started shouting, "That's it Tony, roll the punches, roll, roll,

roll, roll," and he was doing it immaculately. In between rolling he was cracking McCarthy with some lovely counter punches.

And then, all of a sudden – chaos.

A woman was in the ring, with her high heeled shoe in her hand hitting McCarthy on the head!

I couldn't believe it. I'd never experienced anything like it in my life. The referee, Adrian Morgan, jumped in and stopped the fight and moved the woman out of the ring.

It turned out to be Tony's mum, Minna!

I turned to the ref and said, "Are you letting this fight go on?" and he replied that he was so I turned to Dean Powell and got him to start brushing Tony down. As we were getting ready to finish the fight, I looked over to McCarthy's corner and could see they were all arguing.

McCarthy was having a row with his manager and didn't want to come out! In the end, the ref walked over to the corner and asked McCarthy but he stayed put and Tony was declared the winner!

As the decision was being announced, riots started to kick off inside the boxing hall. Bottles were flying at Tony and we all jumped in to shield him. I turned to Terry Dixon and said, "Tel, make us a path through the crowds so we can get back to the changing room." Terry and big James Oyebola walked through, shoving everybody out of the way and then we suddenly realised we were a man down. Mo had been caught up behind us and while trying to defend himself, ended up with about 20 people bundled on top of him.

Thankfully, Terry Dixon and James Oyebola walked over

and started pulling people off Mo like wrapping paper. Finally we managed to make our way back to the changing room.

We didn't want to hang around with what was going on inside the hall and gathered our gear and all piled into my Ford Granada.

The comedy wasn't finished there either.

Just before arriving at the venue I had filled up the car with unleaded petrol. These were the days when unleaded fuel was just being introduced and I didn't think anything of it, thinking my leaded car could function on this stuff.

As we took off from the venue I put my foot down to try and take off like a bat out of hell and leave the hostile crowd behind. We were in mid conversation about Tony's mum coming into the ring, when the car started coughing and jumping like a kangaroo. You have to imagine about 75 stone of tough guys bouncing around inside the car, looking for something to hold on to, thinking, 'What the bloody hell is going on?!'

The day after, the British Boxing Board of Control called us up and declared the fight a 'no contest'. Thankfully in the end, the issue was resolved and Tony had the win on his record.

Understandably but unfairly, if you mention Tony Wilson to anybody, they tend to remember him as the guy whose mother attacked his opponent with a shoe, as opposed to the good boxer he was.

I trained Tony from the start of his pro career. As a person he was a very polite young man, who trained very hard and was very punctual. All I needed to do was smooth him out – shorten his stance a little bit, get him to drop his chin a little and concentrate more on that beautiful long jab he had. Tony also had a great left hook also but his main strength was his jab, which he could hold his opponent at bay with.

It was a pleasure and a privilege to be involved with such a strong fighter and a man full of respect and dedication – as well as a fearsome mother!

****

The roll call of great boxers continued when, in the mid 80s, I took on a man known as 'The Clones Cyclone'. He was a 5ft 6in warrior and he was, in my opinion, one of the best British fighters around.

Barry McGuigan.

McGuigan had every asset needed to be a good boxer. He could fight, he threw crippling body punches, he knew his way around the ring, he had a great engine and most importantly he had plenty of common sense.

How did I hook up with Barry I hear you ask? I was at one of Frank Warren's shows and we had a brief chat after the fights, with no agenda. It was soon after Barry had lost to Steve Cruz and his dad had also passed away during that period, so I offered my condolences, we swapped numbers and that was that really. Or so I thought.

A few days later I received a phone call from Barry, asking if I would like to be his trainer. My initial reaction to myself was, 'What an honour it would be to work together with someone as great as Barry!'

Delighted to have been asked, I quickly agreed and we met up soon after to knuckle down for preparations against Nicky Perez and to carve out the road to success for his comeback.

My first impressions of training Barry? Incredible. His work ethic was relentless, and as with many of the top fighters I had trained, he needed to be pulled back. His punch power was merciless and his work rate was suffocating – as four sparring partners who came down from Manchester to help with the Perez fight quickly found out.

Each sparring partner had their own strength, in terms of speed, power, agility etc, and as they walked into the gym, Barry sized them up with steely-cold eyes. I turned to him and said, "Who do you want first Barry?" He replied, "I'll have him Jim," pointing out the biggest and toughest of the bunch.

After making quick work of that particular boxer, he went through the rest of the three at rapid speed, making sure each and every man well and truly earned their wages.

By the time I had taken on Barry, he was already a great fighter, so I decided to work on some of the more subtle aspects of his boxing such as moving the top half and making sure that he was kept in peak condition without overdoing it. For the Perez fight I was looking to get Barry's timing back as quickly as possible. Being an attacking fighter I didn't want him to appear clumsy and walk into punches bearing in mind that he'd been out of the ring for 22 months.

On the pads, he had fantastic hand speed and incredible co-ordination with combinations – in fact, he was one of the few boxers I trained who could repeat a five-punch combination from training and put it together in a real fight. Barry's brother Dermot also helped with the pad work. It was very clear they had an extremely close bond, and like Barry, he was an absolutely lovely guy and was certainly a great help in getting Barry into peak condition.

Satisfied that Barry was in great shape and with an excellent training camp behind him, we took on Nicky Perez in April, 1988, at the Alexandra Pavilion, Muswell Hill. Perez was a gritty American who had lost to the legendary Julio Cesar Chavez one month earlier and as an ex-world title contender, he was a perfect test for Barry after his two years out of the ring.

Although Perez was still regarded by many as a genuine threat, Barry knocked him out in four rounds. Victim number 30 etched into his boxing record.

After demolishing Perez, we wasted no time and jumped back into the ring two months later to battle a Brazilian by the name of Francisco Tomas De Cruz and Barry demolished him, forcing a stoppage in the fourth round.

Six months later and eager to clock up three victories in the space of eight months, we took on a tough Argentinean by the name of Julio Cesar Miranda.

It was another tough, tough encounter but then Barry was a tough, tough man and his class and strength finally got their rewards a minute after the bell sounded for the eighth round.

Barry landed a terrific overhand right and with his

opponent on the ropes, he started to unload to the body. He then unleashed one great left hook which sent Miranda's head spinning and his gumshield flew about twenty rows back into the crowd.

Ten seconds later, referee Larry O'Connell stepped in and it was all over!

It had turned out to be a tougher fight than me or Barry had expected.

After disposing of Miranda, and maintaining his 80 percent stoppage rate, we decided we would have one more fight before having a crack at Tony Lopez for the IBF world title.

The fight was against none other than my old champion Jim McDonnell and we would be fighting at the G-Mex Centre in Manchester in May, 1989, in front of just under 9,000 boxing fans.

Although Jim was one of my old fighters and a truly lovely bloke, I'm a professional trainer, so it's my job to cut myself off from any emotion between past and present boxers.

You always focus on the job in hand and look out for your fighter's welfare.

Round one was fairly even, with both Barry and Jim trying to size each other up. After about a minute of the second round, Jim threw two long slashing left hooks which opened up a cut over Barry's right eye. The scar tissue from the last fight had tenderised Barry's skin, making it more vulnerable and Jim reopened a cut in that area.

Unfortunately for Barry, we simply couldn't work on the cut for long enough to stop it and the fight was stopped a minute into the fourth round. Minus the cut, the fight was very even and both fighters still had 20 rounds each left in their tanks.

I wasn't happy when referee Mickey Vann stepped in because he didn't give us a chance to work on it. However, looking back, I agree with Mickey's decision because although Ernie Fossey may have been able to patch the cut up, it could have split to twice the size a round later and that's a risk and an injury nobody needs to take.

That turned out to be Barry's last fight.

After retiring as a professional boxer, Barry has thankfully managed to still be involved in the sport. Having been inducted into the International Hall of Fame in 2005, he now manages world title prospect Carl Frampton, who is trained successfully by his son Shane, and who no doubt will be world champion by the time this book is published! Good luck mate.

****

One of the last fighters I trained in the 1980s for five fights, was a Scottish flyweight by the name of Pat Clinton. Pat had done it all as an amateur, including winning the ABAs twice, and by the time we started to train at West Ham for our first fight together, he had already racked up 12 victories, including winning the Scottish flyweight belt.

Our first fight was in March, 1988, where we took on another Scot by the name of Joe Kelly for the vacant British flyweight title, whilst also defending Pat's Scottish area flyweight crown. The fight took place at the York Hall in East London and although I didn't realise it at the time, the fight went down in Scottish history as Pat was the first person to beat a fellow Scot for both the titles – albeit the fight didn't take place in Scotland!

Pat then lost on points to Eyup Can but subsequently stopped Danny Porter and David Afan Jones in five and six rounds respectfully.

A few months later we received the call we were waiting for – a fight for the vacant European title against an unbeaten Italian boxer called Salvatore Fanni, in Cagliari, Italy

Fanni was a much loved idol in Italy at the time so we knew we would be up against it in terms of coming away with a decision. We also knew that we might not receive the warmest of receptions. The night before the fight, the first thing we did was check Pat's weight on the official scales.

He was a fraction over and I certainly wasn't worried as it was the kind of weight he would lose in his sleep and wake up being bang on. First thing we did in the morning was to get Pat back on the scales and I was delighted as his weight was perfect. We then went down for the official weigh-in at 1pm and Pat was suddenly two pounds over.

It made no sense as he hadn't consumed anything and with the fight being on the same day back then, this was not ideal. I didn't want to kick up a fuss though and took Pat to the changing area and made him jog around, while I rubbed every bead of sweat off him until he was two pounds less.

While we were in the changing room with Pat, Bert McCarthy came in and said, "Frankie, Jim – come over and have a look at this canvas."

The canvas was in an awful state, full of lumps and bumps and knowing how good Pat was on his feet we then proceeded to pull the canvas and straighten it out the best we could, in order for Pat to move around the ring without tripping over.

Pat wanted that title badly and after having cooked down to the weight and then cooked down some more, he was a textbook version of what a hungry fighter should look like. He boxed and danced around like Muhammad Ali that night, jabbing Fanni's head off, stepping in and out, side to side and after a few rounds, the unthinkable happened – the Italians started to applaud him.

Pat went on to win – in my books – 11 out of the 12 rounds and incredibly turned what was originally a hostile crowd into a warm bunch of boxing fans. When it was announced that Pat had won the European title we flew into the ring and again, the Italians applauded and showed their appreciation of a masterclass performance.

Although the Fanni fight was our last together, I was delighted to have worked with Pat. He's one of the nicest boxers to ever laced up the gloves and he sincerely deserved every title he received – and that's quite a few!

Life by now was very good. I was training champions, boosting my own self-esteem and helping some amazing boxers reach their potential.

More amazing times were ahead involving plenty of drama.

And some of that drama happened outside the ring.

Round 11

BE YOURSELF

"Jimmy's performance is mesmerising and he can switch from benevolent paternalism to chilling menace without even raising his voice."
– Journalist Harry Mullan reviews 'Real Money' August, 1992

The early 1990s was an extremely busy period for me. I had a big stable of talented fighters that I was trying to prepare so the last thing I needed was somebody asking if they could film a documentary about what life is like for a boxer.

Me or my fighters didn't need the distraction, but I simply couldn't refuse because the man who asked was such a lovely bloke.

As opposed to many East Londoners, film maker Ron Peck was not born into boxing, either as a participant or spectator.

Tension: Mark Kaylor, left, and Errol Christie try and bring forward the start of their upcoming bout, 1985

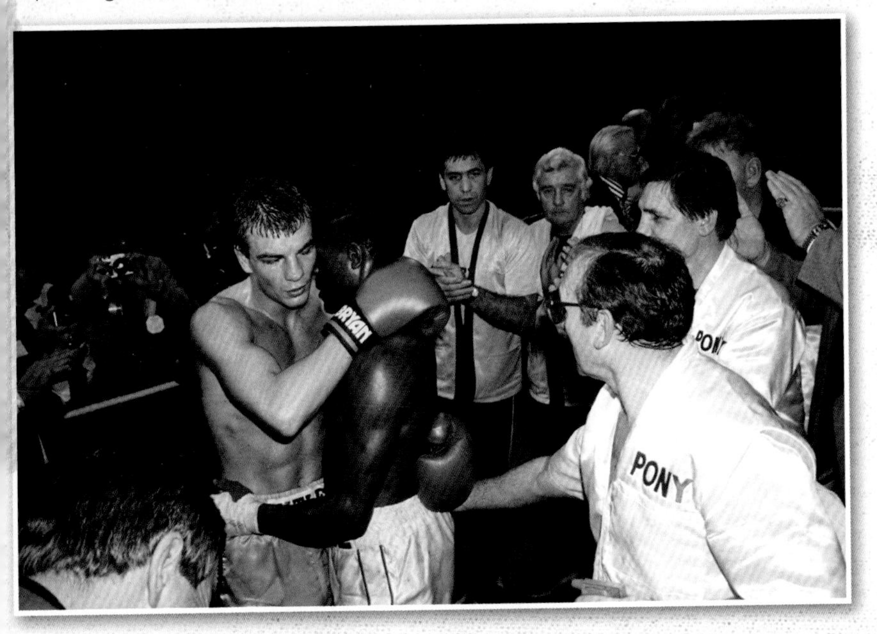

Friends again: Once the fight was over, Kaylor and Christie embraced like the two warriors they were. I'm stood in the background trying to ensure the new-found peace lasts until we can get back to the dressing room

Box office (above): Nigel Benn's rematch with Chris Eubank at Old Trafford in 1993 was a truly epic fight

Pyatt pride: Chris Pyatt wins the WBO middleweight world title after beating Sumbu Kalambay, 1993

The calm: Taping Michael Watson's hands before his life-changing fight with Chris Eubank, 1991

The storm (left): Referee Roy Francis steps in to stop the fight in the 12th round. Michael collapsed soon after

Paying his respects: Muhammad Ali outside St Bartholomew's Hospital, London, after visiting Michael with his twin daughters, Rasheeda and Jamillah, and Michael's mother, Joan

More tragedy: Saying a few words in remembrance of Bradley Stone at the unveiling of his statue at the Peacock Gym, Canning Town – his second home

Happier times: Frankie Simms (seated) is Roy Shaw's unfortunate victim as he gets his hair cut at Mo Hussein's testimonial, 1989

Frank and Wayne: Wayne Alexander, defending one of his many titles, with myself and legendary cut man, Frank Black

Real Money (left): I loved my acting stint as Roy Kane in 'Real Money' although I'm still a far better trainer than actor!

Watchful: I keep an eye on Paolo Roberto (centre) as he spars with Prince Naseem Hamed at the Lennox Lewis Centre, 1999

Crucial moments: Here I'm assessing Joel McIntyre. The 60-second window I get between rounds is an age-old art and can't be taught overnight

Game face: Watching Freddie Luke as he gets ready to fight Nathan Graham for the Southern Area light middleweight title, 2013

Studying (above): Standing back to check technique, footwork and defence. You get a different perspective from outside the ropes looking in

The day job: Putting Kevin Mitchell through his paces on the pads

No detail too small (above, left): Lacing up the gloves for Colin Lynes ahead of a tough sparring session

Unforgettable (above, right): Colin doing the unthinkable and becoming British champion again in 2011

The world's his oyster: Billy Joe Saunders can go as high and as far as he wants

Friends and legends: Still smiling with Mo Hussein and Tony Wilson, 25 years after Tony's mum jumped in the ring, 2014

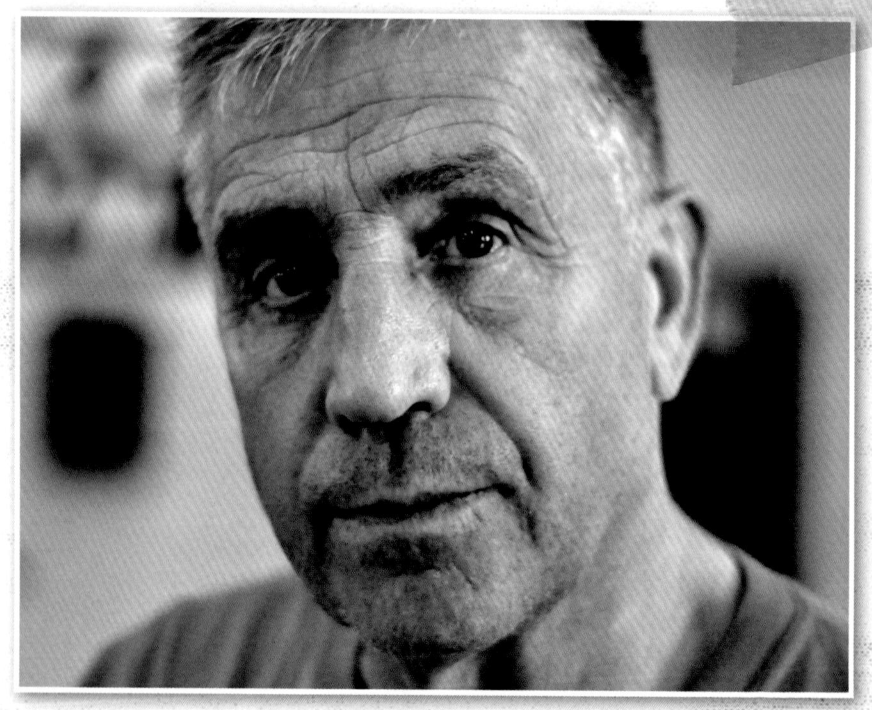

My life: I'm proud of what I've become and how I've taken on the challenges that life has thrown at me. There are plenty more good times ahead – and hopefully plenty more champions to train

His move from leafy Surrey to Bethnal Green in 1975 was just a stone's throw from one of the UK's best known boxing venues, the York Hall. However, before starting to work on this particular documentary, he had never set foot inside the venue to watch a professional bout.

Ron had made a film in 1987 called 'Empire State', which featured the likes of Jamie Foreman and Glen Murphy. The production had a number of characters who were struggling to make a living at the height of Thatcherism and one of the main characters was played by retired, real life boxer Jimmy Flint.

By chance, two of the film's extras turned out to be two fighters I was training at the time, Dean Hollington and one of my sons.

The film premiered at the Mile End ABC cinema and a number of people turned up including Dean Hollington's parents. After the film, Dean's dad told Ron that Dean was going professional with me and that he should come and meet me to see how a boxing gym really works.

Soon after, Ron came down to the Peacock and discussed the idea of filming a documentary called 'Fighters'. I didn't agree straight away though. There was a bit of a turning point that kind of hooked me in. He was talking to my son and Dean Hollington, when I overheard them talking about the script and how it could be staged, and I said to Ron, "People don't talk or act like that in a boxing gym." I gave him a few pointers in terms of what happens in a gym and he said, "Do you want to be in the film?"

That's where my acting "career" began. Another reason

I agreed to take on the part was because it provided a bit of publicity for the fighters and for everybody who was in it, including myself, Terry Lawless and his gym.

The brief we received was as follows. A camera crew would follow the journey of a number of boxers, capturing the pressures a fighter would experience before, during and after a bout. The intention was to provide a never-before-seen insight into boxing.

The documentary would also give an honest view of the discipline and sacrifices involved with the sport and was to be filmed in the East End, reflecting real lives. The project would take 12 months to create, with the end product being around two hours long and aired on Channel 4.

At the time, there were a number of groups who were anti-boxing and had produced documentaries hoping to drum up enough support to get the sport banned, so we wanted to demonstrate boxing's qualities and values.

Once Ron had confirmed his intentions and reassured me about any fears, he took me through how it would work from there onwards.

I had trust in Ron and he never gave me any reason to doubt him in all the time he spent with a camera pointing in mine or anyone else's direction.

I did have one minor concern though – I had never acted before. Although I had been in front of the cameras, it was always for short interviews after fights as a trainer or when I'd boxed as a professional. I certainly hadn't been followed around by film crews for a number of weeks and as a result I expressed my concern to Ron.

He very calmly said to me, "Just carry on and do what you do. Be yourself." That suited me fine as I didn't want to be interrupted while training boxers! Everybody in fact was able to get on and do what they wanted and Ron was almost like a fly on the wall.

He was a very, very polite and nice man. He would always check with me to see if he was overstepping the line at any point and I would always say, "Ron – carry on." There were a few times where I asked him to turn the cameras off to let the boxers get on with their training uninterrupted but the truth is, most of the time he was invisible.

He had the 100 percent trust of everybody who featured in that film and he made sure he never did anything to put that in question.

After making the initial introduction with myself, over the next month, I introduced him to my stable of fighters. The boxers included Bradley Stone, Roy and Jason Rowland, Terry Dixon, Mark Kaylor, Jim Peters and my son.

For those first few weeks, Ron didn't bring a camera crew with him. He wanted to meet the boxers, and gauge their reaction to being asked if they would like to be featured in the film.

At first it seemed a little strange to have somebody walking in to the gym who was not training or being trained, but Ron did well to make himself invisible.

He didn't have a massive camera hanging off his shoulders and an entourage around him, he would simply place himself in one part of the gym with his small hand-held camera, making sure viewers would see a true impression of pro boxers and trainers in action. After an initial introduction, the film throws the viewer right into the atmosphere a boxer and trainer would have experienced in an East London gym over 20 years ago.

I'm featured holding the pads shouting out routines such as, "UPPERCUT, LEFT HAND HOOK, RIGHT HAND. HARDER THIS TIME. NOW GIVE ME DOUBLE LEFT HOOK."

With the likes of Mark Kaylor, Dean Hollington and many other pros banging the bags, skipping rope and working the speedball, the film is as close to boxing a person can experience while sitting in front of a television.

The film allowed people to step into the mind of a boxer to try to give them an idea as to why they would make so many sacrifices and take so many risks in what is a very tough sport.

They all shared one common dream – they returned to the gym, day-in, day-out, with the intention of becoming a champion.

As I said myself in the film, "It takes a special type of person to climb up into that ring, for the real thing. It takes a special type of courage to do that, because it's a one-on-one job in there, not a team effort.

"If you get a 10-year span out of professional boxing, you've done well... If they do make it to be a champion, they need to cash in on those years. It's a very, very hard sport."

The documentary also helped to answer many myths about boxers being a breed of person who are naturally aggressive and have a mentality of wanting to brawl at the drop of a hat. Mark Kaylor played a principal role in the film and at the time he had already fought 45 times as a professional. Although based in California, he made the journey over to be trained by me with the intention of having a couple more fights before making one more attempt to become European champion.

The film allowed Mark to explain how his family life functioned with him as a professional boxer, including concerns from his wife and his own worries as a breadwinner within the very uncertain and unstable financial environment of boxing.

This was also expressed by a number of the boxers featured. There's a financial Catch-22 which comes with this sport. If you want to succeed, you need to dedicate yourself 100 percent and that often means not having the time for another job.

When a date for your fight gets changed or cancelled, this can often see boxers having to borrow money from friends, family or further afield to survive. Some end up walking away from the sport because the financial pressures become too great. The bottom line is – no fight, no money.

Working with Ron also allowed me to have a trip down memory lane.

As a fighter who had trained at the Royal Oak and West Ham Amateur Boxing Club, I gave Ron the tour and I was able to take time to reflect on some of the photos on the wall which showed me winning Schoolboy honours and also point out a number of great fighters who had become champions before and after me. The photos are still on that very same wall at West Ham today. A little more faded than at the time of filming, but still there nonetheless.

In my opinion, the biggest strength about the documentary was its realism. There was no blockbuster 'Rocky' style music playing every time somebody skipped a rope or hit a bag.

In the film, the likes of Dean Hollington, Mark Kaylor and a number of others give you a great insight into what goes on in a boxer's head when facing an opponent. It was an honest glimpse of the psychology that allows a finely tuned athlete to switch off all emotions the second they step through the ropes, right up to the point of the final bell sounding, which is when they change back into a person as opposed to a boxer.

'Fighters' also provided rare footage of the likes of Mark sparring with Michael Watson and a very rare insight, back then, into the dressing room before a fight.

I say "back then", because these days it's quite common to have a camera crew glued to a fighter for the hours leading up to a bout. Up to that point, Terry Lawless had never allowed a camera crew into a dressing room. Ever! At Ron's request, I tackled the subject with Terry and promised that if there was any disruption I would personally sort it out.

By that time, Terry had become so used to seeing the cameras in and around the gym, that he agreed. Ron was incredibly quiet and did an excellent job of capturing key realistic moments throughout a fight night at Basildon Hall, such as me wrapping a boxer's hands while talking them through their game plan.

On watching it back afterwards, there was a moment which made me stop and ponder. Ron Peck is narrating about myself and says, "How many fighters in how many dressing rooms has he seen through the night of a fight?" The answer is – I really don't know!

Certainly quite a few though.

There was however a little episode which happened that night at Basildon Hall which didn't go on script or appear in the film. The guy who Mark Kaylor was going to fight had a pop at Dean Hollington. Dean was only a young lad at the time and had just turned pro, so Mark Kaylor went into the changing room of his opponent and said, "You don't have a go at him. You wait and have a go at me. You understand?"

Nice of Mark to stick up for Dean. The guy backed off and Mark went on to stop him in six rounds later that night!

'Fighters' went on to receive some excellent reviews soon after its release but it was never given the chance to reach its full potential.

Ron had over 160 hours of footage and initially there was talk of turning the documentary into a six or eight part series. Unfortunately, one of the bigwigs at Channel 4 disagreed and that was a massive shame because I believe the documentary reflected the cast as a group of very dedicated boxers, not a bunch of street urchins. A lot of people get the wrong idea that boxers are villains because they fight. The irony of it is that boxing is one of the strongest disciplines on the planet which stops many becoming violent inside and outside of the ring.

What happens in boxing is under controlled conditions

and the film reflected this perfectly. The film was a very true and accurate reflection on how hard boxing is, how lonely it can be and the level of dedication needed to be successful.

****

Four years after 'Fighters', Ron Peck gave me the opportunity to feature in a second movie. I was training Nigel Benn at the time and had gaps of about eight weeks between training camps, so I thought to myself, 'It will be a laugh. Give it a go!'

This time round I would be acting, as opposed to being in a documentary and I would have the chance to act alongside good friends and boxing names such as Micky May and Johnny Eames. I'd never acted in my life at that point, so the prospect of having to act on demand from a script was both exciting and worrying and to top it off, I would be playing a lead role. What had I got myself into?

Ron's inspiration for this movie came through a conversation he'd had with Bradley Stone. After 'Fighters' was done and dusted, Bradley mentioned to Ron that there was another side to boxing.

Bradley was referring to the small time criminal temptations that came hand-in-hand with being a boxer in a tough area. The stresses of not being able to get sponsorship while having little or no income and still trying to pay for boxing training and dietary requirements could often make boxers look to unconventional methods in order to generate cash.

Ron was hooked on the idea and soon after came up with

a title that would reflect the theme.

'Real Money' was born.

As I read the story of a boxing trainer who was trying to keep the young boxers on the straight and narrow, I thought it was something that reflected part of my life and I was comfortable with the script so I agreed to take part within a matter of weeks.

Although the script to 'Real Money' was fictional, each person's role wasn't always a million miles from their natural lives. I was set to play the part of Roy Kane. An ex-prisoner, turned boxing trainer, who worked at the Peacock Gym and who had a son, Bobby, who was a professional boxer.

Sound familiar?

My arch-rival and head villain in the film would be played be none other than Jimmy Flint. Jimmy was the villain (Frankie Chalmers) trying to lure the boxers in with offers of large sums of cash, using them as mules to pick up and deliver 'packages', while also operating a nasty sex trade. When my son in the film starts to have pressure applied from him by Frankie, Roy Kane has to lay down the law.

My son in the film was actually my son in real life, so it didn't take much for me to improvise being the protective father when Frankie Chalmers was putting the frighteners on him.

As important as the scenes with Frankie and my son were, it was sometimes difficult to be serious with my son. There was a scene where I had to pick him up from the police station and we then walk over to the car where I'm supposed to give him a ticking off. Every time I would start with my serious face and tone, my son would look me in the eyes and we would both burst out laughing! Good memories.

As opposed to 'Fighters', which was filmed and set in gymnasiums, 'Real Money' wanted to give a real flavour for the local area of Canning Town.

In fact, when Ron Peck was looking to name the movie, he was actually going to call it, 'Canning Town'. With the majority of the cast coming from the area and with their first-hand knowledge of the issues which were corroding the place, it seemed ideal.

However, in the end, he went with 'Real Money', as it was a more accurate reflection of what he was trying to screen.

On agreeing to taking on the role of Roy Kane, Ron informed us that we would be acting by improvisation.

This basically meant that we wouldn't have to learn a script, but would have guidelines as to how a scene needed to be acted out.

Once I had read the script enough, I was comfortable with the story and I didn't need much by way of coaching. The thing about improvisation is that it's not real, however, the lines are being said by real people, so you can occasionally hit a raw nerve, as you are sometimes getting a genuine reaction.

It may come to a shock to some of you, but I have been known to lose my temper on occasions (!), and there's one scene which I certainly left the onlookers genuinely fearful and wondering, 'Is he still acting?'...

This particular scene involved Roy Kane (myself) and Frankie Chalmers (Jimmy Flint). Both of us were sitting down on comfy chairs and I was trying to tell Frankie in no uncertain terms that he was to back away from my son, or else.

Bear in mind, this is improvisation and here's how the script went...

Roy Kane: *"I'm not trying to put it on ya, but this is my own flesh and blood."*

Frankie Chalmers: *"I understand a little bit, but three times you've told me, you're going to stick it on me."*

Roy Kane: *"Sorry, but..."* (interrupted then by Frankie)

Frankie Chalmers: *"Well you haven't come down here to pray for me have you?"*

Roy Kane: (leaping off the sofa, stepping forward with my arm out and finger pointing at Frankie) *"DON'T TAKE THE FUCKING PISS, COS I'LL FUCKING DO YOU RIGHT NOW. You can have it any way you like."*

Frankie Chalmers: (stands up) *"Now slow down..."*

Roy Kane: (still pointing the finger in Frankie's face, I interrupt)... *"Never mind slow down, you can have it any fucking way you like. Don't take the fucking piss."*

Frankie Chalmers: *"I'm not taking the piss out of anyone."*

Roy Kane: *"Well just sit down and listen to what I've got to say. We're going to do it my way now. Now sit down. IF YOU DON'T SIT DOWN IT'S ON YA."*

At this point I looked over and could see my son and Ron Peck almost trembling as they were wondering if I was being serious at any point.

I then stopped, and calmly said to Ron with a smile on my face, "It depends how far you want to go Ron, because I'm just building up here!"

Ron lets out a nervous laughter, as if to say 'Phew. He's just acting!'

Jimmy Flint would later go on to say to my son and Ron, "It's alright for you two. You didn't have to stand in front of him."

When 'Real Money' was finally aired on Channel 4, it received great feedback as far afield as Italy, and most of the cast were stopped on the street to have their hand shaken or asked for an autograph as a result of their role. In my eyes that made the film a great success.

I certainly had some fun.

****

My final taste of the big screen came in 2008, when I featured in a film documentary called 'The End'. The movie was written, filmed, produced and directed by twins Nicola and Teena Collins, who are the daughters of a good friend of mine, Les Falco.

The twins are certainly no stranger to being in front of the camera, having starred in films such as Guy Richie's 'Snatch' and also being featured in the pages of magazines such as Vogue and Elle, after modelling on the catwalk for the likes of Stella McCartney.

However, this time round, they would be behind the camera looking to capture the magic, as opposed to staring into the lens. Incidentally, if you watch 'Snatch', you will also notice light flyweight boxer Mickey Cantwell sneaking in a performance!

The theme of the film focused on a number of 'ends', such as the end of an era, the end of careers and in some cases, the start of new ones. The common theme between each individual featured in the film was that they all came from the East End.

The old East End.

The film was recorded in black and white, with the majority of the filming being head shots, in order to give a close-up and personal feel to each individual's life and a trip down 'our' memory lane. Characters featured included, the late bare knuckle legend Roy Shaw, my old mate Bobby Reading and a host of other well-known East End figures, including Mickey Taheny, who unfortunately passed away before the premiere was aired.

The film gave the viewer a glimpse of East London, through a number of tough East End characters, but did so in an honest and 'non-Hollywood' manner, and addressed a number of myths about so called 'gangsters'.

In the words of one of the characters, "Gangsterism is a fallacy which is put out there by the newspapers and the films to glamorise something."

Me and my family certainly had first had experience of falling under this branding when I was getting ready for my trial back in the early 1970s, and it was comforting that the general feeling was that the people in the film never glamorised violence – it is the people looking at them who do.

I'm not having a go at gangsters, but my definition of a gangster would be somebody who is involved in something like the mafia. A person who gives their life to the mafia, is loyal to them and when they are nicked, they don't grass on people, they take it – like John Gotti. I wouldn't have liked to live his life, but he was a self-confessed true Mafioso who never grassed on anybody and received a life sentence which he swallowed.

I wasn't alive when Al Capone was about, but I've read about him in books and seen films about him, and he's another example of a proper gangster. If anybody upset them, they wouldn't think anything of killing them.

That was never me.

I was never involved in organised crime and any violence I committed was in revenge for violence against my loved ones.

Another common theme in the film is that nobody likes liberty takers.

My theory is this – if you are respected by people, it's because of the way you are. If you show respect, you usually get it back. However, if you want to frighten people to earn their respect, there's a big difference.

That's the false way of earning respect. Having somebody telling you, "You are a great person, and we love everything about you", when they are saying it out of fear, usually means they don't mean it.

It's best to be respected for what and who you really are. That's my philosophy in life.

One of the cast says, "I respect any man who gets himself

out of bed every morning and feeds his wife and kids... You give people respect they give it back." I'd have to agree.

****

'The End' premiered in April 2009 and received some glowing reviews from the likes of the *Telegraph*, the *Observer* and *London Evening Standard*, not to mention winning a host of awards such as Best UK First Feature at the East End Film Festival.

On its release, it was the fastest selling documentary in the UK at the time. I was glad to have been a part of the film, but even happier that Teena and Nicola Collins had received recognition for all their hard work. Also – a very big thanks to Nicola for the photo on the front of the book which was taken during the making of 'The End'.

A question I've been asked a few times since appearing as an actor is whether I actually ever fancied acting before these opportunities?

The answer is – not really, no. I have however always admired good actors, including the likes of Robert De Niro, Al Pacino and Robert Mitchum. My favourite film is probably 'It's a Wonderful Life' with James Stewart. Can't beat it – especially around Christmas time!

Truth be told, I'm a better boxing trainer than I am an actor, but I certainly had a great deal of fun taking part in the movies. I started acting in my 40s and I was under no illusion that if I was looking to be the next De Niro, I would have needed to have gone to acting school, and my schooling and life has always remained with boxing. This was merely a bit of fun.

I've never been one for doing anything by halves and if I had decided to make a career out of this, I certainly would have needed some kind of schooling. It hasn't always been about money, it's always been more about achievement. If the opportunity came again, with the right script – would I give it a go?... Who knows!

The acting was all a bit of fun and a break from the norm. My priority was boxing – inside and outside of the ring. That was my life. However, for one of my boxers, life almost came to a tragic end.

Round 12

TRAGEDY AND TRIUMPH

"We are just seeing, in fact, that Watson has collapsed in his corner and that is really sad news."
– ITV Sport presenter Jim Rosenthal, 1991

Thirty years ago, a famous four ruled the middleweight division; Hearns, Hagler, Leonard and Duran.

A decade later, those four had been replaced by Eubank, Benn, Watson and Collins.

In the late 1980s there was a young lad from Islington who featured on quite a few of the undercards which my fighters headlined. This same person would end up impressing me even further with his ringcraft by being a sparring partner for Mark Kaylor and coming away with a very respectable performance.

His name was Michael Watson.

The first time I met Michael at the Royal Oak, I was taken

in by how polite he was and how close he was to his family. We used to cross paths on a regular basis but it wasn't until he had his first battle with Chris Eubank in June, 1991, that we officially worked together. He asked me to be his cut man and I gladly agreed.

The fight took place at Earls Court Exhibition Centre and without any bias, I genuinely thought he did enough to win. As the ring announcer spoke into the microphone, "AAAANNNDD STIILLLLL THE MIDDLEWEIGHT CHAMPION OF THE WOOOOORLD", the arena started going mad with disgust over the majority decision which had been granted Eubank's way.

The rematch was being planned within 24 hours.

A couple of days after the fight, Michael contacted me and asked if I could work with him for the rematch without me realising at that point that he wanted me to train him instead of being his cut man. I was delighted to accept because not only was the financial offer good but, more importantly, we got on extremely well.

With less than three months until fight night, we got straight down to work and started the training camp at West Ham Amateur Boxing Club.

The weeks flew by and Michael was in fantastic condition for the fight. He was as fit as he could possibly be and also confident of beating Eubank second time around.

The day of the press conference arrived and Eubank (predictably) appeared with sunglasses and his usual extravagant wardrobe. Michael, unfazed by all the bravado kept asking him, "Take your glasses off when you speak to me Chris", trying to rattle Eubank and show that his circus was having no effect. It was all good clean fun as they both thought they could beat one another. In the grand scheme of things it also helped to sell the bout.

The fight, to be held at White Hart Lane, had been agreed at a catch weight of 11 stone 10 pounds and each fighter came in bang on the limit. Straight after the weigh-in, we all went back to Michael's mum's house in Tottenham, where she prepared a lovely dinner and we had a nice walk afterwards to help relax. On the day of the fight, Michael had arranged for a big stretched limo to take us to the football ground. His friend, DJ Tim Westwood, was also with us and as we pulled up to the football ground, everybody was banging on the windows wishing Michael good luck.

After making it clear to his friends that I wanted everybody out of the changing room, we went through the game plan again. I told him, "Close him down Michael and make him work for three minutes every round." Michael nodded and he looked and felt supremely confident.

We did a little bit of pad work, some shadow boxing and some slow deep breathing to relax. I put a little bit of Vaseline on his face and before you know it, we were walking to the ring in a tight huddle to one of Michael's favourite tracks, 'Momma Said Knock You Out!' I'm not sure how many of the Tottenham fans appreciated Michael's robe with the Arsenal Football Club logo on the back, but the cheer he received when stepping through the ropes was deafening.

Chris finally decided to make his dramatic entrance to Tina Turner's 'Simply The Best', and once everybody had settled down, the referee went through the formalities and the bell rung for the first round.

Michael set a very fast pace from the opening minute and stuck to the game plan of making Chris work for the full three minutes of every round. More of the same followed in the second and third rounds and Michael was starting to take Chris out of his comfort zone by dictating the pace and direction of the fight. Signs of frustration started to appear from the champ by way of wild looping uppercuts and hooks and he was barely connecting with anything.

By round four it was evident that Chris was starting to struggle with Michael's game plan and he looked a little deflated. Michael had been relentless with the jab and straight right and a swelling around Chris's eye had started to form.

Things were looking good.

Rounds five to 10 were very similar. Michael was aggressive, connecting with good shots and kept moving forward. I was so happy with him that I told him to have a rest about round six and catch his breath. That plan lasted about 10 seconds as he went back into flat-out mode and when he came back at the end of the round he said, "Sorry Jim. I couldn't help myself. I feel great in there!" You must remember, Michael took on a fresh and peaking Eubank. This was not an old man on the sliding end of his career. He went on for many years after to reign as a good world champion.

As Michael came out for the eleventh round I told him to, "Hit him round his body and hurt him. Then switch to the head and unload the combinations when you see the gap. Make him work." It was a one-sided fight, Michael was delivering everything to plan and he looked like a dream out there. It was one of the best fights I have ever been involved with.

Up to that point at least.

Michael began working away at the head and body and after a three-shot combination, Chris finally went down.

He looked exhausted more than anything. Michael ran to the neutral corner while Chris started to take the count. Chris made it to his feet and after the referee stepped away from him, he immediately threw the right uppercut which went right through Michael's guard, shook him and he collapsed to the floor.

Michael was beating him, but he didn't beat him.

He beat him over an 11 round fight, but unfortunately it was a 12 round fight as we were about to find out.

As the bell sounded for the end of the round, I realised that I had less than 60 seconds to clear Michael's head. He was standing dazed in the far corner to my right and I remember running to that corner and walking him back.

As I was walking him, I asked, "Are you ok Michael?" I sat him down on the stool in our corner and asked him again, "Are you alright Michael?" He responded calmly, "Jim. I'm fine." The board inspector and Dean Powell were also present and neither noticed any signs for concern.

I told Michael, "LISTEN TO ME. All you need to do is stand up this round and you are champion of the world." I threw some water all over him to shake him up, put on a little bit of Vaseline and the bell sounded for the final round.

The referee made a point of calling both fighters to the

centre of the ring to shake hands, and within seconds of the bell Michael was trapped in that same corner which he had gone down a minute previously. He wasn't taking a great deal of punishment. Most of the punches were off target but the next thing, the referee stepped in and stopped the fight because Michael was not throwing anything back.

I jumped in the ring and was angry at the time, but looking back, I have to say it was a very good decision by a very good referee, Roy Francis. I was hugging Michael, trying to console him. His head was leaning over my shoulder and just as I was about to shout at the referee for stopping it, I felt him collapse in my arms.

I thought he must be exhausted.

****

As I held Michael, fights started to kick off all over the stadium and people were getting in the ring for safety. I now realised the situation with Michael was serious and I needed to rest him down flat.

With all the pandemonium going on around us I couldn't get a doctor in there for what seemed like an eternity and it was actually seven minutes before they showed up.

When they finally did arrive, they didn't know what to do.

They realised he needed to go to hospital but they had no idea that they were wasting precious moments right there and then.

These days, boxing officials insist that an anaesthetist is present at ringside and they can immediately induce a medical coma. This calms the brain down and makes sure any damage is reduced – if treated quickly.

Michael's episode was a major factor in this measure being introduced at all future professional boxing events, with the likes of Spencer Oliver benefiting at a later date. It's just a massive shame Michael couldn't have been a beneficiary of this system on that evening, as opposed to being the pioneer.

Things were going from bad to worst on all fronts. They sent us to the wrong hospital at first, but thankfully we finally reached St Bartholomew Hospital, which is where he would stay in a coma for the next 40 days.

As we arrived at the hospital, Michael's family was waiting and we all prayed together, in the waiting area, while the medical team prepared Michael for brain surgery. The neurosurgeon, Peter Hamlyn, came out to discuss the status quo and explained the procedures Michael would have to undergo.

The prognosis was very bleak.

Michael was in big trouble and needed to be operated on immediately to remove a blood clot from the brain.

The neurosurgeon explained that Michael, should he survive the surgery, would probably never be able to feed himself again and would have very limited physical and mental capabilities.

He discussed the operation in further depth and then came up close to me and said, "Jim. You must not blame yourself. This was not your fault."

It was a terrible, dreadful time and something I would not like to ever repeat.

Michael was a fantastic boxer and he was on the verge of real greatness. More importantly than that though, he was a polite and well respected man who had a loving family. Life can be so unfair and his situation seemed to highlight that in a particularly severe way.

A range of emotions were running through my head and several questions rose rapidly to the surface. Was it time to throw in the towel? Did I need to be part of a sport which could potentially do this to another man? Am I cut out for this anymore?

I stayed at the hospital all night and didn't get a wink of sleep. I decided to make my way home the morning after to take a shower. My wife was waiting and although she didn't know the full story, she provided me with a big hug.

The people from my church had also made their way over to my house and they did something which helped convince me to remain in boxing to this current day.

They said, "Jesus wants you in the gyms. Don't give up. Your work is not finished."

That was the defining moment that made me carry on. I could have easily swayed the other way in terms of my career as a boxing trainer.

I now realised that I must carry on, if anything, just as a tribute to Michael and the dedication he had shown towards his chosen sport.

My work was not over by a long way, but I still walked around with a heavy heart for a long time.

Michael had to undergo six brain surgeries and suffered permanent partial paralysis, but as with his performances against the top fighters, he proved his courage and character once again. He would prove many people wrong about his recovery, including myself and I visited Michael on a regular basis in the years after.

He has a carer by the name of Lennard Ballack, who is a lovely Christian man. Just for the record, you don't need to be a Christian to be a lovely man and you don't need to be a lovely man to be a Christian! I used to go over to his house initially once every fortnight and I used to love my time with him. Seeing his progress first hand, feeding himself, walking, and proving the doctors wrong on so many levels was, and is, fantastic. Seeing him laughing and content with his own progress is worth more than all the money on the planet.

And although he never received the title of world champion, he will always be regarded by many as 'The People's Champion.'

****

If boxing has taught me anything, it's that you have to keep going in life, push through the pain and the hurt and the challenges you face.

You have to get off the canvas and battle back.

So I did just that.

Soon after the Watson tragedy I was back to work at the old Peacock Gym in Freemasons Road and opportunity knocked once again.

Somebody passed me a message with a telephone number on it. The message basically explained that somebody wanted to be trained by myself. The first thing that went through my head was, "I can't take on another six-round fighter as I don't have the money to support them."

I asked Bradley Stone if I could borrow his mobile phone and then called the number. A guy called 'Rolex' Ray Sullivan picked up the phone, and said, "Jimmy. Would you be interested in training Nigel Benn?"

My heart nearly jumped out of my chest.

This was a truly amazing opportunity.

We met up later that evening at my house and discussed terms and conditions. Nigel was very polite and the first thing he did was to ask my wife for her permission for me to train him. He then mentioned that training would be in Tenerife and if she was happy for me to spend that time away from home. My wife said, "That's no problem Nigel." And that was it really!

At the time, I had a big stable of unbeaten fighters but I didn't have a promoter for them. Combined with the fact that I was now taking on a big commitment by way of training Nigel Benn, I decided the best thing was to give them greater opportunities for bouts by releasing the majority of them to Terry Lawless.

The one fighter I needed to have a one-to-one with about this decision was Chris Pyatt. At the time he was Commonwealth champion and I knew he had the talent to become world champion within a short period.

I had spent so many years with Chris, he was like family and I didn't want to leave him in the lurch. I asked him how he felt about the Benn offer was yet another example of why I rate Chris Pyatt as one of the nicest people I've ever crossed paths with. He said, "Jim, you must take it. Frank Black and Dean Powell can take care of me when you're not around, and we both know I'm not earning anywhere near the money you could be getting from Benn. You can't miss the opportunity."

Humbled is not a strong enough word to describe my emotions at that moment.

With everybody happy for me to train with Nigel, I got down to business. The first fight I trained him for was against the existing WBC super middleweight champion, Mauro Galvano, who had beaten Mark Kaylor in March, 1990, for the European belt, and then went on to win the WBC world crown nine months later.

Up to this point, including as an amateur, Nigel had always been a knockout artist. Don't get me wrong, knocking people out left, right and centre is all well and good, until you start to come up against opponents who can not only punch, but who are also able to box.

One of my first tasks with Nigel was turning him into a smarter fighter and getting him in tune with his boxing brain, as opposed to his fighter's instinct. My aim was to get Nigel to relax in the fight, keep his chin down when jabbing and use lateral movement more. Simple as that.

I started working with Nigel as he was making the move up from middle to super middle. He had already held the WBO world title at the lower weight, losing it to his arch-rival, Chris Eubank, but apart from that, the only other fight he had lost at this stage in his career was against Michael

Watson, who stopped Nigel in six rounds in 1989.

I usually tend to have a six-week training camp with my fighters but with the step up in weight, the climate change and the world title on the line, I decided 10 weeks would be a wiser timeframe.

Nigel was an ex-soldier so had no issues with following strict routines. Without fail, he would run up Mount Teide every morning, followed by his deep breathing exercises and then breakfast. After a late morning nap, we would have lunch around 2pm followed by a gym session.

I would be Galvano in front of him on the pads, trying to re-enact the type of moves and scenarios that Nigel would potentially encounter against the Italian.

Then I would have Nigel shadow boxing – bobbing and weaving, throwing right hands and left hooks to the body, followed by the jab, while trying to cut down the imaginary Galvano's ring space.

In addition we hired four sparring partners who between them had strengths as boxers, punchers and movers. With one day off per week, that was the training regime for the next 10 weeks and Nigel followed it down to a tee.

After a great training camp, fight night arrived.

The strategy was to cut the ring off from Galvano and suffocate him. Once in range, Nigel was to roll under his jab and throw the left hook over the top, followed by the right hand over his left lead, before getting in close and working the body to rough him up as much as possible.

As the bell sounded for round one, Nigel jumped on him. Within under 30 seconds it was obvious that Galvano was out of his comfort zone. Nigel was throwing vicious left hooks and right hands at will, and simply not giving him the space to breath.

Every attack Nigel made was booed by the hostile Italian crowd. It was obvious Galvano had met his match and was already resorting to holding, rabbit punches and anything else that could keep him in the fight.

As the bell sounded for the end of round three, Galvano's corner were all standing around their man trying to make an obvious fuss that something was not right. Next thing, they called Joe Cortez over to inspect the damaged eye. It was a bad cut, but certainly not that bad.

If any of my fighters had come back to the corner with a cut like that I would have been straight on it and getting them ready for the next round.

Galvano's team had seen something they could exploit and were looking to use this to the maximum by trying to push for a technical draw as the fight had not gone past three rounds at that point.

The doctor was called over and surprise surprise, the fight was stopped! The minutes that followed were chaos. Nigel's initial reaction was one of joy. He jumped into the corner, climbed the ropes and held his arms up high celebrating what he thought was a new belt round his waist.

I rushed over and told him that although we were ahead on points, they were looking to push for a technical draw. Nigel's reaction was not good.

He was now very angry and was shouting and screaming, "NOOO. NOOO, NO WAY JIM."

One of the guys from ITV came over and asked me for my opinion of what I thought the outcome would be. I told him that we had won the fight and deserved the victory, but I had my doubts, being away from home.

In the meantime, Barry Hearn was having a shouting match with Galvano's team and anybody else who was able to make a decision about the fight. Turns out Barry did a good job arguing the case!

After further confusion, Joe Cortez leant over to me and said, "You've won it Jim."

Seconds later, the news was carried over to Nigel and the celebrations started as he realised he was now a two-weight world champion.

In the immediate interview that followed in the ring with Gary Newbon, Nigel dedicated the win to his brother who had passed away at the young age of 17 and he also looked at the camera and said, "Michael (Watson), that is your belt and nobody can take it away from you. That's from me to you with my love Michael. That's your belt now."

It was an emotional moment for everybody involved.

Seconds later, Chris Eubank appeared, standing ringside giving Nigel the thumbs up for his performance. Nigel, not in the mood for his bravado, stuck his head through the ropes and said, "Now we can do business. You hear me?" The seed was sown.

After wins over Nigel Piper, Mauro Galvano and Lou Gent, it was time to tussle with Eubank again.

With Nigel holding the WBC crown, recognised by many as the best world title, Eubank was hot on our trail, looking for the rematch. After a short negotiation period, the date was set for the October 9, 1993, and the venue was none other than the home of Manchester United Football Club – Old Trafford.

The strategy for this fight was to outwit Eubank before outhitting him, but I was under no illusion that this was going to be a hard fight. I rated Chris Eubank as a very good fighter, with a great chin. The only flaw I spotted, as I had for Michael Watson's fight, was that he didn't like to work nonstop for three minutes every round.

The first time Nigel fought Eubank, he stood there and slugged it out, with his head up in the air. By showing too much heart, he took far too many unnecessary punches and his face came out covered in lumps. Second time round, the intention was to keep his head bobbing and weaving. If you look at the state of him at the end of second fight, the work speaks for itself. The intention was not to sprint around the ring, looking to take Chris down with clubbing shots. Chris was a smart fighter, so I wanted Nigel to stick to his chest, bob and weave in front of him, and work him round the head and the body with hooks. If he stepped back, we were going to jab him, followed by the left hook and right hand.

With a successful training camp completed, it was time to get the circus element of the fight out of the way – the press conference. Eubank pulled up in a pair of jodhpurs, crash helmet and a motorbike. That was Chris Eubank – what can you say?! It was no secret that they hated each other at the time and with little prompting, they gave each other verbals at every available opportunity.

I managed to keep calm and composed and got through the press conference without any confrontation.

Fight night had arrived. It was a cold October evening and 42,000 fans had turned up for what was one of the biggest domestic tear ups in a long time. Love them or hate them, Nigel and Chris's rivalry was the best media machine around in boxing at that time.

When they were in a room together, there was a frenzy of paparazzi and journalists wanting to get caught in the slipstream. They were good for the sport and the size of the audience on that evening reflected that.

With the referee's instructions out of the way, I walked Nigel back to the corner, ducked under the ropes and left him to do the business. From the very outset, Nigel wanted to show a superior level of confidence and get above Eubank's bravado. With Eubank standing in his corner waiting for the bell to sound, he threw a gaze over in Nigel's direction in his distinctive style. Nigel smiled then flexed his lateral muscles, making him look like a cobra. Ten out of 10 for entertainment value!

As the bell sounded, Nigel was the first to make his way over, trying to impose his presence. Although both fighters had moved up from middle to super middle, Nigel naturally walked around at about 12 stone, whereas Chris was about a stone heavier on fight night. That said, it didn't make an ounce of difference. Weight doesn't win a fight; skill, heart and boxing ability does. Nigel was not lacking on any of these fronts.

Nigel was so focused on the job and in such good

condition that he was happy to hunt, trade, work off the back foot or work behind the jab. This was a much different fight to the first one. The strategy of getting into Eubank's personal space and making him work for three minutes was paying off.

The fight was a real tough battle in which both men had moments of superiority. It was two boxers at their physical best doing the job they loved and it shone through.

It was also really, really tight – almost too close to call and as Nigel sat on the stool with about 30 seconds to go before the twelfth and final round, I shouted out to him, "WE WANT THIS LAST ROUND BIG NIGEL. BIIIIIGGG!" Nigel, already pumped up shouted back, "YEAAAAHHH." He then bounced off his stool waiting for the bell and went in search of Eubank.

The final round was pretty even, with both fighters holding their arms up towards the last minute, convinced they had won. As the bell sounded, we got Nigel on the shoulders of one of my corner crew, as we were confident we had done enough to win. Eubank was doing exactly the same as we waited for the result.

One judge scored the fight 115-113 in favour of Nigel.

The second had scored the same but in favour of Eubank. The final judge had it 114-114.

The fight was a draw.

Straight after the verdict had been given, Nigel walked out of the ring in disgust. The thousands in attendance also expressed their disapproval. ITV presenter Gary Newbon quickly came over to me and asked – in the absence of

Nigel – if I could say a few words while sitting next to Chris Eubank on the edge of the ring. I had no problems with that.

I could see Chris was very agitated and after hogging Gary for about two minutes, Gary asked me my views and opinions. I responded by saying I thought it was a close fight but that I believed Nigel had edged it. Chris was not impressed and butted in.

He started to disagree and rant, but Gary stepped in and said, "Chris. You've had your go. Let Jimmy speak now." Truth be told, I was having a giggle to myself, as I knew it would be far too easy to get a reaction from Chris!

As I said, before, no disrespect intended to Chris. He's a great fighter and the rivalry he shared with Nigel made them two of the best known fighters Britain has ever seen.

Nigel wasn't down for long and bounced back with a successful fight against Henry Wharton, when he boxed beautifully, before beating a Paraguayan called Juan Carlos Gimenez on points.

In both fights, Nigel had demonstrated his heart and his talent and although the Gimenez fight was my last with Nigel, we parted on very good terms.

Looking over my shoulder I'm proud to say that I trained Nigel Benn when he was at his peak and for seven successful WBC world title fights. Good memories.

****

Soon after the Henry Wharton contest, but before my last fight with Nigel, the East End community and boxing fraternity was dealt another sickening, horrible blow.

On April 26, 1994, Bradley Stone fought against Richie Wenton for the British super bantamweight title and unfortunately passed away two days later from a blood clot to the brain. He was only 23 years of age.

Bradley was a promising boxer, who had only lost one out of 19 fights at that point, and he was a very well liked person at the Peacock Gym and in the community at large. A short while after Bradley passed away, Martin Bowers and his family made a conscious decision that they wanted to have bronze statue made, which would stand out the front of the Peacock.

A very good boxer called Mickey Cantwell, who was one of Bradley's best mates and who I would go on to train for a world title a few years later, was asked by the Bowers family to be the model.

He would've given anything for Bradley to have been there to do it himself.

Bradley Stone was an extremely hard working boxer and very polite young man, but he was nobody's fool. He was a proper Canning Town boxer who got on with everybody and was no trouble to train.

I knew of his achievements as an amateur when he used to fight for Repton and I trained and managed him for part of his pro career, right up to the point I started training Nigel Benn in 1992.

When the news hit the media about Bradley being taken to hospital it spread like wildfire. It was a very sad time for everybody that knew him and it was also an uncomfortable experience as calls to ban boxing started to rear their heads again. Bradley received an incredible send-off, something seen maybe once in a lifetime.

It was a massive East End funeral with a long line of limos and the street they lived in was like one massive carpet of flowers from one end to the other.

This was my first experience of a boxer dying whom I'd known and people ask me if I considered leaving the sport. But the answer to that is no. Bradley dedicated his life to boxing and if he had seen any of us down in the dumps or considering quitting as a result of his death, he would have been very disappointed.

He inspired many people he came into contact with and his spirit and presence lives on – especially in the form of his statue in Canning Town.

****

With the tragic episodes of Michael Watson and Bradley Stone still fresh, I needed a bit of cheering up.

Cue – Wayne Alexander and Danny Williams.

Both of them had turned pro with Frank Warren in 1995 and had decided they wanted me to be their trainer. I was looking forward to meeting with them.

For two guys who packed serious knockout power and possessed excellent boxing ability, I was surprised with how timid they were, especially the first time we all met at the Peacock. As they walked through the doors, I was doing some pad work with another boxer but I acknowledged their entrance. After a few minutes I gave them another look and told them I would be right over. I could see they were having a chat, but it's only now while getting my life story together that I was given the details of that conversation!

Both Wayne and Danny knew of my past and they also knew of my reputation as a firm trainer so were a bit concerned.

The conversation went as follows:

Wayne Alexander leans over to Danny after my first nod of acknowledgement and says:

"He looks pretty serious Danny."

Danny replies:

"There won't be any laughing or joking with this guy."

After my second look over, Danny says to Wayne:

"Seriously man. What the bloody hell are we doing in here?"

Wayne replies:

"Shut up Danny. He's coming this way..."

I walked over and they stood upright and we shook hands. They explained their aspirations of wanting to be champions and felt that I could make it happen for them. Soon after, I had dates for their debuts later that year and to their surprise, they ended up having a lot of fun!

My first impressions of Danny Williams and Wayne Alexander were very good. I knew Wayne was an ABA champion, recognised as a good boxer and a concussive puncher and I had seen some of his fights. I didn't know a great deal about Danny but I knew he has a very good amateur record. I could see that they liked to do their own thing, but one aspect of training I drilled into them was the need to do groundwork. I'm pretty sure they thought I invented groundwork as they didn't think they had to do any! Sit-ups, push-ups, stretches, you name it. I had them working away on the mats constantly.

I knew they both had boxing ability and could fight, so my job in the early days was to smooth them out a little bit. Strengthen their punches, help out with their lateral movement and work on their defence. Wayne had a terrible habit of lifting his head every time he threw the jab and I would pick him up on it every time. In the end, I got so sick and tired of him having his head up in the air when he jabbed, that I started to shout, "Get your head higher. Higher Wayne, Higher. HIGHER!" The reverse psychology worked. We all had a laugh and most importantly, after a while, he kept his chin down!

Danny was different. I could tell he didn't enjoy being shouted at.

One of my responsibilities as a trainer is to get to know my fighters and understand what can damage them and what can make them stronger. The approach with Danny was to be calm and clear. He didn't like trainers who babbled on and appreciated quick and sharp commands as opposed to long dialogue.

Of the 14 fights Danny had under my wing, he won 12 of them by stoppage. After his first few outings I was already letting everybody know that this guy was a very good heavyweight prospect.

He could punch, he could box, he was smart and to top

it all, was one of the nicest people you could ever meet. However, he also had his temperamental days.

On July 19, 1997, we were fighting on a massive bill at Wembley which featured the likes of Prince Naseem and Johnny Nelson. Danny's opponent was a guy called Roger McKenzie, who had won the Southern Area crown four years before. We knew that we had a few hours to kill before Danny would be fighting, so me and Frank Black sat down with the crowd to catch some of the undercard action and waited for Danny to join us.

Danny arrived a short while after, walked over to our seats and shook our hands. I then said "We've got a bit of time before you're up, do you fancy watching a few of the fights?"

Danny said, "Have you got a minute? I'd like a quick chat." He then dropped the news. "I'm not fighting tonight," he said. I looked at him and said, "What's wrong with you?"

"Nothing," he replied. "I just don't fancy fighting."

I asked him if he was ill, but he said he felt fine – he just didn't want to fight. I turned to him and said, "You can't just walk in here and say you don't want to fight! You need to have a doctor's certificate, you need to inform your manager, there's all sorts of things to consider."

I told him to come with me for a walk around Wembley and I told him what a great fighter he was and the opportunity he was missing. I meant every word. It took me about 45 minutes, but finally he agreed to fight. We went back to the changing room and I did his hand wraps. He had a long face though. I got in the ring and his manager Frank Warren said, "Everything alright Jim?" and I replied, "Yeah. No problems here!" Then Danny turned to me and said, "Give me a slap Jim." I felt like slapping his head off after the last hour of his antics, but I gave him a light slap! He then went out and knocked his opponent out in two rounds!

He had his temperamental days, but he was a very, very good boxer. If the best version of Danny Williams turned up on the night, he was virtually unbeatable. It was therefore no surprise that he went on to win a number of championships belts and in 2004 he knocked out Mike Tyson in four rounds, before going on to fight for the world heavyweight crown against Vitali Klitchko. Although he put up a great fight, Vitali stopped him in the eighth, but Danny returned to England a hero.

He was trained by my old champion Jim McDonnell for those fights, which made me happy twice over.

****

Wayne also had his fair share of championship success and I'm very proud to say that I was with him for 22 of his 27 bouts, during which time he won the Southern Area, British and European titles.

However, the fight I'm proudest of him for was one that he lost.

After a quick one round destruction of journeyman Paul Denton, Wayne was handed his 'Rocky' moment on February 9, 2001.

We received a phone call asking if he would like to step in to challenge tough Namibian Harry Simon for the WBO world middleweight belt... just 24 hours later.

It was a tough, almost impossible, ask, but Wayne was ranked No.3 by the WBO, so it was not as if it was a foregone conclusion that Simon would win.

Wayne was confident in his ability and his record clearly demonstrated, with 12 of his 15 fights at that point of his career ending by stoppage in three rounds and under, he was a destructive puncher and had a chance with any light middleweight or middleweight in the world if he could connect.

After the negotiations for the purses had been sorted, we jumped in my car and headed up to Widnes that evening.

When the weigh-in arrived, I remember Harry Simon looking at Wayne's stomach and noting he was not quite in shape and I knew straight away he would be trying to aim at his midsection. At that particular time, we were training at the Lennox Lewis gym for a defence of Wayne's British title. We were about three weeks away from the defence, so he was not 100 percent. Let me expand on that. He wasn't 100 percent, because I didn't want him to be 100 percent at that point. I didn't want him peaking just yet.

Wayne had no problem making weight as he was a light middleweight and this was a middleweight fight, so we were roughly around the weight anyway.

Simon had held the belt since 1998 and with no training camp and virtually no time to prepare a strategy, or get mentally in the zone, we were aware that this was not going to be easy. Both men came flying out and exchanged blows and Wayne didn't look like a guy who had only had

24 hours notice for the fight.

However, by round four, Simon was starting to land more aggressive punches and when he landed two hooks to the body which sent Wayne onto one knee, Wayne took an eight count. Simon instantly landed a couple more hooks followed by a load of head shots and the referee jumped in and stopped the fight. After the fight, while trying to take Wayne's gloves off, he mentioned how painful both his hands were.

We had to pretty much cut everything off around his knuckles, and do so with extreme caution. It turned out that Wayne had broken both his hands, but he never once complained to me during the fight.

The fact is Simon was too big and too fit. With only a day to prepare, Wayne put up a great fight and gave the champ a good workout.

Absolutely nothing to be ashamed of.

In fact, he went up in the rankings in most of the sanctioning bodies overnight. I was very proud of him and that fight goes to prove the measure of the man.

****

Having taken the 6ft 3in, 18 stone Danny Williams under my wings in 1995, a year later, I was approached by a fiery 5ft 2in, 7 stone warrior, by the name of Mickey Cantwell.

He was looking to challenge none other than the 4ft 10in South African legend, 'Baby' Jake Matlala, for his WBO light flyweight title, and wanted me to train him.

With a good amateur record, including winning the ABAs twice, Mickey had also won the Southern Area title after only eight fights and later went on to win the British belt.

Before jumping in at the deep end, I suggested we tried a week together and if we liked each other we could go from there.

Mickey turned up on the Monday morning and was visibly nervous. I cracked a few jokes and had a bit of a chat to relax him and then we worked on the pads. Within the hour I had him laughing and working at full steam.

The week passed and we were both in no doubt that we gelled.

The Monday after, we got down to business at the Peacock Gym and with three months to go before fight night, we started to work on our attacking strategy.

The plan was to outbox Jake because he was short, stocky and strong. We didn't want to stand around and trade with him for too long, unless it was on our terms. From the word go, Mickey was an absolute dream to coach.

He listened to everything I told him to do inside and outside of the ring and he was a true gentleman before, during and after the training camp.

One night after training he decided to pop in a video tape of an old Matlala fight and thought to himself, 'How the hell am I going to beat this guy?'

He came in the day after and expressed his concerns and I told him he had nothing to worry about and that he just had to stick to the game plan and he'd be fine.

As Mickey was trying to focus himself for the biggest fight

of his life, he was having major financial problems. Things got so bad that his house ended up being repossessed and the press couldn't wait to get involved.

On hearing about the situation, I realised that he would need a shoulder to lean on and a pair of ears to listen. We had a good chat, I gave him some advice on how to handle the media and explained that everything was going to be ok. He listened to me as if I was his dad and I knew everything was going to be fine.

As we started to pick up the training and Mickey started sparring, we both had no doubt that he was going into that boxing ring to win, no longer just to survive.

Before the contest, the press conference was hosted at the plush Four Seasons Hotel on Park Lane. Mickey had been used to press conferences being hosted in pubs, with the smell of lager and cigarettes in the air, the sound of a fruit machine going off in the background, and with a handful of people in attendance.

You should have seen his face when he walked into the lobby! Priceless.

We made our way to the allocated room, where a row of tables had been set up for the fighters and trainers. As Mickey took his place, he got to meet the likes of Prince Naseem Hamed and Steve Collins who were all fighting on the same bill at the New London Arena in Millwall. Mickey loved it!

Baby Jake then walked into the room and this was the first time Mickey had come face-to-face with him.

A few hours before, I had been in a room at the Britannia Hotel with Mickey, cracking jokes and telling him a few boxing stories.

He was laughing, and smiling nonstop. It was essential for him to feel relaxed on entering that room, and when he finally met Matlala, the tension had been drained from him and he stood face to face with peak confidence, ready for action.

At the weigh in the day after, I told Mickey to stand tall. No – I wasn't having a dig at him! He was almost four inches taller than Matlala and I wanted the champ to know that. My confidence in Mickey was now starting to rub off on him and by fight night he was raring to go.

As the bell sounded for round one, Mickey stuck to the game plan of staying behind the jab.

He was a bit fiery and enjoyed a scrap, but this was a world champion he was facing, with an incredible reputation, so he had to make sure he used his skill and space to gain an advantage.

The first three rounds were very competitive, but I gave the edge to Mickey. Neither fighter looked in trouble and both were very confident of their boxing ability. Round four was more eventful.

While in close, Matlala rolled underneath Mickey and head-butted him. It wasn't blatant for a referee to see, but it really didn't look like an accident from where I was standing. I was furious.

As the blood started to roll down Mickey's head, I was trying to get the fight stopped, because if it went to the scorecards Mickey would have won. Despite having a shout at the referee, the fight carried on.

At the end of the round Mickey told me, "After head-butting me in mid-battle, Matlala leaned to my ear and said to me in his thick South African accent 'Sorry Mickey!'"

Thankfully, Mickey had managed to keep himself composed as far as the ninth round. I could tell he was preparing to go to war with Matlala now, so I grabbed a hold of him at the end of the ninth and said, "Listen. LISTEN TO ME! Do NOT have a fight with him. Box him Mickey."

Despite my advice, Mickey did have a bit of a scrap towards the end, but he put on one of the most courageous battles I had seen in a long time.

The decision went to the scorecards and Mickey lost on a split decision. But we had gone in there and delivered a job which everybody had thought was impossible.

Matlala came away that night knowing he'd been in a proper fight and Mickey proved his doubters wrong and gained some new-found respect from those who thought he'd be a pushover.

In my eyes, I was delighted with getting that close to winning and incredibly proud of how Mickey had handled himself against the champ.

After the Matlala fight, both me and Mickey thought that was the end of the road for his boxing. Little did we know that Frank Warren had just lined him up with another world title shot.

This time Mickey would be fighting at straw weight against Filipino, Eric Jamili, for the vacant WBO belt in December, 1997. If the truth be told, I was very concerned about

Mickey dropping down to strawweight, but he assured me he was comfortable making weight and that it would be ok.

And then an issue came up which none of us foresaw. When a fighter is having their hands wrapped, a member of the opposite camp needs to be present to make sure they are happy with the way it has been done.

On returning from seeing Jamili's hands being wrapped, I turned to Mickey and said, "I have some bad news." Mickey said, "Has the fight been called off?"

I said "Steady on Mickey, not that bad. He's a southpaw!" We had been preparing to fight an orthodox fighter and none of us had discovered his stance until that point. Mickey said, "A southpaw? What are we going to do?" I replied, "I don't care if he's a northpaw. You'll beat him."

The first round was explosive, but unfortunately Mickey was on the end of some slicing blows. Jamili caught him with an uppercut that split his nose, caught a nerve and just wouldn't stop bleeding.

Frank Black was cut man that night and he certainly earned his money as Mickey never fully recovered from this punch.

In the second round Jamili cut Mickey's eye and then in the third round he cut his head. It had turned into a bloodbath and Frank, who was one of the best cuts men ever, couldn't stop the bleeding.

I don't think anybody in the world could have done a better job than Frank that night but some cuts just will not stop – and this was one of them.

By the eighth round, referee Mark Nelson from the USA,

stopped it because of the amount of blood loss. It was his first title fight as a referee, so I'm sure he wanted to ensure everything was done correctly, but I was annoyed, as Mickey was starting to get the better of Jamili.

When we got to the changing room and Mickey had been stitched up by the doctor, he turned to me and said, "You would have let me bleed to death in that ring, wouldn't you?" I said, "Yeah. I would have done to let you win that title." I was only joking though. I was just bitter, because he was starting to overcome his opponent and it looked like he was on course for winning the world title.

It was not meant to be though.

I went on to work with Mickey for his last three fights – although for the last two I was not his trainer – and I had the pleasure of seeing him win against Dave Coldwell and challenge unsuccessfully for two more world title shots, including a rematch with Matlala.

He's a fighter that would always leave everything in the ring and it was a sincere pleasure to have had the opportunity to train him.

He is still involved in the boxing scene, training the likes of 2012 Olympic bronze medallist Anthony Ogogo and has a son who is also a professional boxer.

I wish him the best with his journey ahead, as I do all those who I've come in contact with in this sport, including (and especially) Michael Watson, a man who has shown unbelievable courage, determination and strength in the battle that he's faced. His case was a dreadful tragedy that he has turned into a stunning triumph.

His faith has played a big part in his amazing recovery – and it is a faith that I share myself.

Round 13

COCKNEY CHRISTIAN

"Every athlete in training submits to strict discipline in order to be crowned with a wreath that will not last, but we do it for a crown that will last forever."
– Corinthians Ch.9 vs.25

"Jesus was grassed, fitted up and murdered."
– Jimmy Tibbs, 1993

Throughout the Michael Watson incident, the death of Bradley Stone and the various other challenges I've faced before and since then, one of the elements that has allowed me to always keep fighting and bouncing back has been my faith. I was brought up a Roman Catholic because back in those days, if you wanted to attend St Helen's or St Bonaventure's schools, you had to be.

Children of other religions were not accepted and you had to show evidence that you had been christened in a Roman Catholic church. Strict stuff.

While at school, I was taught about God and Jesus. Although I was interested in the lessons, I certainly wasn't an academic and had no real desire to pick up a copy of the Bible when I could be playing football or training down the boxing gym.

Consequently, I left the Catholic schools behind me, became heavily involved with boxing, did my share of ducking and diving and only occasionally went to church.

No disrespect to the church I went to, they were lovely people, but I didn't understand a word they were saying.

More than anything, I just wasn't interested. I found it boring and couldn't wait to get out of there. I probably checked my watch 30 times when I was in church and the service only lasted an hour. However, I felt I had done my duty by attending. Paid my penance so to say.

I didn't know why I was going, but I felt that I needed to go. However, something then happened that changed my entire outlook on faith and religion.

After coming out of prison, I had started earning a good living through training and I had a nice house, four cars and plenty of money.

However, when I look at my life back then, I was happy for one day and miserable for six.

I was lacking direction.

When I was at my fiery peak as a trainer, it was a well known fact that I would be heard having some heated conversations while on the phone negotiating with the matchmakers, trying to get my fighters their bouts.

Then I had a defining day.

Every Saturday afternoon, like clockwork, I used to go to the Golden Lion down the Barking Road and meet with my mates for a few drinks.

The only exception to this rule would be if I had a fighter who had a big bout coming up then I would be at the gym getting the boxer prepared.

This particular morning I was sitting in my television room having a fag and a cup of tea thinking to myself, 'I'll go down the Golden Lion and have a bit of breakfast and a few drinks'.

As I was sitting there, out of nowhere, I started to think about death.

I've never, ever been frightened to die. My outlook on life up to that point was whether you are rich, poor, free or a slave, we are all going to die.

But as I sat there, I started to think to myself, 'What's going to happen to me when I die? Where will I go?' I know I'd been calling myself a Catholic for many years, but I started asking myself, 'Is there really a God?' I started feeling really uncomfortable and was trying to work out what had brought all this on.

I was 44 years of age and for some unknown reason I was trying to work out if there was a heaven and a hell.

I'd never read a Bible in my life up to that point, but couldn't stop thinking about the 'hell' part of my thoughts, which circled around my head constantly.

It was starting to rattle me. I snapped out of it and thought to myself, 'Get in that shower Jim and then get down to the pub and have that drink'.

Freshly showered, I arrived at the Golden Lion and joined my mates. Unfortunately, it hadn't distracted me enough from my thoughts at the house and the same question kept going round in my head, 'Where will I go when I die?'

I knew I needed to speak to somebody about this and although I've got one of the closest families on the planet, I knew this was something I couldn't discuss with them, mainly because I didn't want them to think I was losing it.

The week after, I was at the gym training my fighters but I couldn't shift the thoughts running through my head. I needed somebody I could open up to about how I felt inside.

This went on for a few weeks and I thought to myself, 'I'm going to speak to Mo Hussein'. As well as being a very good fighter, he was also devout Muslim and he took his faith very seriously.

I was nervous about approaching him at first but then I asked if I could have a few minutes with him, knowing he wouldn't laugh at me, I asked him, "What happens when we die Mo?"

He put his hand on my shoulder and said, "We all go to heaven in the end." I was so pleased to hear that. It was like a big weight off my shoulders.

****

A few more weeks passed and one Monday morning this

guy sticks his head through the door at West Ham Amateur Boxing Club. His name was Benny Stafford. I knew Benny as his son used to train at the club now and then.

I remembered that years before, a mate came up to me and told me that Benny had become a born again Christian so when he asked if he could train at the gym, I agreed. He had boxed as a youth and had his own routine when working out, so I used to leave him to it. I knew he had his faith but I actually felt like telling him not to bring it up in the gym as I had lots of fights coming up and the boys needed to concentrate.

I didn't say anything but for the next few weeks, Benny could see what I was like – shouting down the phone at matchmakers, sometimes getting into heated discussions with my fighters in the gym and using language that was so blue it was untrue.

On one occasion, I slammed the phone down so hard it almost bounced around the office. That's when Benny said "Jim – you need the peace of Jesus." I looked at him disgruntled and growled, "What?"

He repeated himself and I said, "Benny, haven't I got enough problems trying get these boys fights?" He repeated himself again, but I walked out of the office while he was still in mid-flow.

Benny didn't know how I was feeling about this heaven and hell business.

Nobody knew because I'd kept it to myself. As I walked out of the office I thought, 'What does he mean by the peace of Jesus?' So I walked back in and was angry, but at that point I didn't know why I was angry. I asked him, "How long has this 'born again' thing of yours been around. Five years, eight, 10? And don't tell me all about Jesus as I'm a Catholic."

I asked him how long Jesus has been around and he said that if I was a Catholic I should know the answer to that. I thought to myself, 'Now he's giving me the right hump!' He asked me again about how long Jesus has been around and my mind was blank.

I was looking through the glass partitions making out that I wasn't paying attention and that I was pretending to be looking at the fighters but in reality I was still trying to give him the answer.

I then turned to Benny and said, "I don't know." He then replied about 2,000 years. I thought to myself, 'You should have known that one!' I felt like I'd been mugged right off and wasn't sure if the Lord was doing it to me.

Next time he came in, he brought me a Bible. I started having a good read and for every little detail I didn't fully understand, I would ask Benny. He would break it down to me in a way which helped me to understand the morals of each story and the lessons to be learnt.

I soon started to get into the routine of going round to see Benny in the morning, wanting to know more about being a born again Christian.

Somehow, from the moment Benny stuck his head through that door, I knew from the bottom of my heart he had it right and I had it wrong. The whole experience made me feel sick to be honest. Nobody had ever told me how I needed to invite Jesus into my life.

My enthusiasm and commitment to wanting to understand more about Jesus was now at a peak. I couldn't wait to finish training so I could phone Benny and ask more questions. However, he couldn't answer all my queries so he took us to see a friend of his who he thought could.

Now remember – I've had a gun pointed at me, I've been blown up in a car, I've been cut, I've done a long prison sentence, I've seen my dad get sentenced to a 15-year stretch and never complain once, but I'd never shed a tear in public. Nobody has ever made me cry in front of them, no matter who they were or how big they were.

I had a number of questions I needed to ask this guy, because in my mind the Lord Jesus was breaking me down. Benny kept telling me that I needed to let Jesus into my life to get peace, but I kept saying "I can't see him. How can Jesus do all this for me?"

It made no sense.

We arrived at this guy's house and I didn't want to beat around the bush as I had so many questions to ask him.

In my mind I was thinking, "I'll turn this guy inside out." Me, being the worldly man I was, thought I would ask him so many questions that he simply wouldn't have the answers and will be coming back with responses like "I don't know. Leave it to the Lord. I don't know."

All of a sudden, a strange feeling came over me. Do you remember when you were a little kid and you would hit your head or hurt yourself and you wanted to be cuddled by the closest person to you, such as your mum or your dad?

That's how I suddenly felt. I had to sit down and I felt like a little child.

I put my cup of tea to one side and started to cry. I then took out my handkerchief and started sobbing heavily into that. I found myself shouting out "NOOO, NOOO," because I couldn't stop crying. This went on for about 30 seconds. Benny and this guy just sat there and didn't say anything. I didn't drink my tea. I got up and apologised, shook hands with Benny and his mate, and left.

I saw him later that day though, and I still had so many questions.

If I committed to God, could I still go for a drink with my mates? Could I still stay in boxing and train fighters? Could I live a normal life?

I had so many questions and concerns and Benny calmly turned to me and said "You can do what you like. Leave it to Jesus and don't try to change yourself."

I did trust this guy and believed I had nothing to lose. That night I went home and said that prayer. It was a prayer from the heart, asking Jesus to be my saviour.

I told my wife the next day and she said, "I wonder how long that will last? Not even Jesus Christ himself will change him."

My son turned to my wife and said, "What's the matter with the old man? Is he cracking up?"

I woke up the day after making that commitment to the Lord in 1990 and I felt no different. However, I knew in my heart what I had done and by sharing what I had done with my family I felt relieved on a number of levels.

Now I knew I had to find a church to be fed. I don't mean grub, but spiritual food, valuable knowledge. My wife bumped into a lady called Lynne, who she used to go to school with and hadn't seen for a number of years. They got talking and Lynne told Claudette that her whole family were born again Christians. Claudette turned to Lynne and said, "My Jimmy is one of them."

Lynne asked which church I was going to and Claudette explained I was looking for one. Lynne suggested I came to their church in Ilford. Eric, Lynne's husband, gave me a call to arrange for me to go round on the Sunday evening to see the church, but as I had never spoken to this guy before, I almost hung up because I thought it was a prank call.

But I went to the church on the Sunday and have never looked back since.

****

Let me tell you what Jesus has done for me and how real he is. I used to smoke a little bit of cannabis and loved it. My wife would to say to me, "You'll never be able to turn that up", and I used to say, "Don't be stupid woman, I can turn it up any time I like. I train champions."

In fact, the second I got out of there I fancied a joint. But I thought to myself, 'Why should I give it up?' I kept it to myself in the privacy of my own home, I would never smoke in somebody else's house and if I was at the pub and I wanted a joint I would walk outside.

Then one day, about a month after I became a Christian,

I started to feel a little bit guilty. I knew I couldn't turn it up. In fact, I enjoyed smoking a joint and didn't even pray to turn it up.

One day, this guy came over and offered me a bit of gear for Christmas but I turned him down. As he drove away I thought to myself, 'What have I done? I've gotta have a smoke for Christmas.' I knew how to get hold of him so I planned on calling him and getting some brought over.

The day after, I was sitting in the garden rolling a joint and I spoke to Jesus and I said, "You are the only one who can stop me."

I smoked that joint and the next morning I went to my stash and tipped it into the toilet. I've never smoked cannabis from that day onwards.

The decision was effortless.

A similar thing happened to me on holiday. I was in Spain with my wife and looked over at the bed cabinet where I had 400 cigarettes. I decided to have a cup of tea and normally I would have a fag with it. I picked up the packet and told myself that I was stopping smoking.

I've never touched one since. My addiction to tobacco left me right at that moment. The Lord takes away what he knows he needs to take away from you. He gives you what you need, not what you want.

****

Over the years, there's been a number of boxers I have worked with who have also been touched by Jesus. There was a lad called Jimmy Clark who I was training for a fight in 1990 at the London Arena. After the weigh-in, I took him back to my house so he could relax for a couple of hours. When I got upstairs I picked up the Bible to get some confidence and reassurance and prayed that Jimmy would be safe in the ring.

After waking up from a nap around 5pm, I made me and Jimmy a cup of tea and we headed off to the London Arena. As we were driving over, Jimmy said to me, "I could have been a good footballer you know, but my dad used to hide my boots." I looked over at him and said, "You would have earned more money in football than in this game."

Jimmy then said, "Maybe it was meant to be eh?" I kept thinking he was talking a bit strange and that something wasn't quite right.

We arrived at the London Arena about an hour earlier than we needed to and I suggested we went for a cup of coffee. As we were walking through the 12,000-seater venue, Jimmy stopped dead in his tracks. I turned and looked at him and there were tears rolling down his face. I asked him, "What's the matter mate?" He replied, "I want to know about Jesus but I don't know what to do."

Bearing in mind I'd ask Jesus for a sign that afternoon, he had come up with the goods by 6pm. No messing around. I told Jimmy that if Jesus didn't want him to fight then we wouldn't have reached the arena.

I told him to pull himself together and I would tell him all about Jesus after the fight.

Fight time was drawing closer, so I did Jimmy's hand

wraps and then did Bradley Stone's. Whilst doing Bradley's wraps I could see Jimmy was doing his warm up a little too vigorously.

I walked over, told him to sit down and I put my hands on his knees and said to him, "You ok?" He said, "I can feel the Holy Spirit running through me." Jimmy went on to win the fight that evening.

Mark Kaylor is another one. He was over from the USA getting ready for a fight and came over to my house to discuss the possibility of winning another title. Out of nowhere, he says, "I hear you are a born again Christian Jim. Is that true?"

I confirmed that I was and Mark announced that he had trouble with forgiveness.

I told him that he had to forgive people, just like I'd forgiven those who had done me harm over the years.

That doesn't mean to say I wanted to be around those people, but I could look them in the eyes and forgive them. Mark sat down on my sofa and it looked like he had shrunk. He turned to me and said, "I can feel Jesus right now."

Mark left my house that evening and went round to the houses of those people he felt he couldn't forgive and forgave them. A turnaround in literally a matter of hours.

He went back to the USA and had that feeling for about three weeks and while I was on the phone to him, his wife jumped on the line and said, "What have you done to my husband? I liked him the way he was."

Funnily enough, she's now born again.

Mark then jumped back on the line and said he was losing

that feeling. I told him he needed to mix with Christians and 'get fed'. I told him next time he was in England to come and see me and I would take him round the church.

Nigel Benn was another one and I distinctly remember the moment when he openly expressed his belief in Jesus.

I was at the Conference Centre in Wembley with Wayne Alexander, in August, 2000, the night he knocked out Paul Denton in one round.

As we were going back to the dressing room, I heard somebody shouting out, "Oi Jim. JIMMY." I looked round and it was Nigel Benn. He said very enthusiastically, "It's real mate. It's real." I knew what he meant straight away. Wayne turned to me and said, "Is that Nigel Benn?" I said, "Yeah. He's coming down to the dressing room." Wayne said, "Any chance I can get his autograph?" When Nigel came into the dressing room, all he did was talk about Jesus. After about 10 minutes I said, "Nigel, Wayne wants your autograph." He gladly obliged and that was that. To this day he is still a very dedicated Christian and believer in his faith.

****

The first church I went to after being born again was a Pentecostal church. It was very lively, very happy clappy, but true born again believers who were happy to spread the word of God.

I also attended a Lutheran church and a number of others. I personally don't pay too much attention or time worrying about which denomination the church I attend is branded with. In fact, I wouldn't consider myself to be dedicated to any one of them. To me it's knowing more about Jesus and speaking to people who allow me to get a better understanding of my faith.

A lot has happened in my life. When I came out of prison, at the back of my mind I did want revenge for what those people had done to me and my family.

In my heart I felt I needed to get some kind of payback to even the score and also to be at peace with myself but, in fact, that was actually the total opposite of what I needed.

I even had offers from people asking if I wanted them to carry out the revenge for me but I always refused. More than anything, I didn't want to take a chance, especially knowing the consequences first hand, and when I became a Christian, God helped take any remaining anger away from me.

****

You can't force faith on anybody. You can talk to people about it, but it's up to them whether or not they decide to pursue. Sometimes people will be frank with me and say, "Jim, you're a terrific bloke, but I'm not really interested."

I'll respond by saying, "That's no problem", and I'll never bring the subject up with them again. I hate being pestered about anything, so the last thing I would want to do is keep on at somebody who doesn't want to hear.

From my experience though, once somebody has asked me more about Jesus, most of them come back.

Not all of them, but a great number.

They have to want it. You can't force it on them. When that person gets it, and makes that true commitment, it's my responsibility to nurture them through it. People often ask me after making the commitment, "What do I do now?"

I tell them "Nothing. Your faith will lead you."

I don't walk into the gym and put my hands up to get everybody's attention and say, "Who wants to know about Jesus today?" As a born again Christian myself that would put me right off. You should never ram anything down anybody's throat. If I mention Jesus, it will be at an appropriate time. If I see somebody down, or there's a story which can be told to add value in their lives, I'll tell that story.

It's probably not a macho thing to say you are a born again Christian, but to stand up and be counted certainly shows a big strength of character.

****

When the boxing fraternity found out, I can imagine they laughed at me to be honest. I had built up a reputation as a very disciplined trainer with a very strict manner so many believed that being a Christian was an image that simply didn't suit me and that wouldn't last.

Twenty plus years later, they have realised that I have stood the test of time.

In the words of the former British and Commonwealth middleweight champion, Mark Kaylor, "The two go together well. You can be a tough guy and a Christian.

There's nothing in the rule book that says you can't."

When I became born again, it made headlines in the *News of the World*. I didn't realise I was causing such a storm. I was on the way to visit somebody in prison with Benny Stafford, when I saw the paper. I thought to myself, 'Blimey. If people didn't know I was a born again Christian, they certainly will now', but I didn't mind.

I know I'm not perfect, but if compare myself to where I was before getting Jesus in my life, I feel very lucky. Take for example the way I valued people and wealth. When I came out of prison I was 29. I used to go out most nights and worked myself to the bone during the day.

The scrapyard business was paying me a wonderful living and although I had a big house and four cars, I still wasn't happy.

If I saw my wife looking unhappy, I would try to make it up by giving her money or gifts and I would say, "What are you moaning for, you have everything you want?" Although on the surface she made out the gifts made her happy, underneath she was becoming more and more miserable.

Don't get me wrong, my wife still enjoys receiving a gift. The difference now is that I don't give her gifts out of guilt.

The main thing I wasn't giving her was a bit more love. That was the essential gift that I was not offering in abundance. I was very selfish. It was all about me. Material wealth was starting to rule my life and having a negative effect on my relationship with the mother of my kids and the lady who had stood by me through thick and thin.

In the end we are all going to end up in the dirt six feet

under, or in the furnace. The material things we consider to be of value are not a true reflection of our wealth. I felt very ashamed of myself. But not any more.

****

Being born again has also helped me as a boxing trainer. Don't all laugh at once, but I'm serious when I say I have became a calmer character.

I argue less and the days of screaming, shouting and throwing furniture around the office are long gone. I understood why I did that back then and now I understand why I no longer need to.

Giving encouragement to a boxer is far more important than shouting at them. As long as they are listening to my instructions and producing the results, why should I use a more aggressive tone?

There are far more born again Christians out there than you would imagine. Ask your friends and work colleagues if they are born again, or if they know somebody who is, and you'll be surprised just how many people surface. Most will never say, simply because they value Jesus as their own gift in life.

If you tell people you are a born again Christian, most will either run a mile, listen to you suspiciously or embrace the fact that you have a belief in something other than football or boxing.

I don't go round standing on a soapbox preaching the word of Jesus but neither do I shy away from the fact that

I'm born again. Either way, I'm content with the impact it's had on me, my family and my training career.

Round 14

CURRENT CROP

"One big thing Jimmy has taught me, is that if you don't get hit, you don't get hurt. If you don't get hurt, the chances of making mistakes are far reduced."
– Billy Joe Saunders 2013

Anyhow, back to the boxing.

The one constant in my training career – as I think this book proves – is just how dedicated and brilliant the fighters have been who I've worked with.

That extends right up to today.

Although I no longer train Kevin Mitchell, he was, and is, a fine fighter and I was proud to have him at my gym.

I first met Kevin at the Lennox Lewis gym in London and although he was only 13 at the time, he already punched the pads like a man at that age. He'd been trained by my old mate Micky May who is a legend at West Ham Amateur Boxing Club, having trained over 100 champions. As I was writing this book, I'm very sad to say Micky passed away. He will be dearly missed by West Ham Amateur Boxing Club and the boxing fraternity at large. I'll see you one day on the other side mate.

Me and Kevin officially started working with each other in 2009. At that point he'd already fought 29 times as a professional and had held several titles including the British, Commonwealth and Inter-Continental belts. He was contemplating training in the USA and had been approached by Freddie Roach to get him ready for the Breidis Prescott fight, to challenge for the WBO Inter-Continental lightweight title.

With his brother Vinny already training at the Peacock Gym with me and my son, he decided that he would be far more comfortable working with East Enders than going to America. After a quick chat at the TKO gym, Kevin asked my son if I would train him so we cracked on and started from there.

Going into the Prescott fight, Kevin was rated an underdog by many. Prescott had knocked out Amir Khan in 54 seconds and went on to beat a tough fighter by way of Humberto Toledo.

Prescott had only lost to Saul Alvarez and Tim Bradley so many boxing pundits were not sure if Kevin was ready for somebody of this calibre.

Although Prescott looked more like a natural middleweight and with a three-inch height advantage to boot, many were forgetting that Kevin was unbeaten in 29 fights, with 23 knockouts, and that he was a very fine boxer.

It would be the latter which would confuse Prescott and defy most of the boxing media, as everybody thought the bout would be an almighty tear up.

The move up in weight from super featherweight to lightweight ensured that Kevin would have no problems making weight, but also meant that when he did connect there would be added venom.

However, the strategy for the fight wasn't based on trying to stop Prescott but to pick him to pieces and take his heart away from him. The motto was, "Make him miss and make him pay." The sparring went perfectly for this fight as I'd arranged for tall strong guys to spar with Kevin who would jump into the ring for a round or two before being rotated with another fresh opponent to make sure he was being worked to his maximum.

By the end of the training camp Kevin was ready for a world champion, never mind Prescott.

The fight was scheduled for December, 2009, at the Metro Radio Arena in Newcastle. As well as being a title bout, the fight was also an eliminator for the WBO world lightweight belt, so there was a great deal of pressure on both fighters to perform.

The press conference took place a few days before and was pretty entertaining. The first day we all sat down Kevin was pretty quiet, whereas 'Team Prescott' were trying to get under our skin.

The day after was the weigh-in and I turned round

to Kevin and said, "Stop being so polite. Be how you normally are!"

At that point Kevin started giving as good as he was getting and we all started getting into a heated war of words. Prescott turned to Kevin and said, "I'm going to knock you out in two rounds." Kevin looked at me and then looked back to Prescott and said, "How? Will you have a shotgun with you?!" All good clean fun!

My advice for the fight was simple, "Put the jab in his face, keep making him miss, keep moving the head, keep feigning, get some flurries going then move off. Don't move off backwards in straight lines, move off at angles."

This is how we had trained in the gym and it was no different to how he would perform that night.

By round nine, Prescott was showing visible signs of tiring. Having run after Kevin for nearly 20 minutes, chasing him into each corner and missing with big shots, the fight was now being based in the centre of the ring, which saw Kevin working some lovely counters.

As round 11 started, we knew that this was new territory for Prescott and it was visible that Kevin's engine was looking the fresher of the two.

Prescott's corner were obviously also concerned, as they had shoved so much ice down his shorts to wake him up that the referee had to stop the opening minute on three occasions to kick the cubes off the canvas, which gradually kept falling out! None of this fazed Kevin as he stuck to the game plan and kept working behind the jab and moving.

After touching gloves for the final round, it was obvious

that Prescott's corner had told him he needed the knockout to win.

Kevin continued to box Prescott's head off, tying him up when needed and landing some beautiful straight right hands off the one two combination. He even had time to fit in an Ali shuffle before the bell rung for the end of the fight. It was no surprise that Kevin won a heavy points decision on all three scorecards and he was now the new WBO Inter-Continental lightweight champion.

Not only did he have a belt, but he was now recognised by the boxing authorities as a genuine contender for world level boxing.

We all walked away happy, but Kevin was especially able to hold his head up high after an outstanding performance. Amir Khan was supposed to be headlining that night, but with a first round stoppage win, it turned out that Kevin's fight was the crowd pleaser, especially after he'd beaten the fighter who had stopped Khan in such dramatic fashion.

With a world title fight now a certainty, in February, 2010, at Wembley Arena, Kevin had a warm-up bout against another tough Colombian called Ignacio Mendoza. Hardly breaking a sweat, Kevin knocked out Mendoza heavily in round two and we now set our sights on fighting the Australian gladiator, Michael Katsidis, at Upton Park in July.

Kevin's a massive West Ham fan, so this was a dream come true for him. As we walked out in front of an 18,000 strong crowd with fans singing "Walking in a Mitchell Wonderland", the highs were about to hit rock-bottom lows.

Katsidis destroyed Kevin and the fight was over in three

rounds. I was furious. I knew he could have won this fight if he had showed his previous level of discipline, but the plan crumbled before we even entered the ring.

At the press conference afterwards, which was printed in *Boxing News*, I couldn't hold back when asked if I was happy with the preparations for this fight.

"If you're asking me honestly, no I wasn't. You've got to live the life and he did not prepare the way he did for Prescott," I said.

We all walked away from this fight with a bad taste in our mouth and it would take a while before regrouping. Kevin had gone from hero to zero and I needed to get him back in the 'champions' frame of mind again.

****

John Murray was being touted as the next world champion and many had written Kevin off because of his loss to Katsidis. I knew in my heart that if Kevin followed my advice like he did for the Prescott fight, he would not only have won the Katsidis bout, but he would also come out victorious against Murray.

The fight was scheduled for July, 2011, and they would be fighting for the vacant WBO Inter-Continental lightweight title, at the Echo Arena in Liverpool. Once I was satisfied that Kevin was physically fit and had put the Katsidis fight behind him, we started to prepare immediately.

The strategy for Murray was to get inside his opponent with plenty of feigning. We didn't want him to run from

Murray too much because that's what he liked. I didn't want to give him the opportunity to put Kevin on the back foot and part of the strategy would be to make a mess of him on the inside and find the openings.

Kevin fought like a dream that night, making Murray miss often while also finding his target time and time again.

After starting round eight by absorbing a few of Murray's punches, Kevin then landed a beautiful combination, finishing with a left hook to the head which put Murray to the canvas. Murray just about made the count, before Kevin launched in with a three-punch attack which was swiftly followed by the referee calling the fight off!

Winning another title belt in my eyes was not the greatest victory here, it was the show he put on that night.

I never forget Frank Warren after that fight saying, "Kevin, That's the best I've ever seen you box." I have to agree. I think that was his best ever performance, even to this day. This ended up being the fight that gave him a shot for the world title a second time.

However, before facing the WBO lightweight champ Ricky Burns, Kevin had a warm-up fight against Felix Lora in February, 2012. Boxing to orders, Kevin dominated the fight. In all honesty he could have taken him out early, but I told him to back off and get some rounds under his belt. In the last round, he started to unload on Lora and shook him.

He could have finished it right there, but instead he stood back and let him recover and carried on boxing until the bell rung. He knew he had won the fight, and saw no reason in hurting his opponent more than he needed to. This was just a tune-up and Kevin showed his class and the signs of a true pro with the way he behaved that night. Unsurprisingly, he won 98-92.

Unfortunately in September later that year, Kevin was unsuccessful in his bid to take the world title from Ricky Burns. The training camp had gone extremely well, but the plan didn't unfold to its full potential that evening. The better man won and that's that really.

Kevin is one of the nicest people I've had the pleasure of working with and I sincerely believe, at the time of writing this book, he's still good enough to win a world title.

****

One of my most recently crowned champions is a gifted boxer by the name of Freddie Luke Turner.

I was first introduced to Freddie when he was about 15 back in 2003 when he was boxing for West Ham as an amateur. His record was already impressive, having won the junior ABAs, the NABCs, and the Four Nations gold medal.

Even at that age, Freddie's strength was already showing. Listening to my instructions, I had him in the ring with pros such as Matthew Marsh and Martin Power and he was able to handle himself very well.

By the age of 17 we started training at the Peacock and TKO gyms, preparing for the senior ABAs. Although he lost in the quarter-finals, Freddie gave a very good account of himself and pushed Frankie Gavin to his limits. Freddie didn't lose by a big margin and that gave him a lot of credit in the amateurs. Soon after, he had to take a year out due to injuries but in 2009, Freddie went one step further and reached the semis against Bradley Skeete who was fighting for Repton.

During the gap between the Gavin and Skeete fights, Freddie had taken on a very physically demanding job as a full-time labourer on a building site.

Although delighted that Freddie was earning good money and had landed himself full-time work, my concern as a boxing trainer is always that my boxer enters that ring in peak condition, for no other reason than their own safety.

A couple of weeks before the senior ABAs, I said to Freddie, "You have the ABAs coming up and you are one of the favourites. If you win this we can turn pro and move on." I told him to make sure the week before he started to ease off a little, but more importantly to take two full days off before the fight. Freddie's replied, "Of course Jim!" But he didn't.

On the night of the fight I went to the changing rooms to check on Freddie but I couldn't instantly spot him. With the room full of fighters all wearing their matching tracksuits, I asked the head coach where Freddie was and he pointed to the corner. I'm not joking, but when I looked over, I thought it was an old tramp who had rocked up and fallen asleep. I woke him up and said, "You haven't been at work today have you?" and he said, "No Jim. I've had a day off."

Freddie had sparred with Bradley Skeete a few weeks earlier and had handled him very well, but in order to beat him in an ABA semi-final, Freddie needed to be 100 percent, which he was obviously not.

In the build-up to this fight, I had been telling everybody how good Freddie looked in training, how proud I was of him and that he had a chance of progressing far in the ABAs, possibly even win this time round. Well – he lost the first round, won the second and lost the third.

Freddie told me it just wasn't his night and I left it there. I then found out from somebody else that he had in fact been at work all week, including the day of the fight.

I told him I was disappointed and we parted company for a little while. If he wanted to go to work all day then that's fine, but don't waste my time in that case.

****

Within a short time, I started to see Freddie at the Peacock and we would always chat. I couldn't stay disappointed at him for long, simply because he's such a nice guy. On asking if I could train him again I looked at him and said, "Do you want me to train you again?" He said yes and we got back down to business.

I really respected his strength of character in coming back to me and admitting he had done wrong.

Freddie made his pro debut in February, 2010, and won his first eight fights, dropping only one round in all his points victories.

In the late summer of 2013, we were told that Freddie would be fighting against a much tougher opponent called Nathan Graham, challenging him for his Southern Area title.

I then had to sit him down and have an honest conversation about how he would need to strike the correct balance between working and boxing training in order to be successful.

I knew how much his day job took out of him and I would never ask a boxer to give up their employment, especially with the current shortage of paid work out there.

However, we both knew that he would need to take some time out to dedicate himself to this fight and live and breathe the life of a pro boxer during the length of the eight week training camp.

My thoughts on Freddie had always been that he was a good boxer but he'd never had the time to do it properly. This occasion was different. He was there whenever I wanted him there and did everything I said. I had him in the gym every other day for sparring and the days in between I would have him shadow boxing in preparation for his training the day after.

He did his road work immaculately and his ground work the same and was pretty much at fighting weight about three weeks before the bout.

On October 18, 2013, we stepped through the ropes at the York Hall with the intention of Freddie beating a champion and walking away as onc himself.

As the bell rang for the first round it was clear that Nathan was calm and composed compared to Freddie, who was a little jumpy and eager to get going.

After about a minute, it dawned on him that he could potentially be fighting for half an hour (which he did!) and that he needed to relax and just remember what we had practiced during the camp.

Towards the end of the eighth round, just as Graham was walking into him, Freddie put him down with a crunching left uppercut and a right hook. They unfortunately clashed heads around the moment of the last punch, but more frustrating for Freddie was the bell ringing just before he could have jumped on Graham and perhaps stopped him.

As the bell rang for round nine, Freddie came out relaxed and confident but maybe a little too confident and he took his eye off the ball for a moment which in boxing is enough time for a fight to be over.

This was enough of a gap for Graham to get back in and he hit Freddie with a great right hand, bang on the chin. I knew Graham was a mature fighter who knew the game but I also didn't think he was a big puncher.

It wasn't a knockout punch that caught Freddie, it simply caught him point blank on the chin and would have knocked anybody down.

Bearing in mind Freddie had never been hurt in sparring and had never been down as an amateur or a professional, here he was sitting on the canvas listening to the referee counting over him.

Freddie took the count, walked to the referee and showed he was ok. A little bit of luck did come our way though. As Nathan's punch landed, Freddie's gumshield came flying out and the ref couldn't find it!

It turned out to be in Graham's corner, so he brought it back to be washed, then the house second accidentally dropped it on the floor. We received a bit of stick afterwards from people saying we took a long time, but as the ref confirmed, it wasn't our fault. Just one of those things.

Although the knockdown happened early in the round, Freddie made his way through it, he fought back hard and had Graham on the back foot.

The crowd were all standing and cheering for what was a fantastic fight and a great round.

As Freddie came back for the end of the ninth, I told him, "Fred – Clear your head. Next round, go out there and use your footwork. Slip and slide and stay out of trouble. You've won the fight. Don't get caught again. Go out there and box his head off."

And he did! At the end of the three minutes, the score was announced, 94-93 in Freddie's favour – "AND THE NEEEEEEEEEWW, SOUTHERN AREA CHAMPION!"

I was over the moon. I was so proud of him because of the way he trained and the way he listened before and during the fight. He had a big following of fans present that night and the second the result was announced, York Hall erupted in delight.

Freddie never blew once – he fought back when he got knocked down and he showed true grit, which I knew he already had.

He's got the chin, the talent and the bottle and most importantly he can really fight.

I still stick by my original comments and I genuinely believe that Freddie has the ability, courage and character to win a British title.

Hopefully I can be at his side when he reaches that goal and I can watch him celebrate what would be a fantastic and well deserved achievement.

****

At the time of writing this book, Colin Lynes has fought 48 times and won the IBO Inter-Continental, the British, European and IBO world light welterweight belts.

I've known Colin since 1998 but it wasn't until 2010 that he called me and said, "Jimmy, I'd like you to hear me out and give me a chance. I don't believe I'm finished as a boxer just yet."

Without hesitation I took him on. He came down to the TKO gym, we did a session and we never looked back.

Colin was his own manager, so I told him to sort himself a fight and that I would be straight on board when he had an opponent and a date.

Sure enough, he came back with February, 2011, against the former light middleweight Commonwealth champion Bradley Pryce, at the Olympia in Liverpool.

Colin used the ring space and his ringcraft to put on a lovely performance and won the bout 78-76. This got people thinking that Colin Lynes still had what it took.

Four months later we had to prepare for a completely different format of fighting – we would be taking part in the rapid fire Prizefighter competition at York Hall. Although he blasted his first opponent 30-27, he lost a split decision against Moroccan born Yassine El Maachi and failed to progress. A few weeks after the El Maachi fight, we were at the gym when Colin received a phone call from Matchroom saying that Lee Purdy's next fight had fallen through and asking whether he would like to have a shot at the British welterweight title.

Lee was being touted as a contender for bigger and better titles and as far as many were concerned, Colin was a stepping stone. The game plan from our side was not to fight Purdy, but to box him. Keep behind that jab and counter Lee with everything he did. Jab, right hands, left hooks, but mainly the jab.

On the night of the fight, Colin was the big underdog. I think we all realised that if I he didn't do it that night, he wasn't going to get another shot – possibly ever again.

However, on this night, the underdog turned the tables and became the favourite. In fact, Colin was so far ahead and hitting Purdy with so many unanswered shots that I was worried Colin might get overconfident and go for the knockout.

Thankfully he listened to me and when the opportunity did come to unload, he took it and floored Lee in round 10, giving him a two-point advantage on the scorecards.

For the 12th and final round, I said, "Last round Colin", and he was pumped up and replied, "LET'S GO JIM!" He knew what to do and went on to win by majority decision. I was very proud of Colin that night and he went on to receive the recognition he deserved and he most importantly proved to himself that he certainly still did have a lot to offer the boxing game. This was his 14th title fight and many said afterwards that Colin peaked that night, including himself. That was one of mine and my son's greatest achievements in boxing.

Colin is the template of how a fighter should conduct themselves inside and outside of the ring. His preparations are immaculate and his respect for other boxers is the sign of a true gentleman. He acts as a great mentor to many boxers in and around Canning Town, including Billy Joe Saunders, Billy Morgan and Freddie Luke Turner.

****

Talking of Billy Joe Saunders, we started working together after he came back from the 2008 Olympics.

He was a very talented amateur boxer, winning about 50 senior fights nonstop, and my first impressions of him were that he could achieve anything. He comes from a heritage of good boxing stock from the travelling community, and his great grandfather Absolom Beeney was a famous bare knuckle champion while Billy's father was also an amateur boxer.

When I first started working with Bill he used to slap a little bit with his punches, because he was boxing to bag points in the amateurs.

Then once you have the points, you can dance around and run away so they can't catch you up. I'm not saying this system is bad for boxing but in my day the amateur scoring method was more closely linked to professional boxing than it is now. When an amateur wants to turn pro now, they have a much bigger gap to bridge. Nowadays, if you hit with a body punch, they don't always score it, unless you knock your opponent down with a body punch, then they have to score it.

I found that I had to settle him down and get his southpaw jab going to find his range. At that point, nine times out of 10, Billy Joe would want to back his man up.

I had to teach him that there would be times when he would have an opponent who would want to hunt him down and when that did happen, his instinct of stepping in and throwing the jab would leave him exposed for a right hand. He had to let the person come in for him to find his range.

It's about strategy, it's definitely not about getting caught into a tear up.

Initially he would be going in with a few journeymen who certainly knew how to pace themselves, so it was essential to get him used to the long haul which he'd not been used to as an amateur.

A few things that struck me very quickly on working on his jab were his hand speed, accuracy and ability to move after throwing a punch.

His power was not staggering, but with every fight Billy Joe has had as a pro, his strength has improved. Within no time he was hooking off the jab and putting the shoulder in and slipping – not to mention his great ability to make his opponent punch into fresh air.

Aware that he could handle himself, I put him with the likes of George Groves and Darren Barker – top quality sparring partners.

They were better than him at that stage, which was to be expected, but he learned a lot off them and was always very confident.

Something else that struck me about Billy Joe was his sense of humour. Bill may come across as quite a serious person on the television so I think it's worth clarifying that off screen and out of the gym he's one of the biggest jokers out there! Here's just one example. We were all meeting up at Hainault Forest for a run and I always like to arrive early. Unbeknownst to me, Bill arrived and parked up, but I couldn't see his motor in the car park.

Next thing I received a phone call from him. I said, "Where are you Bill?" He said, "I'm in hospital Jim. I broke my leg playing football." I didn't want to overreact on the phone, but I was shaking my head and saying, "Noooo. Noooo." Bill then said, "They reckon I'll be out for three months Jim. When I'm well again I'll give you a call." Then out of the corner of my eye I see Billy Joe stepping out of his car. I jumped out of mine laughing, swearing and shouting at him in hysterics!

****

Bill won his first 10 fights without any stress or strain and with only three of his opponents lasting the distance. However, in my eyes, he really started to perform as his competition became stiffer and that first test came in November, 2011, against Gary Boulden for his middleweight Southern Area belt at Wembley Arena.

We knew Gary was a very durable fighter and it was going to be tough to stop him. It took the first few rounds for Bill to realise that this was not a journeyman and he was in the ring with somebody who could throw punches back at him and who was not willing to hand over their championship belt easily. It's not like it was a massive shock to Bill but he realised that he needed to start thinking and start boxing. On this occasion he couldn't simply stop Gary as he had done with most of his previous opponents.

Although Bill won the fight comfortably 99-92, I think he could have boxed better and we were all guilty of underestimating Gary Boulden. From here onwards we really started to knuckle down.

In Bill's next fight he knocked out Tommy Tolan in just 67 seconds, before beating Tony Hill to become the new Commonwealth middleweight champion! Bill threw 33 unanswered punches against Hill, and Richie Davies stopped the fight after just 30 seconds of the first round.

Veteran Bradley Pryce was next up and Bill was faultless. As opposed to the Boulden fight, Bill had a clear strategy throughout the bout.

Once a fighter like Billy Joe Saunders gets thinking in the ring, there's very few people who can beat him. The ability to change direction in a fight with plans A, B, C, D and E in your back pocket shows the mark of a great fighter and that's exactly what he was that night. His accuracy with the jab and the unloading of combinations which followed were simply too much for Bradley and two judges had it 120-108, whilst the other had it 120-109. I couldn't have asked for any more. He was outstanding and had proved the critics wrong on a number of fronts.

In September, 2012, we moved the bar up another notch and took on a genuine threat by way of the Australian middleweight champion, Jarrod Fletcher.

This man had won an outstanding amount of silverware as an amateur – and I mean outstanding. It's worth looking him up on the internet if you are not familiar with his achievements. Soon before turning pro, he won the gold medal at the Commonwealth Games in 2006, beating James DeGale along the way and in the final he beat the hard hitting current day world light heavyweight champion Adonis Stevenson. By the time he was fighting Bill at York Hall he was 12-0 and a very good boxer.

At the weigh-in, Fletcher was standing there as a proper mature grown man, bulging with muscles, whereas Billy Joe was 23, still a little boy in relative terms, and still carrying some puppy fat on him. Fletcher looked at him as if to say, "Not tonight son. You are too young." Bill looked at him knowing exactly what he was thinking and knew he had the edge on him. Fletcher was the one in the end who looked away! Muscles don't win fights, it's all about who will make the first mistake.

In the first round both fighters exchanged their jabs in the centre of the ring but it was Bill who was the marginally sharper of the two and landed a nice straight left after about a minute.

It wasn't a hurting shot, but it had enough for Fletcher to tap his gloves in recognition of the punch. I would say that Bill's speed and accuracy made the round more eye-catching in his favour and no disrespect to Fletcher, but he simply struggled to touch Bill during the round.

As Billy Joe came back to the corner for the end of the round, I told him to keep the jab going but follow it up with a left uppercut. "Keep boxing him Bill and don't get caught in a tear up."

The first minute and 42 seconds of the second were identical to the first round, when suddenly Billy Joe threw a beautiful long left hook which landed flush on the right hand side of Fletcher's jaw and rocked him instantly, forcing him to cover up on the ropes.

For the next 30 seconds Bill unloaded on Fletcher until he was forced to the canvas to take an eight count. The second the count was over he sprinted back over to Fletcher and this time stopped him with another nonstop attack, finishing with a crunching right hook.

Billy Joe had picked up a small cut over his right eye, but Fletcher looked far worse with a badly bloodied nose and more importantly was far too dazed to carry on. The referee did the right thing by stepping in and stopping the fight.

Nick Blackwell was next up, in December, 2012, and Billy Joe's Commonwealth belt was on the line, in addition to the both of them fighting for the vacant British middleweight belt. Billy tussled and won a tight contest fight before then beating former Commonwealth champion Matthew Hall in a very heavy points victory.

After that, in July, 2013, he put in the best performance of his career, facing the unbeaten Irish middleweight champion, Gary O'Sullivan, also known as 'Spike'.

They would be fighting for the WBO international middleweight title at Wembley Arena.

Bill looked in tremendous shape and despite all the hype and the comments, he wasn't rattled for one moment. One of the journalists came over to me and said, "O'Sullivan believes he's going to knock Billy Joe out in five rounds. What's your thoughts on that?" I replied, "Everyone wants to knock him out. I don't know why though. He's a nice fella!"

The atmosphere at Wembley that night was fantastic. There were 10 fights including the likes of Tom Baker, Bradley Saunders, Frank Buglioni and Bradley Skeete.

Within seconds of the bell sounding for round one Bill imposed his presence with double and triple jabs and kept circling to O'Sullivan's left, making sure that his right hand would not give Bill any problems.

Just under a minute into the round, Bill let a five-punch combination go, finishing with a right hook to the body, which Spike tapped his gloves in recognition and smiled as if to say, "I felt that last one."

About 10 seconds later he unleashed two left hooks off the same hand, followed by a right hook and then triple jabbed before unloading another combination. Bill's work rate was incredible and the Mohican cut O'Sullivan was being suffocated by the speed and accuracy which Bill was throwing his way.

As the rounds progressed, O'Sullivan was simply unable to nail Bill's speed and movement and by the time Bill walked back to the corner for the end of round 11, he looked as fresh as he had at the beginning of the fight. I told him, "He's gonna come at ya. Make him miss and stick that jab in his face right away." Bill replied, "Don't worry – I'll be dancing."

Our comments pretty much summed up how the last round went. Spike came out like a bull and Billy Joe kept moving away in an unpredictable pattern, throwing out the jab and countering with combinations off the back foot before bouncing off in another direction.

Many compared his leg work in that last round to Sugar Ray Leonard!

It came as no surprise that Bill won by a landslide and while he was at it, added the WBO international belt to his British and Commonwealth straps. Bill went on to successfully defend his British title against John Ryder and I have no doubt he will eventually become a world champion.

When Billy Joe is on form, he's like a young Muhammad Ali and shows moments of brilliance in every fight. That talent will never go away.

And I'm convinced that he can go as far and as high as he wants to. He has the lot and is a fantastic and dedicated young fighter.

****

I'd also like to give a mention to a Canning Town boxer who fought earlier that evening, who is trained by my son. This story is a prime example of the importance and the power of taking time out to speak with boxers.

Billy Morgan is one of the nicest young fighters on the pro circuit, a real well-mannered gentleman and on this occasion he was boxing for the ninth time as a professional with an unbeaten record of eight straight wins behind him.

He was fighting against a boxer by the name of Ashley Mayall and they suffered a nasty accidental clash of heads in the third round which resulted in Billy having a massive gash over his left eyebrow.

The fight was stopped by the referee on the recommendation of the doctor that the cut was beyond repair. Billy was noticeably upset walking around the ring, because he was concerned he would lose the fight and suffer his first loss. Thankfully, the decision went to the scorecards and he had done enough to win the bout on a technical decision 30-28. However, afterwards, in the changing room it was obvious that he was still very upset, focusing on how long the cut would put him out for.

I wasn't working Billy's corner that night as cut man, but it doesn't matter who was, because they were never going to stop that cut on his eyebrow.

After the medic had stitched up his eye, I sat him down and said, "Bill. You're a young man and you're gonna heal up. You're not going to be out two months, you will probably be out four weeks and in six months time you're not even gonna know that cut was there. You will come back stronger, have a couple of fights and then you will fight for the Southern Area Title. That's what's gonna happen Bill."

He paused for a second, looked up at me and then thanked me with a new and genuine look of calm about him.

In my day, if you got beat, you got beat. Nobody analysed it. Things have change thankfully. I'm not saying for one moment that I have more heart or sympathy for fighters than the trainers had back then. They were all sad back then as well! But it wasn't common practice to console a fighter if he had lost.

****

As I'm mentioning cuts, now seems the right time to pay tribute to Frank Black, who passed away in 2008.

He was a great man, inside and outside of boxing and one whom I had many a laugh with. I'd known Frank from when I was a boxer, as he'd worked my corner. He was a true part of East London heritage and, in a similar way to Dean Powell, he featured in more world champions corners than I can remember.

I had my fair share of winding Frank up in the Peacock Gym when mobile phones first started to come out. I'd wait until he was at the other end of the gym and with my number withheld, I'd call him. The second he was about to pick it up, I'd stop calling!

Sometimes he would have the phone in his pocket having a cup of tea and I'd start to call it. After about three or four times, the phone would fall out of his hand in pure frustration as he was trying to get to it faster and faster. In the end he sussed it was me, and Frank would always see the funny side. A fantastic sense of humour and a wonderful man.

I had some big laughs with him over the years, but I also

want to say one thing about Frank – he was one of the best cut men out there. I learnt a lot from him on how to assess and treat cuts and I will never forget how welcome he made me feel when I became a part of the Lawless team back in 1981 as a relative novice.

An unsung hero and a massive loss to the boxing fraternity.

****

Another terrible blow, to boxing and to his family, was the passing of Dean Powell in September, 2013.

People spend too much time talking about how people die, so I would like to talk about how Dean lived.

The first time I met Dean was at the Royal Oak in 1985. Frank Bruno was getting ready for a world title shot against Tim Witherspoon and back in those days Terry Lawless let very few people into the gym when boxers were in deep training.

However, there was something warming about this tall, skinny, 19-year-old lad, with a strong Brummy accent, so Terry sat down with Dean and had a long chat with him.

Dean explained to Terry that he wanted to make boxing his life and asked if there was anybody he could shadow. Terry pointed over in my direction.

At the time, I was giving Adrian Elliot a ticking off for not doing his ground work. I was shouting at Adrian, telling him, "Horace Notace has done his ground work, Frank Bruno and Mark Kaylor have done theirs, why haven't you done yours?"

I could see Dean was a having a bit of a giggle as 6ft 2in heavyweight Adrian bowed his head and nodded.

I noticed something about Dean back then. He had a massive willingness to learn and he also had a fantastic memory. It didn't take him long to get to grips with the responsibilities of working a corner but his real area of expertise became the art of matchmaking.

Over the years, I would trust his judgement implicitly when it came to boxing knowledge.

Within a few years of shadowing the likes of myself, Terry Lawless and Frank Black, Dean proved that he was able to train and work the corner for pretty much any fighter. We worked together on some of the best fights ever to have taken place on British soil, such as the Benn versus Eubank rematch.

If you watch the fight, before the end of the 12th round, Dean can be heard shouting to Nigel, "These are the most important three minutes of your life." Reg Gutteridge then makes a reference, "Listen to young Dean Powell firing Nigel up."

In the 20 years that followed, Dean went on to motivate a host of other boxers, including the likes of Joe Calzaghe, Amir Khan and Dereck Chisora.

When he worked in a corner, he showed every boxer the complete and utter respect they were due. He didn't care what level they were operating at. If you were a world champion defending your title or a journeyman, Dean would always shout out the right words at you when you most needed them and make you feel like Muhammad Ali.

I don't have enough time to go through every boxer Dean ever worked with but you know who you are and you have your special moments to cherish.

Dean was 100 percent dedicated to achieving results, but 200 percent committed to not letting anybody down.

You could call him at any time of the day and he would pick up the phone. If you needed advice, he would never rush with a response and he always knew what to say.

He was one of the good guys.

Back when he first started, he would be looking over mine, Terry Lawless and Frank Black's shoulders and he would ask for advice as he tried to pick up the tricks of the trade. It's hard to believe that was 25 years ago. Dean went on to become known as a premier figure within the sport, not just within the UK, but worldwide.

I'd like to finish on an upbeat note about Dean. The boxing game is well known for its blood, sweat and tears, but it also comes with its laughs and I shared many of those with Dean.

On one occasion, we had a boxer called Johnny Graham at the Royal Oak who had a flat nose – a proper pug and a lovely fella. I had initially trained Johnny, then Dean took over and on this occasion he asked me to give him a leg up because he'd just been knocked out in the first round when fighting for the vacant light heavyweight Southern Area title. I put him in to spar with Mark Kaylor one day and he was jabbing Kaylor's head off.

I suddenly shouted out, "HOLD ON. STOP RIGHT THERE." I asked John to walk over to me in the corner and took his head guard off. Dean looked over in concern thinking Johnny had been cut. As I took off the head guard I said, "Thank God for that. I thought that was Sugar Ray Leonard underneath there."

Everybody in the gym exploded into laughter and it's a story that me and Dean laughed about many more times in the years that followed.

I'm not a huge lover of funerals if the truth be told and I can't imagine they rate highly in anyone's book.

I'm glad to say that Dean did leave us all with great memories of his final exit from the church.

Dean was a mod through and through and he also had a passion for Mini Coopers. He loved them so much that his voicemail on his mobile phone was straight out of the movie 'The Italian Job'.

After an excellent service which featured eulogies and readings from the likes of Mickey Cantwell, myself, Frank Warren and a fantastic tribute from Jim Rosenthal, the congregation stood up to walk outside.

You must try and picture 1,000 people, mainly from the boxing fraternity, with tears in their eyes and long faces for obvious reasons and then suddenly looking around the church in shock as the following came through the speakers at full volume – "YOU'RE ONLY SUPPOSED TO BLOW THE BLOODY DOORS OFF!", followed by the theme tune from 'The Italian Job.'

Laughter echoed around the packed church and a round of applause quickly followed. As we walked out of the church, there were three minis, again, like 'The Italian Job', parked by the hearse and a stunning parade of his mates on Vespas and mopeds. His friends were his extended family outside of boxing and it was a fitting and uplifting tribute to a great man.

RIP mate.

****

Most of the boxers mentioned in this chapter are still being trained by myself today and I'm hopeful they will climb higher championship heights than they have already reached.

There's an old expression – when you teach, two people learn. I have enjoyed teaching as much as I have learning and you're never too old to try and improve yourself and also help those around you improve as well.

Round 15

FINAL WORDS

"How would I describe Jimmy? As a person, respectful, a grafter, and above all a great friend. He was a talented fighter who never reached his prime but he's done it all as a trainer. British boxing had a big saviour when Jimmy Tibbs arrived on the scene."
– Micky May, 2013

So that is my life story.

Writing this book has unearthed a lot of old emotions and memories. Some of them great, most of them good – and a few bad ones too.

Ultimately, I want to be remembered for my boxing, and I think I will be. There has been no real secret to my success. Hard work, patience, discipline, an understanding of what it takes to get between those ropes and trade punches with another man and a willingness to always work and better myself. That will never change.

You will find me in the gym every day, trying to get the best out of my boxers – whether they be the next big thing, a world champion or somewhere in between.

Today, tomorrow, yesterday – I'm always working, striving, trying to get better, better, better.

You will have noticed that London, and East London in particular, is mentioned heavily in this book – and I make no apologies for that.

Although Canning Town, as I remember it from many years ago, has changed dramatically, it's good to see that the local council are trying to rescue some of its heritage. Rumour has it that a new Rathbone Street market is in the planning and a year after Terry Spinks died in 2012, the Mayor of Newham unveiled a new street sign on Silvertown Way called 'Terry Spinks Place' not far from the Peacock Gym. A very fitting tribute to a man who helped put and keep Canning Town on the map for many years.

Hopefully, Canning Town's best years are still ahead of it.

****

The 'troubled times' scarred me mentally and physically.

I may have used the expression, "things got out of hand", on a few occasions and I do not use this expression lightly.

Every time I wanted to bail out, another episode would kick off and blind rage would unfortunately get the better of me. The way I responded to my brother having his throat cut, or me and my young son almost being killed by a bomb, cannot be tolerated, praised or condoned.

However, I ask you to walk in my shoes for those episodes and think to yourself how you might have reacted.

For those of you who came up with a solution of walking away or not looking for revenge – I applaud you.

I wish I'd had the ability to walk away but, back then, events meant I'd gone past the point of no return. As Dwight D. Eisenhower said, "War settles nothing", and I can testify to this first hand.

There are further anecdotes mentioned by various authors that are factually incorrect but I do not wish to drag out a chapter of my life creating a long list to say "I've set everything straight."

If I started low blowing other authors from years gone by, it would pay testament to the fact that I have not moved on from their comments or come to terms with the events which happened over 40 years ago.

The truth is I have moved on.

What's done is done and as far as I'm concerned that chapter of my life is closed and finished.

Let's leave the past where it sits best. In the past.

When asked if have flashbacks of when I spent a birthday or a Christmas in prison, the answer is, "Of course." I was inside for 365 days of each year for almost five years. For each day on the calendar there is a memory I can relate to when I was inside.

It's like having the inside of your brain tattooed. After a while you learn to live with it, but the memories are permanently there to remind you. However, I've learned to use the memories of prison positively.

When I'm feeling down or work starts to get on top of me and I start to get stressed with something, I think to myself, 'It's better than doing bird.'

My years spent in a prison cell have actually helped me realise what is important to in life – those I cared about most, but also those who cared about me.

I'm not saying every decision I have made in my life since I left prison has been correct but on the whole I've made many more correct decisions than bad ones. I have spent more time smiling and laughing than I have spent being angry or sad and that's good enough for me.

****

I've been involved with boxing for over 55 years and at the age of 67 I can say with conviction that it's still a massive part of my life.

Boxing will never leave my blood and I would never want it to. I see myself as a lucky man to be part of one of the largest fraternities on the planet and one where I hope I'm recognised for my attempts to help past, present and future generations of boxers.

As long as there's decent fighters around who want me to train them and I'm still fit and healthy, I'm still available for a long time to come.

There's 18 weight categories in boxing and I've trained fighters in and each every one of them. I'm also proud to say

I've trained boxers to reach Area, British, Commonwealth, Inter-Continental, European and World titles.

Have I peaked? I doubt I will ever peak. The day I believe I've peaked is the day I will lose all enthusiasm for the sport and for life.

With over five decades of boxing in my blood, the most common question I'm asked is, "Jim – how much has boxing changed over the years from when you first got involved?" Compared to when I first started out as a pro, "safety first" has become a major part of the boxing world's outlook, which in my opinion is a great thing.

Two ambulances, three doctors and an anaesthetist are present at each fight.

If something happens, all we have to do is stand back and leave it to the experts. Also, back in my days, they used 6oz horsehair boxing gloves for everyone, in every weight division, which almost allowed your knuckles to come out of the glove!

You would only get good gloves if you were fighting for a title. Nowadays, if you are fighting professionally, from minimum weight up to welterweight (147 pounds), you use 8oz and above that you use 10oz.

The science behind the gloves has improved incredibly as a result of major testing and research and is improving all the time.

One thing that certainly changed boxing on a number of fronts was the decrease in the number of championship rounds from 15 to 12.

I was training fighters during the transitional period and

the views and opinions were very mixed. They brought the change in for safety reasons and you cannot argue with that.

But there will always be something special about those guys who did take part in those epic 15 round battles.

When I was a kid, everybody wanted to fight the full 15 and when the distance was reduced from 45 minutes to 36 minutes a little bit of shine was taken off the achievement of winning over the total distance.

****

Although boxing has evolved, the way I operate hasn't differed too much down the years.

In between a round I will have about 40 seconds, tops, depending on which corner the boxer finishes at the end of a round.

If they are at the furthest point from my corner, I will jump into the ring and walk him back to the corner as fast as I can. Without giving off any vibes of panic or fuss, I will wipe him down with a towel, let him have a couple of deep breaths and then take out his gumshield before giving him a drink. As I'm giving the drink, I'm assessing if he has any damage to his face and then will put some on some Vaseline.

The gumshield then goes back in, I will then give him instructions for his next round which is based on what he's done right or wrong in the last round.

Then he's ready to go out again. It will probably take you longer to read this description, than the speed this all happens in reality in between each round.

And who said men can't multi-task?!

I'm a lot calmer than I used to be too. I like to play golf and fish and I also practise deep breathing, something I learned from watching Mark Rowe, the man I fought twice in the amateurs.

If you have wind in your lungs, you have stamina. At the age of 67, I get up every morning at 5am, have a cup of tea and then do six sets of 10 deep, slow breaths, by which time my lungs start working like a fire blower and I'm ready for my day.

****

As the years have gone on, I have become set in my ways on certain things (boxing not being one of them), but I still appreciate a pleasant surprise.

When I was getting ready to turn 60, I said to Claudette that we would go for a nice meal and I would pay for the booze and she could pay for the food. Just a small affair. Me, Claudette, my cousin, her husband and their son.

It was a lovely summer's day and she told me I had to wear a suit. Well, I hadn't worn a pair of jeans in almost 40 years and wasn't going to start now, but I asked her why I needed to wear a suit when it was so hot and suggested a pair of slacks and a nice shirt.

Claudette insisted I wore the suit, so I thought, 'Ok. Anything for the easy life!' When my cousin's son arrived, he was wearing jeans and I felt a little overdressed!

We stepped outside and I realised that somebody had hired

a van out. I thought it had been hired so that we could all have a drink. We drive off to the restaurant in Hornchurch and my cousin's husband turned to driver and said, "There might be a few other people by the time we get there."

Before he could get the next word out my cousin gave him a hard elbow in the ribs, which certainly stopped him saying another word! I wondered at the time why she had done that though. When we got to the restaurant they all jumped out quickly and I thought, 'Ok – don't worry, I'll pick up the cab fare!' I turned round to the driver and he said, "It's already been paid for." I was now getting suspicious.

As I walked to the front door of the restaurant, the manager walked over and said, "Mr Tibbs – this way please." As I walked in, the whole family was there waiting for me. It was brilliant and I will never forget that day. Claudette had made a lovely cake with me training Chris Pyatt on the top of it and having my family around me was sincerely the best birthday I could have asked for.

If that is the kind of surprises I've got left to look forward to then the more the merrier.

I live my life now with greater inner freedom than ever before and have reached heights I could have only dreamed of when I was sat in that prison cell.

I'd like to be remembered for being an honest and fair man to work with.

I know I'm not always right, but I'd like for people to remember me in years to come as somebody who held their hands up when he knew he was wrong.

For many years I lived wondering 'what might have been?'

But now I'm at peace with myself and I'm happy with what I've become, who I've been and the journey it's taken to get here.

And that journey is not over, not by a long way.